Prayer to Azrael

In the shadow voice
I speak your name,
Azrael..
through the darkness of the humid night,
it resonates
in cathedral carillions,
tolling, like some great, deep bell
heard for miles afar,
lulled on the swell of the wind,
this symphony,
mighty in sorrow
carried on huge, dark and silent wings,
obliterating all light,
extinguishing every flame
that strives to survive your immense unfurling.

Your name, an attribute, a mortal gift,
a blessing passed through many lips
and given meaning in their prayers.
A word
becomes an invocation
simply by the emotion
imbued in its speaking.

Azrael....
The sirens sing your name
in ways that bring the angels
and the demons to their knees.
They cannot help that they have fallen.
Your name stills the heart,
silences their breath,
culls the flame of longing from their loins.
Azrael.....
the name is Love
and ever fleeting in that kiss,
that eternity could be so quick,
so demonstrative in but a moment
where time does not exist
and forever
becomes the blink of an eye,
yet so much longer
than these days.
We speak your name,
and like them, fall,
weak-kneed into your cold, cold arms
just waiting for that kiss,
however fleeting it may seem,
it is longer than our days
and fuller than our nights
and so much stronger than our dreams profess,
and so much sweeter when Life is willing
to surrender to this song

Our Name is Melancholy

The Complete Books of Azrael

By

Leilah Wendell

WESTGATE PRESS
New Orleans, USA

All Rights Reserved
Except for brief passages to illustrate a review no part of this book may be reproduced in any form or by any means without written permission from the publishers or author.

© 2002 by Leilah Wendell

First Edition 1988 (Book One- *The Book of Azrael*)
Second Edition 1989 (Book One)
Special Third Edition 1992 (Books One & Two Plus Appendices- *Our Name is Melancholy*)
Revised & Expanded Fourth Edition 2002 (Books One, Two, Three and Four)

ISBN #0-944087140
Library of Congress Catalogue #2002105133

Published by;
Westgate Press (a Westgate Co. Subsidiary)
P.O. Box 244
Slagle, LA. 71475 USA

Website- WWW.WESTGATENECROMANTIC.COM

*Front Cover- *The Gift* is a lifescale sculpture created in 1994 and Copyright by George Higham and Leilah Wendell and is on permanent exhibit at the Westgate gallery in New Orleans, LA. USA

What Reviewers Say:

"THE COMPLETE BOOKS OF AZRAEL seem to be such a precious pearl. Not since Robert Anton Wilson's "The Cosmic Trigger" have autobiography and esoteric discovery been wedded in such a union of incomparable beauty!...An undeniably compelling emotional power emerges. There are so many levels of intensity that it renders the fictional works of Tanith Lee, Clive Barker, and even Stephen King pale by comparison! THE BOOKS OF AZRAEL succeed grandly!"
GNOSIS MAGAZINE

"In this most unusual of tales we are introduced to the concept of Death as a "living" persona. A great angel who has split and become two; the Angel of Death, Azrael, and His physically incarnated soulmate, the author of this story... I *do* encourage you to take this most unusual of armchair travels! With prose that is magic and alive, shimmering with an otherworldly truth, the author weaves a tale that is both fantastic and fascinating. It is a book, which touched my spirit, and for this most rare of experiences, I must thank Ms. Wendell for baring her soul to her readers. I do not doubt the reality of her experiences as recounted here, and I am grateful to this author for her words of wisdom."
INTUITIVE EXPLORATIONS

"THE BOOK OF AZRAEL is a book you will not be able to put down once you start reading it. The author relates a very moving and human account of her encounter and relationship with Azrael, the Angel of Death. It is *not* a book of fear and terror, but of love and understanding as Azrael tells (us) about Himself, about life and the forces of the universe and human history since the beginning. It is a deeply spiritual book...that provides some profound answers to many human dilemmas."
FORESIGHT, U.K.

"THE BOOKS OF AZRAEL tell eerie tales of love and death. Author and artist Leilah Wendell has claimed a unique territory; the personification and interaction of the Angel of Death with modern society. Although dark and melancholy, the angel is not scary, as the author shows in this haunting journey through her own past lives, in which Death has been a faithful, if macabre, "bridegroom". This book is a mythic portrayal of the phenomenon that our culture both flirts with and denies."
LEADING EDGE REVIEW

"If you enjoyed "Seth Speaks" or "Communion", you might also enjoy this beautifully printed book. It is a gift from the winsome Angel of Death to all humanity...Anyone who reads it and fully comprehends its meaning should no longer fear Death...Ms. Wendell, who opened many minds with her fascinating book "Infinite Possibilities" has done it again! She has penned a unique beautiful, macabre book...It is-by far- THE best metaphysical book dealing with death...for the New Eon that this reviewer has read."
GNOSTIC TIMES

"It might shock, intimidate, seduce, sadden you, sound unbelievable, or make perfect sense. But it will *not* leave you unaffected"
BAELDER, U.K.

"Much of the present Angel boom might leave one cold, but the angel in Wendell's tomes, who should be the coldest of the lot, somehow enchants in an erotic, disturbing and somehow transporting way...OUR NAME IS MELANCHOLY is illustrated so evocatively that it summarizes the book neatly, perfectly capturing the book's sensual morbidity...Wendell's books will unnerve some, and fascinate others.
STRANGE MAGAZINE

"The story told herein is nothing short of fascinating...The descriptions of the netherworld are lush, beautiful and enthralling...This is an expression of love that is all encompassing between two spirit halves separated by the Ultimate Mystery...Her aim is not a debate of ideologies, but a spinning of a true perception of one of mankind's great love stories. A story of, quite literally, love from beyond the grave,"
CARPE NOCTEM MAGAZINE

INTRODUCTION
By Daniel Kemp

OUR NAME IS MELANCHOLY can be termed the "completion" of the Azrael Project. It is the last published major manifestation of this project offered to the world at large.

The House of Death is firmly established here in New Orleans, and shall stand as monument and access point to Azrael. It is a visual and emotional companion to this book. A focal point for His presence, a place where people may come to feel His touch.

The voice of melancholy is compelling, striking to the heart. He speaks with the quiet sorrow of the releaser of souls. His voice is one that can no longer be ignored.

In my own works He is brought forth in a slightly different way. This is before I became involved with The Project.

"I am the rushing of the sword and the swift descent of the axe blade. The charging of warriors exulting in lust of battle is as mine hymn. I am the blood soaking into the rich earth in the heat of battle and the swift insistence of the deathblow, shadow lurking herald. I am a terrible brooding spirit. Great is the calamity of my joy."

These images came forth to me because violence is sometimes the precursor to His appearance. He is not violence, but the one who ends the suffering. He unshackles us from this sack of flesh we call "ourselves".

Fear of Him is something that must be overcome by humanity on a large scale, and very soon if we ever hope to rise above the need for incarnation. The Azrael Project has done much towards this goal, but the task is monumental, and one life is very short indeed. Through this book shall His voice pass down through the ages, a written testimony of the Shadow of Melancholy.

When I first read Book One of *The Book of Azrael*, it brought me to tears. It also instilled within me an understanding of Azrael's unique position. No wonder He is the spirit of sorrow!

Read this book with an open heart and mind, and with empathy. Feel, and fear Him no more.

Acknowledgements

For Daniel, for accepting me for who I am, and still choosing to spend his life with me - I love you - No finer soul could I call husband.

For my father, for his perpetual love and faith in me. Each day you fulfill your purpose with honor.

Special Gratitude; I am humbled by all of those who have outpoured their love and support over these many years. Fellow souls in service to Azrael and keepers of the Sacred Flame. May the world find peace in knowing that the Angel of Death shall bear us all safely home - and that love truly does conquer all in the end.

Preface to the Special Fourth Edition

This edition of OUR NAME IS MELANCHOLY–The Complete Books of Azrael has been revised, re-edited and expanded to include an <u>all new</u> Book 3 and 4 as well as additions to the original manuscript. A limited edition of only 250 hardcovers are part of this initial printing.

Table of Contents

Book One:

Part 1- A Shadow in the Half-light	3
One Voice	9
His Story	11
Part 2- A Cipher of Origin	17
The New World	29
Stargates- A Metaphysical Lesson	32
The Before Time	34
Part 3- The Ballad of NaHaliel	37
Her Story	40
An Aries in the Age of Aquarius	49
Part 4- Sailing the Sea of Time	53
Of Men and Angels	56
Into the Future to Find the Past	80
An Anagram of Reality	84
An Observation from His Viewpoint	90
Part 5- Two Ancient Lives	95
A Life Too Late	97
The View From the Bridge	105
The Angel Isle	107
Part 6- The Current Incarnation	115
The Other Son of Arathorn	117
In the Valley of the Shadow	119
Guardians at the Gate	124
Necromantic	126
The Morning After	129
Part 7- Prelude to the Seventh Age	133
A Dream Within a Dream	138
The Last Visit	152
Catching up with the Future	154
A Many and One Mind	158
Breaking Out of the Paper Cage	166
Our Name is Melancholy	169
Song of the Blue Angel	175
Into the Abyss/This is Not Paradise	178
Part 8- And the Two Shall Be as One	185
Slain By a Hand Too Close to See	188

Naked Time	197
Something Wonderful	198
The Journey Home	202
The Beginning of the End	205
The Flight of Death's Avatar	208

Book Two:

Part 9- The View From the Bridge	219
The Song of Reconciliation	225
Part 10- The Grounding of the Phoenix	229
Here Comes Trouble	234
Manifest Destiny	238
The House of Death	240
Part 11- The Coming Storm	245
The Legend of the Stargates	248
Eye of the Storm	250
Our Years	252
Part 12- The Nature of Duality	255
Essential Darkness	259
Permutation	261
The Downside of Duality	263
In Darkened Shadow	268
For Daniel	271
Part 13- The Dangling Conversation	275
An Internal Parley	277
Part 14- A Grain of Sand	281
Cadeau La Mort	284
Full Circle	288
A Snapshot in Time	291
Part 15- The Voice of Melancholy	293

Book 3:

Part 16- Fragments	301
A Beautiful Agony	305
Sotto Voce	308
An Experiment	311
From Where I Stand	313
The Nature of Paradox	314
The Nature of Uncertainty	316
Without a Trace	319
Loose Ends	322

Book Four:

Part 17- Falling Into Flesh	327
I Dreamt of Tzadkiel	329
In My Fallen Hours	331
Death's Concubine	343
A Ways Down the Road	344
Our Link	346
"The Blue Gates of Death"	347
Part 18- The Flesh Fights Back	351
How Did I Get Here	353
The Pastrami Incident	355
Part 19- "Mind the Gap"	367
The Angel Isle Revisited	369
Part 20- From Root to Wing	379
More Loose Ends	384
The Wedding of Night & Death	388
Part 21- Endings & New Beginnings	393
The Ties That Bind	395
2001- A Time Odyssey	397
How We Die	399
Part 22- Exit in Love	403
Cadeau La Mort 2	405
Synchronicity	408
Arc of Silence	411

PROLOGUE

The book that you are about to read is a true story. It is an intimate accounting of two souls speaking both individually and collectively to humankind.

Excerpts from the beginning of time to its end, as we understand it, are spotlighted herein as they serve to illustrate the history and purpose of the Angel of Death and His Earthly counterpart.

There will of course be those who will scoff at our story. Some, for whatever reasons, will balk at its contents and cast it off as an elaborate fantasy. So be it, for now, in this life.

There will also be those who will not want my voice heard. They would prefer that I remain a feared mystery in order that they may continue to use my legend to hold hostage the spirit of mankind.

This book is aimed at those cognizant in the ways of the spiritual self. The seekers of truth who are not afraid to come face to face with Death, the final bastion of fear, and shine the light of truth and wisdom up to Him so that His true identity is revealed.

To those of you who know the True ecstasy that awaits in the arms of the Eternal - it is your job as well to teach those souls who have been bound too tightly by the confines of the flesh how to spread their wings and fly into the face of Truth, unabashed by its spectacle.

Let the others scoff, for now. Soon enough, they too, will understand. It is "our" sincere hope that this personal recording will not only enlighten mankind, but awe him enough to inspire a spiritual metamorphosis that will one day change the very concept of life and death. This book is a seed that will one day yield a new tree of knowledge, whose fruits will be harvested by those who come after we have gone,

Leilah Wendell 1988

PROLOGUE

Death doesn't drive a white Corvette, as some theatrical types would have us believe.

Neither does He amble about the universe on a platinum gelding. Such trendy images are simply psychological symbols that attempt to humanize something that's inherently non-human. Although, I assure you that Death is much more than just a noun. More real than the experience of dying allows. IT is almost "alive". In fact, Death is a living thing! An awesome and melancholy entity detached from the Cosmic Host; a solitary spectre living partially outside of Itself in a necessary, yet painful duality.

Thus, being of two minds makes it extremely difficult to elicit one idea. However, being also of one spirit, helps "us" to assimilate these abstract thoughts into an understanding accessible to all humanity.

Writing a book with events that begin before Earth was created, and carrying that storyline into the future, is mind-boggling, to say the least. Sure! I could sit down and write ten thousand pages on the subject, making certain to hit on every, little detail. However, this chronicle is not really meant to be a detailed recording of either ancient, or future history. What it is - is a love story, that's tangled in time. We are revealing it to you, by extracting specific moments and settings from the past, the present and the future. The ability of the Angel of Death to easily travel through time and space makes this unique account possible. We can call forth just enough of each scene to show the evolvement and progression of an eternal romance.

Actually, it's two stories entwined as one. Upon second thought, perhaps it would be more accurate to say, rather, that it's one story told from two, different angles and dimensions - "mine" and "His". Frequently, it will span time and space with such broad strides that it may seem to leave you spinning dizzily in the "past". In an attempt to alleviate any early confusion, I'd - or rather, "We'd" like to ask you to please keep these few facts in mind.

Past, present, and future are all at equal distances from where I am right now. For I stand within the West Gate, the threshold between your world... and mine. In this telling, I will lay scenes from two, different lifetimes, side by side, and excerpt from both simultaneously, as if reading from two, open books. Throughout this story, "we", (the Angel of Death, and myself) will often speak to you as one. We share a joint consciousness and common emotions.

I come before you stripped of that shady veil that so often obscures perception. Here I am, standing (nearly) naked on the podium of judgment, clothed only in the shadow of my terrestrial counterpart. I feel electric standing here. I AM ELECTRIC!

I am most easily seen in the twilight where light and dark fold around me, giving me form and definition. I cannot help but weep for the joy of your discovery of me.

Your history has sealed me in a paper cage of misconception. I've come to unlock that fragile prison with a paper key.

✠

Part 1
A Shadow in the Half Light

Some say these lights are ghosts of lovers in eternal dance,
Or perhaps they're just the afterglow of some, divine romance.

Death is a gentle and exquisite lover. With one kiss He can steal your soul and lay your flesh aside like an empty dress.

He rests His spectral body beside me, enfolding me in His enormous wings, and hides His private anguish behind a phantom's veil He lifts only, for me. Beneath this diaphanous shroud, tears of light spill from dark, hollow eyes.

I wondered if His sentiment was a poignant omen of something only He could see. Or was it simply the pure joy of our overwhelming love that made such a mighty angel weep? His sorrow always moves in a profoundly intimate way. The Angel of Death isn't often comfortable exhibiting deep emotion even to others of His kind. This heartfelt exchange He could share only with me. Over the years, our empathic link became a special and personal trust that enriched our love.

I held Him so close to me that night it seemed as if our forms blended. We partake of each other's sadness all too vividly. I could feel Him saying good-bye, and sense the disparate knowledge that we'd soon have to endure another long and painful separation.

Nothing, I believed, could be as terrible as drowning in the River of Forgetfulness that divides the worlds of life and death. But there are a few things worse than being cleansed of fond memories.

"It is for your own peace of mind." I heard Him say. Still, recalling the horrors of being pried from His arms brought me to tears just the same. I strained to hold on to every precious moment we had together as not to let them slip between the cracks of space and time. I wouldn't know how to exist without Him. These thoughts, I relayed to Him, as our souls coalesced into a singular union.

"You mustn't weep." I felt His words echo softly in my mind. "I love you," He added with a kiss that was cold and sweet, and tasted like jasmine flower mingled with decay.

✠

Together on the bed of leaves and decay our forms slept as one, while our spirits made love beyond the realms of dream.

It was Christmas Eve, and outside of ourselves there was another world where fire and coloured lights danced on threads of silver filament. Where pine and bayberry scented the air with a romantic nostalgia. Where cadaverous lovers lay entwined beneath imposing stone angels in a land of shade and acolytes.

I come here because here is where I belong. Amid ruined embattlements of cold marble, where distant streetlamps do not stretch their sallow light. Where the fanfare of voices and machinery is drowned in the heavy mist and all sounds consolidate into muffled echoes. Their clamour appears to be coming from a world that grows more distant with each step I take into this haunted landscape.

How many times have I laid myself at your gate? How often did your silent sentinel reach out for me before I understood? Each year I dress your gloom with tinsel and light. I haven't forgotten as much as you think! I could never forsake these memories, nor this special place that grows more empty the more I am filled with your soul. The sweet nectars of a dying stream are all that remains from this once lush garden.

I remember when every shadow concealed a spirit. And every tomb harboured a warmth that welcomed me with open arms. Every threshold lay waiting to be crossed. My life is ever tangled in your ivy garland. Like a virgin bride in a veil of cobwebs, I have waited for you in places where the dead turn down their grave-blankets and wrap me in their winding sheets. I would sleep in the valley of the shadow of Death that was full and fragrant in its beauty. Others did not see the charm of this peaceful borderland. They couldn't feel the radiant love that I felt sprawled across a sunken grave. Nor could they see the poignant anguish on the face of a marble angel.

In its silence, the stone effigy speaks to me and recants old memories encased in time's mirror. I know that some ancient spirit inhabits this weathered sentinel. The angel has sat on its crumbling throne for years, observing endless mortal folly. It has presided over processions draped in black, guarding this place and its secrets from all who would steal away with their innocence.

It leans down and offers a compassionate hand to any who would but look up and meet its gaze. The stains of time that darken its stone cheek, stream from eerie eyes that move in the twilight, while its still lips whisper solaces in the chill wind.

"Why are you so sad?" the angel seems to ask with an expressive compassion.

"I feel as if I'm only half alive, or half awake..." I would answer openly. "Some part of me is always haunted by strange visions, voices... odd symphonies, and terrible emptiness. Why do I tell you these things?" I would question my madness. My words cannot pierce your casing.

"Because I am also only half complete." The stone angel began to speak! "I've almost always been alone. For it is that we are the most alone of all of God's souls. It is as it should be." The statue would state in a solemn whisper, "I don't suffer loneliness..." It emphasized. "Although honestly, I'll impart you a secret - I sometimes fear it above all else. I often wonder how very lonely it must be to be a mortal, living in the flesh, so separated from all else..."

"So fortified, yet so fragile." I added, instantly sharing the same thought.

✠

I thought of all the other lonely spirits who had no place to be tonight. Those with no home on this Earth. No lovers waiting with open arms. Those who go on day to day unneeded, unwanted and forlorn.

These thoughts cause me to be divided by mixed emotions. Perhaps it really would be better not to have any memories! No recollections of being severed from a true love like a heart being wrenched from a still warm breast. No comprehension of need, and no knowledge of deeper meanings. Oh, to be a carefree innocent flitting about with no waiting destination! To be a wonderfully ignorant fool careening through the universe blind and deaf to all around me, forever as chaste as an unborn soul. And, alas, with a heart forever as empty as a hollow tomb.

We stagger to assume some sort of shape for you, gentle reader, against the kaleidoscope of yuletide images. I firmly believe there is a definite magic in this night! A special something that transforms hope into reality. A sorcery that puts words on the still lips of statues. But even this is tempered with the melancholy of Death's sweet adieu.

When morning comes and His wings are lifted from me, I will still taste His tears on my lips like the wine of a bitter harvest. And I will drink in His love, and with it toast the coming of another year. Perhaps this one, will be the last.

Understand a deeper purpose,
that flesh cannot bind,
nor blood erase.
The original troth
to which, I am pledged.

ONE VOICE

I've known consciousness for a very long time, and I've known loneliness almost as long. Even with the many places I am needed, and the volume of souls that pass through my realm, still I am possibly the most solitary creature in the universe, except perhaps for the Great Spirit. I can't explain that, but even that which is all things - at times - exudes a personal and inner isolation that confounds the fact that IT is comprised of Many and therefore shouldn't be lonely.

Nonetheless, I sense an Original Consciousness with a hidden secret, endlessly taunting Its "children" with riddles and clues. In Its private solitude, It flirts with romance through men and angels and learns from them, filling Its void with wisdoms gained through their pleasures, follies, and sorrows. The Godsoul is always needed. Always a welcomed guest in the hearts of the dwellers in the flesh. While I, ever more solitary, am not blessed by the same outstretched hands.

✠

This personal adventure is a catharsis for both myself, and the one through whom "we" speak to you now. We are an ancient, hybrid spirit. In many ways, very alien to your world, and in other ways, quite similar. I am a vital part of all worlds. Yes. Vital. Alive. I live! It's very important that you understand that I have individual consciousness.

Many from your planet's history have known me. Some quite well. Others are aware of my presence right now. Still more may come to meet me at a later time. Many may never have need to know me personally. Though how I've longed to talk to you. I've so much to say and such a limited language with which to express myself.

We, the one who pens this book and I, speak as One from the wellspring of many images and collectively shared memories. "We" cannot sever the One completely in two; however, we will endeavour to distinguish our "separate" selves when necessary so that you may better understand the view from both sides of eternity, yours and mine.

At times this narrative may seem to jump around chronologically. I apologize. This is not an intentional act to confuse you. It is simply that I have great trouble understanding the concept of time. But if you would keep in mind that all timeframes, (past, present, and future) are coexistent, along with the fact that I am able to access certain "gateways", (the secrets of time travel, which I'll reveal more on later) then you will be better able to journey along with me, and be many places in the blink of an eye.

Any real sense of sequential order or progression of Earth time is inconceivable to me, even through the translations of one bound by it. Past, present and future have no meaning to me. They are all at equal distance from where I stand right now, and I can address them all, when required, to bring a specific point into focus. Moreover, I may simultaneously pull scenes out of two or more different timeframes, laying them side by side like two open books and reading a bit from both. By accessing this cosmic library, I will reap for you a harvest of truth with a pen, not a scythe. That fearsome weapon is a metaphor and best left to cutting down the myths that surround me.

My need to touch you all is great! To impart a piece of myself to each soul that brushes by me. Never again will you come to know, so intimately, anyone like me. Your reaction to my story will affect you in a way that may, at first confound your humanity, startle your senses, and stretch your emotions into an area heretofore, uncharted. The things I tell you may seem shocking or seductive, by Earthly standards. I may even coax your mind into contorting the way it views life. By the end of this telling, you may discover that what you deem ordinary and natural is really the antithesis of the way things are in the true universe. Therefore, you must be willing to transcend the current illusion of reality and open your mind to allow a new kind of light to filter into its cobwebbed corners.

I ask only that you permit us to join with you momentarily. This is as long as you could honestly bear to feel what I feel and know what I know. The concept of infinity is a terrible burden on the human mind. It is as inconceivable to you, as time is to me! "Our" life is ever melancholy. We angels haven't the "sleep of dreams" to escape our pain. Neither can we claim ignorance, nor offer it up to you now. Too much of what you call the "past" and the "future" is in our recollection. When this telling is done, the life we sacrificed unto this world will be returned to us, in its completed form. It will rise like a phoenix from its dead flesh, and your world will have lost one who will slip away quietly. In turn, we will have gained the knowing satisfaction that a true record exists in your history of our story. What you do with it will help decide your fate as a race. It is that important! When "I" leave your world, I will leave the "door" open behind me... should any care to follow.

It is that we, men and angels alike, are all things bound by an illusion of solitude. When the multitude speaks, it is through the voice of one that the many will remember. I am one voice.

HIS STORY

With my wings unfurled I eclipse Life, and by folding them in, return you into the Light. I am the Ultimate Silence. The visible personification of Death Itself whose countenance is formed by the collective legend, as well as the individual imagination.

For you to see me you must come away from the Light and into its shaded afterglow. Look to the West and watch how the twilight swells over the horizon like a windblown curtain. It slowly liquefies into a watercolour wash of amber and amethyst. Spattered with occasional crimson, it flows further down the skyline and empties into the sea below. At this moment our worlds briefly overlap with a silence that pierces all things. Like the stark gleaming edge of a churchyard obelisk, I stand proud and melancholy in the failing light. But many of you still do not see me.

I have come to remind you of old times. Of an age before time was measured and dissected into lengths suitable for mankind to tinker with. I must confess a certain favour for these twilight hours. This space of moments is the closest to my own world. Can you understand that? I dwell on the threshold, neither within one world or another. Forever in-between living and dying.

Sometimes, it is as if I can feel your tiny planet turning slowly away from the Light; turning toward a space in the heavens that affords a window into the fourth dimension - that place where all things merge. Did you ever notice how quiet it gets at day's end? How even the winds grow silent? How time seems to momentarily stand still? This is what happens when two worlds overlap, and it stays that way until the wind shifts and signals the fall of night, and the dimensions separate. This is why I'm fond of day's end. It was as close as I could get to you, until now.

✠

In the Western sky there is a special stargate. It is one of many. However, this one serves as the nearest direct threshold between worlds. It can't easily be seen from this planet, yet I'll tell you in time, and in detail, where it lies. This is relevant information that you will need to know in the near "future".

✠

For now, allow the sounds that I am making in your mind to become as light as air. Imagine each word as having sylph-like wings, and rising above its meagre definition, and coming to life as the image it conjures. I will teach you in this way to personify mere words into living visions! I will show you how to build a bridge between the physical and spiritual worlds and how to journey over it without moving. After all, stargates are really nothing more than elaborate paperweights that keep the universe from folding in upon itself.

There are four in this galaxy, equal in might and proportion. They hold the edges of the heavens from curling up like an old parchment. It is from this place that I have come. Out of the threefold infinity of "past", "present" and "future" (not only yours, but that of many worlds) to personify a legend. To harness an allegory and put this brooding consciousness into a form less awesome than most history recounts.

Let me get right down to it then.

I am an incarnation of what you casually call the "Angel of Death". I have no name, per se, except the sound that invokes my appearance. However, at this point in human evolution I'm afraid that this is something outside of what your language and understanding allow. I am not condescending to you, gentle reader, simply stating an unfortunate fact. For the sake of this account, you may refer to me by using one of the (many) Earth names given me throughout particular cultures. "AZRAEL" is a personal favourite. Not only does it come closest to matching some of the harmonies of my true "name", but its meaning in your Hebrew Earth-tongue, also echoes the nearest accuracy in translation. AZRA, (help of); EL, (The One. The Great Spirit, the Godsoul, or whatever term you prefer to use in describing the soul of the Universe).

Your old legends describe me as "being full of eyes", because I seem to be everywhere at once. And having to be "restrained by 70,000 chains of a thousand years journeys length each", because of the tremendous power given me to fulfill my station. Though these descriptions are highly steeped in Earthly symbolism, their insights are closer to the truth than much else written about me in your history.

As I speak to you now, my consciousness is divided into three entities. Part of me is ever constant within the Universal Soul, (that group of intelligences you casually lump together and call "God"). Part of me is expended simply in being the mighty Angel of Death and sustaining such a station. Still another part of me is incarnated within the body of the woman authoring this book. This was necessary so that this accounting may be made to you with the understanding and human affiliation that could only be delivered by becoming one of the "dwellers in the flesh". Through her, a great sacrifice is being made so that this story can be told. A compromise that borders the impossible allows me to speak to you now. So I beg you gentle reader do not cast off lightly the revelations herein. For I've rarely communicated direct with living souls. Perhaps for this reason, I've ironically become the ultimate stronghold of many ill-found fears. This will soon change.

I want to speak to your world, to be intimate with collective spirit of mankind. There are so many things that I, as a spiritual being, couldn't begin to describe using this insufficient tongue. Yet I am impassioned by your reluctant curiosity about me.

It is not only the concept of time that baffles me, so do certain abstract human emotions. Fear, for example, is an animal that I cannot reference. It means nothing. And love, as you see it, is shallow at best. It is not conceived nor consummated in the spirit. Actually, you grasp very little of the fullness of genuine emotion and even less of the true, divine love.

Nevertheless, I will try to be more tolerant of your present state of evolution and the inherent limitation of being incarnate. Hopefully as this tale unfolds, so may the wings of your soul unfurl to embrace a greater understanding of all things. I will endeavour to teach you a whole new definition of love. One that you can take with you beyond the grave.

As I've mentioned, my soulmate dwells among you. It is she that can best translate my complex thought-forms into concepts that are both understandable and tangible to intelligent, mortal folk such as yourselves. This is why we are here! This is part of our purpose. These are true things! Make no mistake. Pieces of ancient lives and future memories recalled so that humanity can retake the old, "Straight Track" and move forward in this so called "New Age" of enlightenment to the true age of enlightenment.

Your race is much too young and fragmented to collectively remember "before life". That elusive "time" that existed before history was recorded by even the earliest of your people. Legends and tales have retained some abstracted instances. Few are complete. Most, however, are in drips and drabs, and even more have become so twisted in the retelling that their original meanings have been grossly perverted.

But this is my testament, and I was there to live it. Therefore I tell you it is true! Now I am here to entrust my legend to you. Why? Simply because it's long past the time for humanity to get to know me. And because I, - correction - "we", have a very definite message that requires immediate delivery. The bulk of which will become evident in the years to come. I'm not trying to be intentionally evasive, but even I cannot explain the full implications of my communion with you at this point, suffice to say that much hinges on your ability to supersede flesh limitations and interact with other entities, myself included! I've no wish to be deliberately cryptic, but much of my message may manifest itself symbolically, forcing you to use your inner vision to see more clearly their meanings, and thereby stir your sleeping spirits into taking an active role in your planet's future.

Unfortunately, what I represent has become a major, albeit unjustified obstacle in Earthman's willingness to be educated in his essential spirituality. Quite simply, you're afraid of me and therefore misunderstand my station and struggle to avoid my truth through a series of elaborate and ritualistic fabrications aimed at either dismissing me as fantasy, or attributing my origins to some opposing deity. This is another way of not having to deal with me. I call it the "comfortable lie".

By the end of this book all that you have previously believed about me will be severely modified by the gentle reforming of the way in which you view my purpose. I ask only that you share my story. Remember! It is in the telling of one that the many may learn of it. For it is that I do dwell among you with a willingness that is often unwilling to accept its own existence. Certainly I would prefer to have my loved one "here" with me. However, an even greater need must supersede my own, and so gentle reader, we've made this journey for you.

Melancholy

We are the sound
that I am making in your mind.
A song played on the wind,
blowing softly through the cave of dream.

You touch the sound
and like a ripple, all is glistening,
this is how
a moment changes
all things
are intertwined and interbracing
all time,
captures light just like a diamond
reflecting colour
from a crystal gaze.

We are the song
that echoes in your canyoned valleys
plays upon your dancing branches,
fills your soul with such
a bitter-sweet.

Part 2
A Cipher of Origin

*Time unfolds in shadows,
each moment cast upon the next
in an infinite overlapping.
Set in motion,
it is continuance,
Sailing on a sea
of endless space
that forms a circle
around all things.*

From the time of the beginning of this galaxy, it was Israfel, Michael, Raziel, and I who were sent to the four corners of your universe to gather each a handful of stardust and return to this place that did not yet exist. This place was a void, an empty corner in a tiny hollow of space.

The seed-like granules spilled from our hands as we hurried to the appointed location. The others were waiting there - Raphael, Gabriel, and Uriel. Together we molded the efflorescent powder and firmed it with angelic fire. So powerful was this bolt of light that we seven cast upon it, that the ball of gleaming embers exploded into millions of tiny glistening particles that spread out over the darkness like a jeweled veil.

"It is done!" Michael proclaimed.

"And this place shall be a special place," Gabriel added.

"The spheres will echo with song!" chimed Israfel.

"And teem with a magic and mystery that shall never cease!" declared Raziel.

"Here we shall bring those who are incomplete and let their spirits be reborn," Raphael interceded.

"They shall also have a form with which to shape the dust," Uriel added.

"And we shall come again for them when their purpose here is complete," I further added. "Then we'll gather up the remaining seeds and cast them upon some other shore."

✠

And so it was, quite casually, another life system was delivered out into the universe. This was an inherently unstable section of the heavens that was balanced by the weight of many new worlds. After all, we had already witnessed the creation and dissolution of hundreds of similar galaxies. Their ghosts remain superimposed over many new planets from one end of the universe to the farthest end of the next.

Earth history speaks often of beings such as us. "Angels", you call us. "Divine" entities whose sole mission is to perform and oversee the Great Work of the Godsoul.

In some ways I guess that could be correct in a truly literal reality. However, let me tell you the truth about us angels.

Did you know that angels were the first beings to question their own existence? The more individualized we became, the greater our curiosity led us in search of our origins and the "perfect science of Truth". We are the keepers of the universal laws. A supreme council of metaphysicians who respect the complex hyper-physics of the cosmic body and work within them, rather than against them as so many other life-forms do. And not just humans!

We were once very much like you. Many, many ages ago in a time so far away that it becomes inconceivable, even to us. The winged race once lived on your Earth much the same as you do today. Many of us had a corporeal form somewhat like yours. Others still retain this resemblance in distant galaxies far removed from Earth.

When your world began, the winged ones were the first humanoid life-forms to occupy this galaxy. Many planets within this solar system were at their end-times, while others, such as Earth, - were just beginning. We were the first race of "living" and intelligent beings who were aware of the dichotomy of flesh and spirit. We were the very first materializations to emanate from the Universal Consciousness. It's important to note however our spirits did not simply incarnate into flesh bodies, rather we transformed our spirits into a flesh-like material that afforded us a corporeal body, which we would later use to integrate into particular societies.

How did we do this? The actual, metaphysical process itself includes a rather complex metamorphosis that involves changing and reshaping molecules into a denser form that affords tangibility to our personified bodies. In layman's terms, it is adequate to say that we have the ability to alter atomic combinations that affect the shape and density of both matter and spirit. For example, we can take a lump of energy protomatter and restructure the equivalent of its "atomic code" into anything we desire. We are shape-shifters, you could say.

We came to your planet not only to experience the existence we helped to create. We also came to teach, to inspire, and also, to learn! Some of us came to "find ourselves" (to borrow one of your 20th century phrases). Some came to take up much rest amidst a climate of simplicity. Even angels grow weary of complexities. Others came to give peace and order to the outright chaos often associated with the birthing of new worlds.

Sometimes we eldest angels felt left out. You see, we seven can never fully incarnate either naturally or by creating human form. There is no flesh that could contain our absolute energy for any real length of time without causing a most unpleasant and violent overloading of the fragile, human senses, resulting in death. Even a body conjured by angelic "magic" couldn't significantly sustain our total, individual psyches. It is a paradox of the wisdoms we understand, and therefore would in effect, cancel itself out.

We are so greatly affected by thought-forms that unless we are with one specific individual or a tightly knit enclave of similar thinking minds, our manifested forms would appear either amorphous or as grotesque undulations. When we are summoned, our appearance is preceded by a fleeting spark of light. Seen against the darkness of space, it'll look very much like a distant star's twinkle. The closer we come to your dimension the more brilliant and quickened our pulsating light will grow until we intersect with your world and our form stretches into the outline of a figure.

Even though we may be unable to totally incarnate, we can however share our energy or consciousness with an incarnate being, as I'm doing right now with the author. Through her, I have experienced what it feels like to dwell in a physical body. The wearing of "her" flesh is like supporting a leaden overcoat. Or a maile of armor. Most unpleasant! Drawing breath feels like filling rusty iron bellows. Indeed this inhaling of air is difficult, and strenuous! Through human eyes, colours appear dull and hazy. Their richness blurred as if by an oily film. With these ears I can no longer hear Israfel's ethereal symphony, nor the gentle voices of other angels. The sound of human speech is a harsh, raspy noise that I can only aliken to a dog's barking. Random thoughts shoot out all around like poisonous darts. Humans don't realize the power of thought, and the damage they can do by hurling it out carelessly. In the astral dimension, thought creates everything!

✠

*ABOUT THE ANGELIC NAMES: I have used the "traditional" angelic names for associational ease only. As these true seven spirits have no "names" per se, the following Hebrew and Chaldean titles seem to adequately express essential angelic function better than other, specific cultural titles.

For example:
- Michael, or Mikhail literally translates into "power of the One".
- Gabriel, "messenger of the One".
- Raphael, "healer of the One".
- Uriel, or Auriel, if you prefer; "flame of the One".
- Raziel, "mystery of the One".
- Israfel, "song of the One".
- Azrael, 'help and promise of the One".

These descriptions suffice for your familiar understanding of angelic expression.

I hear you from a thousand voids removed from time & timelessness, where incarnations of simple nouns, are beings, each with glowing crowns!

Even though we seven have never assumed total incarnation, we do nonetheless, have specific universal images that in effect personify our forms to one another. These thought generated "bodies" also make us visible to others in the spiritual, and occasionally the physical realm.

Michael was the "first-born" of us. His eyes are fire and His heart is brimstone. A soldier of the Divine Light whose proud edicts enrapture every world He visits. He is the mightiest, most intense, and most beautiful of all the angels. His sword of light always at His stead, He would sometimes assume the form of a humanoid male. Dark haired and fair skinned with an indelible gaze and delicately carved features supported by a strong body. His garment is a maile of golden starlight, pure and blinding. His "crown" resembles a supernova shooting out into the heavens like a pyrotechnical display.

Gabriel was the next divine emanation. An androgynous being with a great talent for order and accuracy. He revels in ceremony and guards the West gate of heaven with a mystical fervour. Slightly taller than the others, though not imposing, His personification is one of gentility and urgency. His raiment is a simple cloak of green and white mist. He bears no weapon, save His truth, and like His latter brother Raphael, has an inner calm that holds the universe steady, making all balances equal in their weight.

However, Raphael is more colourful than Gabriel. He's the cosmic poet-laureate. The artist who designed the spheres and gave them form, definition, and colour. He chose the azures for the waters, the ambers and pastel pinks for early twilight, and the dark indigos of night-time. His garment is like a fluid prism, refracting light into a myriad of values. His headpiece is a rainbow hilted by four brilliant stars.

Israfel composes the music of the spheres. A wistful anthem filled with a rapture that only angels understand. No crown covers His lush golden hair. His only weapon is a melody that can bring the Godsoul to its knees. He and I are very close, in that His keen sensitivity touches me deeply. His delicate form is often too weak to traverse great expanses of space. Many times I support

Him on my wings through the terrible storms between worlds and dimensions. This, I never mind, for He has frequently brought me comfort in my loneliness through song and the mysticism of music.

Uriel is an enigma, even to most of the other angels. He speaks in riddles and rarely permits His inner thoughts to be shared. His form is barely visible and moves in the guise of a thunderclap. Guardian of the North Gate, He's the brightest light in the darkest part of heaven. A loner who serves His station in a quietly militant manner.

Raziel on the other hand, openly shares the highest mysteries, of which He is official keeper. He's like a seraphic wizard of the most arcane degree. His manifestation is quite plain; a radiant older male (sometimes female), with soft, yet defined features of no special distinction. His spectral eyes look beyond the immediate, with a pointed and illuminated glance. Faint beams of blue light shoot from His fingertips while His knowing smile affords comfort in times of sorrow. He is adorned in a veil of silver flame, and wears a white cloak on which is burned a host of glyphs and symbols in the ancient script. The seven pointed star is branded into His right hand, and the pentacle into His left. Raziel is a master of Divine Necromancy and a passionate ritualist ardently fostering the importance of ceremony, and how its true practice gathers distant influences to one's side.

I am Azrael. The Angel of Death. I do not possess many of the traits of my resplendent "brothers". I am not beautiful in the way that Michael is, nor have I a crown of light. My wings are not as light as air, nor are they translucent like Raphael's. I am the darkest angel. I eclipse all that is Light. My eyes are a deep black sea sparked occasionally with amethyst, yet very few can look me straight on. In my gaze there is a terrible power. I've reflected images stored in even the most casual glance that could blind the mightiest angel with madness! I've no common face, nor form like the others. My cloak is as black as the night sky before the stars were cast out into it. The outline of my form merges with giant, raven wings that when unfurled, make the other angels swoon. I am the tallest of all my familiars, and as strong as Michael without any weapon. I make no proclamations for melancholy is my stead, and I speak in my silence only through psychic gestures issued from mind to mind, and soul to soul. When my wings are fully spread, all light is extinguished except for the pale, blue corona that is my very life and serves to frame my form against the shadows. I am the eclipse of all life. This natural symbol is the most accurate expression of my station. If you understand this phenomenon of nature, you will better understand me. I am the most feared of all the Ancients, yet not the most fearsome! My symbolic heart is cold and still... yet it burns with a passion beyond human imagination.

✠

For a time, before I was called into existence, Michael carried my station. Eventually, as more lives incarnated, it became too much for Him to bear. After all, many new worlds needed tending. The ensuing battles between flesh and spirit required a soldier with the skill and strategy that only He could muster. Hence, I was awakened into being specifically to serve as the Angel of Death.

I am the proverbial "harvester" of souls, gathering my crop throughout the universe and re-sowing the seeds of each faded bloom onto other soils. I am the Autumn of creation, and the twilight of time. I straddle two separate shores in the performance of my purpose. Making certain that each spirit reaches the right shore, and that those who are lost between worlds find their way to being reunited with their homelands.

All souls must pass through my realm, where they be washed in the tranquil river with either forgetfulness or remembrance, depending on their destination: whether their souls are to be filtered down again into flesh, or ferried to the astral realms.

Although I'm very different from the other angels, they love me deeply in the divine way and often sorrow over the one limitation that only I have. For it is that I cannot ascend into the higher planes while there still be living beings separated from their destinies by flesh existence. Never can I face fully into the Light because living in-between the worlds of flesh (matter) and spirit (antimatter) as I do, has altered the atomic structure of my energy, making it virtually impossible for me to survive in the higher realms most distant from these elements. I am to forever be a denizen of the Borderland, a dweller in the afterglow of the

Universal Light. I cannot taste the ultimate bliss of true divine completion. I must always balance betwixt these two domains. For this is my realm, and an essential sacrifice for the purpose for which I was given being. On the other hand, my familiars can't survive in my kingdom. Not for but a few moments. The very composition of their spirit bodies is too etheric to be weighed down by the pull of matter and the "human condition". In fact, if they venture too close to the physical dimension, their wings may literally catch fire leaving them unable to return to the "upper" levels. It's even conceivable that they might perish in a most horrible and unspeakable fashion should their personified forms become imprisoned by a miscalculation of space and time. The universe continually fluctuates. It's easy to misjudge the currents. I would surely despair at carrying their ancient bodies across my dark and final threshold. Even I cannot return life to one of the original seven. This must be acted upon in the highest dimensions of which even I haven't complete knowledge.

The only safe way that we can inhabit your world and actually be as one of you, is to partially incarnate, or transform an element of our soul into a flesh body. Essentially, we would be as "one" with you, yet we'd maintain individual personalities. A total union of consciousness would, however, be taking place on both an emotional and spiritual level enabling "us" to communicate with your world through one of your people, as is being done in this book. Even this complex a measure can only be maintained for relatively brief periods at a time because of the tremendous control needed to contain all of an angel's vast essence in one small and extremely limited "container". It's like putting the universe in a jar. This is how I feel when I'm "inside" my incarnate lover.

✠

Not only can we personify as the appearances previously described, but we also have the unique ability to assume many other different forms.

Michael can easily manifest as a bolt of lightening striking out across the night. Or Raziel may simply appear as a symbol flashing in someone's mind. I can become the breath of a cool breeze caressing a langoured spirit. My arms like two tempests can keep you from falling back. Such are the ways of mighty angels.

When I was invoked, I was kissed with an intentional darkness. One that would render me free from the dangers of the lower realms... and one that would also forbid me from entering the mightiest kingdoms. This "darkening" forced me to dwell alone. The more worlds that were created, the less my familiars would frequent my haunted domain. Much new work needed to be done. Many new confrontations required their immediate attention.

There soon came a time when many, yet lesser angels were summoned from their celestial wombs. Awakened into a new life by the hearkening of their old names. The four gates of the universe burst open, and soon a bright legion illuminated the heavens. Thousands of handfuls of dust were cast out into the infinite darkness as new worlds sprung up everywhere. Their forms were myriad. Some never took complete shape and they exploded from within releasing an immeasurable number of smaller "seed" planets.

Some life grew from the waters of Raphael's creation. Planets giving birth to greenery which lifted up and out of its heaving colossus. Liquefied rock was cast in the cooling seas as life grew from within the planet. Life was also deposited on various worlds, brought from other galaxies, other dimensions, and other universes.

"Here. Look at this new world!" Michael would point proudly as we flew over a forming orb.

"Behold." He lifted His mighty sword of Light and aimed it at the small planet below us. A wild brilliance shot out from its point, accompanied by timely thundering that shook the heavens and cracked open the darkness. Countless angels came out of the stargates and gathered to watch the incredible spectacle. They came from every corner of the universe and began forming a large circle around the planet. Their flapping wings created such a tempest that the seas rose up and roared. The ground swirled into writhing shapes as the globe began to levitate off of its axis and turn toward the West Gate, where it slowly settled into a tilted position. The glowing ring of angels then dispersed, dropping back into the mezzanine of space. There, they waited and watched as Gabriel beckoned at each of the four universal gates. First to the North Gate He hailed:

"Come forth all souls abandoned by your former worlds. Here is a new place awaiting your command!" He then flew to the Southern-most gate and cried,

"Come forth all my brethren empty of spirit! Here is a place where you might be replenished of promise."

The East Gate was next.

"Come forth all spirits in turmoil! Here is a place to mend your ragged wings and shine with the mightiest of us again."

And finally Gabriel hailed to the Western Gate:

"Come forth and touch this new existence! Be all reformed and remade from the dusts that we've collected from your former worlds upon their grand completion."

The spectral gates swung wide open and there-from issued a great legion of ragged souls. Some barely bright enough to be seen. Others too brilliant to behold. Some merely faint sparks dashing across the horizon like windblown embers. Their combined forms showered upon the new world and looked like a million stars falling from the darkness. Their resplendence rained into the seas, and over the land until the planet's surface glowed with what appeared to be, from this distance, a sea of dancing candle flames.

✠

This is a personified expression of how your world began. "A cipher of origin", Raziel likes to call it. Representative ciphers passed down into mortal minds by the angels. There are no intentional allusions to any other Earth chronicles. If certain images seem to vaguely overlap, it's simply because some of the angelic symbols are often universal in translation. This little orb that you call Earth is only your temporary home. It's really just a speck of dust in the proverbial "cosmic fold", but it's also quite a special place. Not just because you think so, but because upon this rather isolated globe, the spirit of my bride would complete our final incarnation.

It would take however, three previous Earthbound lives to gather all the necessary information and knowledge to afford enough wisdom to fulfill our final purpose to your world, in our fourth life, the one we are enduring now to bring this tale. We would go from being one entity, into two - and then back into one when this incarnation ends. It is no coincidence that the true turning of a "New Age" will coincide with our reunion.

THE NEW WORLD

Many lengthy intervals of time had passed but Earth was still fairly young, as planets go. The divine teachings were still fresh in the minds of lives that were settled there. They had learned well how to effectively apply universal laws and practice the angelic runes. We gave direct instruction to specific beings: Certain "elder" souls with strong ties to the Universal Soul.

Great societies were cultivated and introduced to "younger" spirits that kept coming from even more remote distances across the galaxy. The news of this new place traveled faster than we expected. It became a sign of hope to forlorn souls, and nourishment for the spiritually starving among us. Many of our kind ached for a new opportunity to add to our original purpose. Our consciousness was expanding with the growth of the universe, and as with all growth, comes change. Our original stations had to be updated and revised to accommodate the evolvement of our knowledge. The more we understood, the greater our yearning to be complete. For this reason, many angels took form and chose to dwell upon the new planet in the hope that this world may afford them the key to completion.

Some who had either lost or forsaken their old worlds through various reasons, found a home here. They were eager to try for a second chance at a meaningful existence, and a new challenge with which to put their accumulated wisdoms into action. What good is knowledge and wisdom if it can't be utilized?

Many of us were simply lonesome and greatly desired news of other dimensions and ardent interaction with the souls that brought it.

It wasn't long before impressive monoliths were lifted up out of the settling dust and erected as precise "temples". Here, at these charged locations, the most highly evolved souls (those older spirits who've been able to retain ancient lessons) could come and receive direct divine instruction regarding the building of the "New World".

As time continued, clearly defined and accurate aerial maps were painstakingly etched across the planet's surface so that other beings and energies traversing the galaxy would recognize the familiar markings of each distinctive crest. Following their intricate patterns would lead to vast colonies awaiting them with friendly welcomes.

✠

High upon the ancient thrones of Ursa Major we would sit beholding the facets of this newly forged jewel. Our work here was nearly complete, for now. It would soon be time for us to return into the three-fold infinity and allow the seeds that we had planted to evolve into even newer forms of life.

Israfel bid us farewell and returned to His complex orchestrations. Allowing for the additional spheres, He choreographed each new and colourful globe in time with the laborous compositions of the Universal Mind. More notes, as it were, were being added every day and constantly augmented by the transient spirits of dead planets. All of these facets had to be scored into the cosmic ballet for it to continue to play out smoothly.

Raphael and Uriel were already on their way back to "guarding" their respective gates. It's a difficult job restraining the furies that bulge forth from behind them. The energies that are attracted and repelled by the cosmic cycles, very much like two powerful and moving magnets that sometimes get too close to each other. It takes great talent to balance these vital forces.

Gabriel was following behind them, leaving a trail of green mist that spiraled higher and higher until it faded out of sight. "How marvelous!" He thought aloud. "The power of THE WORD on these mortal ears!" Gabriel seemed pleased with himself.

Michael was standing on Earth's highest peak. From its awkward loft, He gallantly hurled His flaming sword down into an anxious crowd below. A tower of fire shot up from the ground where it landed, point down in the soil. The onlookers gasped in awe and quickly gathered together, making a circle around the fiery needle.

"This is the flame of creation." Michael roared from the mountain. "From where this place came, it shall one day be returned, and like the phoenix from the world before, it'll rise again on another shore!" (Michael enjoys poetic endings.)

Raziel was below mingling with the people. He didn't join the circle, instead, He walked over to the sword and grasped it by its golden hilt, lifting it from the flame. The brilliance of the crystal blade projected out an image unfamiliar to most of the crowd. It was a star with seven points, each radiating out into infinite space. Raziel stood inside the image and declared;

"This is the most sacred of all seals that I do cast upon this place that all Her mysteries may work together as one." He did not offer any further explanations. With that, the smoky image melted and began to sink into the soils like acid burning its way right into the core of the planet.

Raziel then ascended from the throng, making gesture toward me as He passed.

"Go ye, my dark brother," He whispered, "and complete the seal." Slowly I began to emerge from the shadows.

"Look Him not straight on." Raziel cautioned the crowd firmly. "For surely thou wouldst swoon away!"

"Don't be afraid." I countered with gentility as I formed the shadows into a cloak. "I'll take no one from this place today. But I will return, for each of you, soon, and shall endow each with the knowledge that all will come to thirst for when your time is near. Only I can navigate the twisted river that divides this shore from the shores of the Eternal. Only I can recast your dust into the cosmic waters, and only I can lead you home again. Mine is the River of Forgetfulness and the River of Memory. I will wash you with new life, and old."

I opened my cloak of darkness and swept the huddled flock into my cool embrace.

"Know this, that you are all beloved," I whispered, "not only by my kinsmen, but by me as well! Come to know me..." I suggested kindly "...and you will never again fear my station".

"We must go now." Raziel called to me. His shrill voice shattering the moments' intimacy. I offered a parting gesture as the congregation fell back allowing me ample space within which to fully expand my wings and leap gracefully into the sky. My billowing form eclipsed the Sun as I passed in front of it. It made me appear even more like a black cut-out in the sky. Michael and Raziel haloed my ascending image, affording a backlit penumbra that cast a strange pallor on the faces below.

"Now they can more easily see your image," Michael said, as His aura glowed with brightness and warmth.

Our consecration of the planet was complete.

"Hail to this neophyte world!" Raziel concluded by tracing a symbol in the air.

All we could do now was back away and let Nature take its course.

STARGATES: A METAPHYSICAL LESSON

So many are the days of infinity that time is a non-existent force in the astral world. Thus, the very concept of it grows increasingly elusive with the aging of each soul, human as well as angelic. We can never really understand what it means to be subject to the whim of time. Nevertheless, as extremely empathetic spirits, many of us can easily experience the anguish that this barrier inflicts on the dwellers in the flesh. Especially in the waiting! The waiting for cognizance of purpose, for hope, guidance, divine love... and for Death.

If it wasn't for knowing how to use the stargates, we, too, would be subject to life in only one timeframe.

A stargate isn't really a place, nor is it a "thing". It's more of a space between dimensions within worlds - a threshold, if you will. They aren't always in the same place, location-wise. They are as transient as any other celestial formation.

There's more than one in your galaxy, yet less than eight in all. A stargate bows only to speed, sound, or light, and only at certain universal times and for specific affiliations. Occasionally it may appear stationary, but only for the most fleeting of moments.

The most prominent one in your solar system is the Orion Threshold, located generally within what you call the "belt". For those of you who reduce everything to mathematics, its numerical identity is 6.996.5. It has three pivotal points, or angles of deflection if you prefer. They are essentially "stars" comprised of subatomic materials invisible to human eyes.

Basically, this is how they work: as light from your Sun hits the first point, it is bounced off the second and onto the third where the purified beam is returned to point one. It looks something like this in configuration:

This causes a transformation of the space within the triangle, specifically within the centermost area, creating what we call "three-fold infinity" where all times and spaces are accessible simply by penetrating the center point at diverse speeds, angles and Solar moments. In plain speech, it's a doorway to all that was, is, and will be anywhere in the universe. All timeframes overlap in a stargate. This is how we are able to be many places at once or traverse great distances in what you would term, "the blink of an eye".

Earth-people are not yet ready to use the stargates. Too much needs doing on the planet first. Some of your people have however, trespassed, quite accidentally into the gates. You see, there are other doorways similar to stargates right on the surface of your own planet. These, too, are changeable. I'll tell you more about them later on.

Meanwhile, you first must realize that the universe is alive. It's actually a gigantic body with many cells and individualized energies. What you call "time" and "space" aren't simple influences. They've actually evolved a consciousness all their own. They are binary intelligences, joined together by a bridge of energy. The kind of psionic force that holds both the "great body" intact, and carries psychic emissions that link mankind with the Godsoul are one and the same. These charged links are made of energy from beyond the stargates which is absorbed within each cell until it's equated there. The power is then dispersed outward at a particular idea or thought-form off of which it's again reflected and refracted at the object that collects the energy and animates its purpose.

✠

The force that motivates mankind to evolve and the force that creates "miracles" uses the same power source at varying levels of focus and concentration. A practical result of this cosmic equation would be in finding the right combination of elements for actuating a bridge between time and space. And then we could all travel freely between dimensions. Time would no longer hold humanity back from bursting forth into the future - or the past, as need be. Two worlds could easily converge on the surface of Earth itself. And all souls could step in and out of many realities as easily as walking from one room into the next.

THE BEFORE TIME

Did you know that there exists an actual place before physical existence? A place where souls live prior to being incarnated into any flesh world. It isn't a bleak oblivion nor a formless void, but rather, a vast expanse of infinite diversity. A universe within a universe, so immense that its size is unimaginable. It's as varied as it is large, and in as many ways visually similar to the physical universe, and in as many ways, strikingly different.

In this astral world, all of man's rules are shattered. The Earthly laws of physics do not apply. The atmosphere is malleable and can be plied and molded into anything within the realm of individual conception. Thought creates everything here. It is a place conducive to the purest form of all direct creation. I think it, therefore it is!

There are places draped in total darkness, and places bordering them bathed in blinding, white light. The evidence of many worlds and many life-forms creates a contrast of the utmost awe.

My part of this world is an overcast region. A land of eternal afterglow. A supernal blending of amethyst and lampblack bathed in an eerie half-light. Mine is a beautifully cool and gentle valley where the shadows stand high like lofty sentinels. They preside over a lich-lit river whose haunted tranquility divides two distinct worlds. The ballad of the West wind plays a beautiful and constant requiem on the thin, twisted branches of silver trees. Their limbs appear sinuous and webbed as if striving to perform some difficult ballet.

I exist here alone. Where the lamp of the Will-o-wisp dances on the water and hollow eyes peer up from its crystalline depth. Although many pass this way, none belong. And even though I gather many spirits, none are mine to keep. The air here is enchantingly sweet with Jasmine Nocturne. There are fields of it as well as other exotic things which are equally as potent. Sometimes it becomes so quiet that the silence itself is deafening! The atmosphere frequently undulates with the combined rhythm of a million heartbeats struggling to maintain life's last moments. That shows how close my world lays to yours. It's actually a very narrow river that separates us. Still, it's wider than the space that divides the ancient world from that which is future.

So much of your past is your future. I wish I could make you understand this. The secrets locked in ancient history are necessary tools for the future. I can help you restore their power, and at the same time refresh your collective memory by retelling tales that have not found their way into Earth legend. I can see all times at once, therefore I know much of what was and what will be. As I speak to you now, the important keys will have long been lost in your world. Lost due to neglect, misinformation, false prophecies, and simple ignorance. So many vital cosmic doctrines and networks of power have crumbled thereby disrupting the natural currents of energy that serve both to maintain vital harmony between flesh and spirit (mankind and the Godsoul), and link present life with the "before time".

It is to assist you in this great reunion that I have chosen to speak with you now. It's no coincidence that the seeds of reconciliation with the universe are planted simultaneously with the rejoining of myself with my soulmate. I can't emphasize enough the importance of this concurrence. The revealing of our romance is our combined attempt to measurably further man's comprehension of Divine Love. By showing you a broader overview of your history, I hope you can get a fuller understanding of all things contained in it, including the relevance of our story.

Gentle reader, try to understand, I've dwelt solitary for too long, and it's drawing against my ability to perform in my station. I beseech your compassion, and your comprehension. The one I have put in your world must return to me soon with the certain knowledge that our purpose here is done. I will not allow "her" to be taken from me again.

In the flesh she must draw strength and purpose from me, and I must also draw life and love from her. Therefore, we grow weak as a whole, and the closer we come to closing the circle of reunion, the less we can afford such weakness. Each day we require more and more strength to push against the polarities that try to keep us apart. These are the same forces that divided the dwellers in the flesh from the Godsoul. Our continuance must come from somewhere. I'm hoping that it comes from the faith of all Keepers of our Legend.

Death's Reflection

Realizing a form out of thought
I am comprised of the dust
He has shaped around this soul we share.

I am the reflection of His spirit,
Made solid by the power of His love.
A sculpture fashioned through many incarnations
That came to life one night
When the lightning kissed its lips
And the dust rose up
And gathered around this form
Sealing its wings within the clay.

Molded in His gentle hand
And fired in the kilns of hell,
I am made of Him
So that I could withstand
Both worlds
And not waver
In the presence of the shadow
That our purpose casts Upon all living things.

Part 3

The Ballad of Nahaliel

> *Running to, running from.*
> *In His shadow, I've become*
> *Both blinded and embraced the same*
> *By His darkness and His flame!*

omeone recently asked me if I'd be willing to die for what I believe in. I answered by telling him that I've died many times before, for the very same beliefs, and that this time would at least be the most purposeful death of any. After all, Death is my lover, I told him, rather smugly. And if it must be that I relinquish this life, I would comply by willingly laying my body aside like a worn overcoat and falling unbridled into Azrael's lovingly cool embrace.

Here in this garden of stone, beneath the painterly colours of day's end, nature is the catalyst that transmutes shadow into form. The darkening sky is a celestial alchemist, sculpting a Philosopher's stone into this grand and fantastic marble sentinel that stares out soulfully over the lesser cherubs in its keep. Its ancient hand reaches out like a brooding metaphor, soliciting to any who would dare accept its fatal touch. The angel peers down at me with dark eyes that seem to search my spirit for reason. The mysteries of life and death contort its stoic face, and at the same time extol a gentleness on its silent lips.

This stone effigy is my counsel in this Earthly life. It oversees the very wording of this story. Marble wings thunder in my imagination, and black weatherworn stains spill from the sad, lonely eyes. I am spellbound by this weird image, and haunted by this electric, grey place. The lilting whispers of unseen ghosts in tune with the mild breeze as it plays upon the tree-limbs like a subtle rhapsody in D minor. The strange melody is an ever constant backdrop to "our" legend. Exaggerated spectres of twilight shadow gather closely around me as I enter the words you are reading now.

I often come to places like this. Not only to write, but to draw nourishment from a familiar welcome that only makes me feel more homesick for the life I had in "the valley of the shadow". A hush more loud than death fills my head. There is joy here in this field of crooked stones. An excitement that baffles the normal psyche. I can feel my Dark Angel's loving hand and His cold kiss set softly on my lips as if to say, "Thank you for wanting to tell my story".

The sunken grave becomes like a warm bed beneath the statue's spreading shadow. The night will soon consume us both in dream and recollection.

Gentle reader, it is on this lampblack canvas that I can trace electric visions and animate them for you. My story will breathe life into the dead. From this garden of stone, a fatal yet loving hand extends out to you. We are proof that love can survive the grave. Our souls are evidence of this eternal Truth.

HER STORY

It is now April of 1987 and I've been tiptoeing around this book for over fifteen years, not knowing whether the world was ready to hear from Death. Let alone believe in the personification of this ultimate and final "taboo". Little did I know, that whether the world was ready or not was irrelevant, as He would speak anyway. And had been doing so through me for as long as I can remember. (Those of you familiar with my past work, will have no trouble agreeing with this.)

✠

At this point in my life, I no longer struggle with trying to make others believe in Him. I've grown too comfortably complacent with the cliché, "Truth is indeed, stranger than fiction".

I'm not going to dwell on furnishing caches of historical reference to His existence. A bibliography is provided for those of you seeking further confirmation, along with a brief dissertation of personification, in general.

His truth was pushing through me long before I was ready to acknowledge or understand what was happening, or who "we" were. And quite honestly, when this realization was finally made, I was unsure of my own ability to effectively express His words when I was growing all too close to Him to remain a truly, objective vehicle.

Lately, I often wonder where His consciousness stops and mine begins. This is how unified our thoughts have become.

"So, then," He tells me, "We shall speak... as One! Jointly formulate the emotions and transform them into words stretching language to the farthest reaches of each words' definition."

I am called Na'Haliel, an earthly equivalent to the expression of my spiritual name. I live among you, as one of you. This isn't the first lifetime I've had on Earth, in fact, it's my fourth! And thankfully, my last.

My present physical incarnation doesn't really lend itself to revealing my identity. My stature isn't imposing, nor is my countenance striking. Neither does the depth of my gaze lend itself to madness, as His can easily do. Still, when you first meet me, you may not be awe-struck, simply haunted by an indescribable paradox. Something "different" stands before you but you can't quite grasp exactly what it is that's unique.

Most people experience a queer unease in my presence. I don't respond in the usual way to suggestions or concepts. I've genuine difficulty fathoming the often trivial things that are regarded with great importance. For instance, I draw no pleasure from the touching of warm flesh, nor do I appreciate the weird mystique surrounding physical attraction. Other than providing more bodies for souls seeking incarnation, what can possibly be gained by the simple pressing of dust against dust? How, I wonder, do those who practice this bizarre "lovemaking" expect to express their love when they're in spirit form? What will they do without their precious bodies to clothe their "nakedness"?

It seems to us that in the physical world, so much valuable energy is expended on the futility of matter. It's no wonder mankind hasn't yet risen from the worship of his tangibles.

✠

Call me "Lady Death," everyone else does. It's a moniker I picked up working in the morgue. Actually, it's an alias that I've grown quite fond of.

I live inside the shadows of life and only frequent certain daylight hours because I must. The reclusive life appeals to me, although this chronicle deems it an ironic impossibility.

I've got precious little in common with other flesh dwellers except that I reluctantly seem to be one of them. I've lived among you for these many years, in many forms, for many reasons. May you never have to know what it feels like being an ancient spirit forced into the meager confines of the flesh. May you never have cognizance of such torment! It's such a severely, limited prison. Especially when your mind retains the images of being a truly free spirit. I am the half-life of a greater union, with clear recollection of being torn from a peaceful realm and pushed into this world to teach a class that few will attend, and even less understand, at least in this lifetime.

My life is one of extreme frustration and private madness: By no means a contented way to live, however necessary. The transformations involved require much personal torment and sacrifice. Many basic human instincts go against who and what I grew to become.

The primary instinct of survival was the first thing to go. I grew away from the common light, toward a brilliance that many couldn't see. I didn't blossom with familiar passions, needs or desires. Energies that would've normally been expended physically, were turned in, toward more spiritual pursuits. My sunlight was more distant, harder to feel. My soul would reach out while my body would pull away. I viewed the flesh as my enemy: one that had to be defeated, and eventually overcome by its astral counterpart. It mustn't enjoy "pleasures" better reserved for the soul. My flesh is expendable. I live with the continued understanding that I can be "withdrawn" from this world at any moment. I've waited for this as one does for a lover returning from a thousand year war. I often think, perhaps, He wouldn't just come and take me. Instead, He might call to me and expect me to find a way to free my own soul from this shackled life. Moreover, it is possible that I may be asked to sacrifice my own life as final proof of love for Him.

Everyday is a testing. Each new life afforded me the ability to revoke my legacy. Every time we're reborn, we are each given the chance to revise our destiny. The Angel of Death knew this. And He'd watch me be continually tempted by the immediate delights that the physical world offers. He couldn't prevent my choices nor alter my decisions. He could only observe, and hope that my love for Him would be strong enough to override generations of human instinct.

When the inner metamorphosis began, it was a subconscious process that caused a domino effect on both the spiritual and physical levels. Gently peeling away the thick skin that covered my memory of other lives and exposing the skeleton on which its truth was built.

The idea that we were not two separate beings but one entity exploded into my reality like a bomb. How was I to deal with this fact? What do I do with this knowledge? How do I live the life of a paradox? What do I do now?

As the revealing progressed, I began to recoup some sanity by discovering that even though I am essentially a part of Azrael's soul, we still maintain some segregated consciousness. In other words, even though we are true "soulmates", and two halves of a mighty One, we do have individual minds.

I am His voice in this world and I translate His message into language, albeit inadequate, it's all I've got to work with. More often I'm transliterating his complex emotions and symbolic gestures from arcane hieroglyphics into everyday English. You will learn that angels don't really speak as we understand speech and semantics. Rather, they elicit thoughts and thought-forms from mind to mind using a highly evolved telepathic code of images, sensations and emotions. Each person's psyche deciphers these images uniquely, depending on his or her relation to its significance in the "Great Plan".

It's a complicated task, condensing such demonstrative passions into blasé diction. I require a more intense language with which to work. A dialect wherein the mention of a simple word would immediately conjure that image into life. A tongue that would, in effect, personify itself. Each colourful sentence creating its meaning. Breathing life into an image no matter how fantastic, and animating the vision like a total sensory hologram. But all I have is words on a page. I'll try my best to stretch their imagery and make you "feel".

To simply say that I love the Angel of Death, is at best, a paltry understatement. But what more mighty word have I to offer, other than love? I do love Him, ever so deeply, and with a rapture whose comprehension is above any spoken or written word. It is a love beyond the reaches of such inferior powers as Time and Space. It's an ancient romance that promises ecstasy, yet too often delivers despair. Our love is a legend, recalled in a tear, a mythical voice that sighs in the night with poignant yearning. When we reach out for each other across the bridge of time, it's the "Life-force" that often keeps us from touching. So many worlds cry out, that our world frequently goes untended. When we are able to find one another across the "great divide", He enters my spirit and we actually do become one being. Our love is then consummated in an astral orgasm that is far beyond Earthly description. Ours is a union that's both absolute and divine. And if I only knew how many steps between the walls of the universe there are contained in a thousand journeys there, only then could I ever begin, in words, to tell you how much I love Him.

✠

In His varied appearances, it's the more traditional personification that I confess to prefer. I'm sure you know the one.

Perhaps it's the grandeur of the awe He inspires looking as He does, like the winged darkness with a brooding splendour. Or His electric glance, like a bottomless amethyst backlit by a coruscating lamplight. This resplendence is both His macabre grace and majesty.

When you first behold His spectacle, you can't help but fall to your knees appalled by His beauty. Your psyche has no choice but to remain speechless there until His skeleton-like hand bids welcome. He is so dreadfully beautiful that the human mind cannot easily reconcile the power of His image. Hence, it often goes black in attempting to comprehend the vision before it.

Because it's often so very long between our times together, we must constantly draw upon a seemingly bottomless well of stored moments, in order to sustain the flame our soul requires for basic existence and nourishment in this isolated world. Ours is a symbiotic love. Each relying on the other for energy and strength, as well as inner peace, the hardest of all to maintain. I can't tell you how many times my "well" has been dangerously empty. On many occasions my passionate offerings exceed reciprocation. Or we would be too far "out of synch" to commune on a spiritual level. Sometimes, it's as if there's a stone wall pressed up between us. Each clinging to it, hearing the cries of the other, yet both unable to penetrate it even with the most powerful weapon in our trust; our love! It would seem that even mighty angels have certain limitations.

Nevertheless, He always manages to find some small or esoteric way of eventually reaching me so as to let me know that He does feel my residual love. Communiqués are found in even the most coincidental things. A specific song dominating a radio dial. Strangers approaching me with the most uncanny statements. Books and other literature with related themes literally falling into my hands. Children that can barely speak, casually tossing out mind-boggling announcements. And more of this kind of "communication", usually through others.

✠

The Angel of Death is an uncommon lover. Impassioned with a gentle fury that surpasses anything that the physical realm has to offer. He is a spiritual lover, and nothing that humanity equates with intimacy can be measured against the boundless limits of a Divine Romance. He doesn't touch me in the way that you understand "touch" yet He embraces me completely. The kiss of Death is not the futile pressing of flesh, but rather the sensation of two spirits coming into a powerful alignment by sharing the awesome energy of an ancient bonding, such as ours.

He is mine, and mine alone in this way. We desire no other. We are soulmates bound together by an eternal trust. There exists no force in the universe, any universe that could break this invincible troth. It's already endured the horrors of many lifetimes. But I would still suffer the torment of a hundred hellish nightmares to save Him from shedding but one tear. I would as willingly cut the still beating heart from my breast, and offer Him my last life if it would in any more validate my love... and He knows that.

Melodramatic? Of course it is. But true. All He need do is reach out for me and I'd take His hand and never let go, not ever.

And you, gentle reader, could espy our legend going down like the velveteen curtain on a Wagnerian crescendo. Our fading forms are backed by a gallant and grand finale churned up out of the deep throat of a musty pipe organ. Our romance is a metaphoric feast for the purple pen! So, if I wax a trifle florid now and then, just bear with me, I never promised I'd be objective in this telling. Besides, don't all lovers strive for the most flamboyant and descriptive adjectives? A purple pen is certainly the natural complimentary to the lampblack image I'm evoking in this tale.

This book isn't written to please the literary establishment. It's written because the Angel of Death and I desire to share our story with you.

Our romance will not end with the death of my flesh. Quite the contrary. It blossoms eternal in the afterlife. Truthfully, the flesh stands in the way of our complete reunion. Albeit the vehicle of my purpose here, I still long to escape this elastic cage. I cry out for us both. I AM A FREE SPIRIT encased in a lead shell! My wings are painfully bound by blood and bone, while my spirit is tethered to this Earth by a tangled web of the Godsoul's weaving. Our plea is neither seeking, nor requiring your sympathy. We solicit only for your understanding. I am not born of this world, nor are you for that matter! Only human flesh be made of its elements.

It was long before I was ever incarnated into any physical existence that I was "betrothed" to Azrael - "Isaro El" in the ancient tongue of the first world. It means, "the promised one". Originally, we were completely one being. Soulmates, as I've indicated, but in the fullest sense of the word. Even now, our spirits continue to vibrate to one chord. We still harness one energy, and one overall purpose. We can never be separated completely in two.

✠

"Till death do us part." A rather bleak forecast for human love, wouldn't you agree? No wonder people tend to fear dying. Is this unfortunate lie the reason humans opt for physical closeness rather than spiritual rapture? Well, it certainly fosters the temporary attitude towards earthly love. There is no truth to this lie that the grave divides true, spiritually attached lovers. And nothing can divide soulmates. There is no parting in death for those who are capable of experiencing their love in spiritual terms only. And, being in the flesh has no bearing on such an eternal romance. This kind of bonding supersedes the physical deceptions so often mistaken for true emotion by incarnate beings. Here's the real problem: human consummation of love originates in the flesh, and may, at best, slightly stimulate the surface of spiritual awareness. Whereas the love between "soulmates" is consummated completely on the spiritual level with only faint traces welling up into the flesh. We do not require physical bodies to experience each other's love!

It took me quite a while to understand that. In fact, I've come to realize that we are gravely limited by the flesh as to just how deep our expression of love can go. And, that the body actually hinders the ability of soulmates to spiritually unite. It's like making love while wearing suits of armor.

✠

In the time before our individualities were extracted, we were a completed entity; a unified consciousness that had never yet experienced the kind of separation that physical incarnation would later force upon us. We were the quintessential lovers. And even now, so much a part of the tangible world, our souls are still interacting on a level incomprehensible to flesh beings. We are still One, and remain One at all times: even when there's no direct flow of images or emotions between us. We're very much like two sides of the same coin.

When He's "inside" me it feels as if I'm intoxicated by a strange opiate; as if my body floats weightless between worlds. As I begin to share His visions, everything around me seems to crystallize, and I get the sensation that I'm moving in slow motion and everything around me is accelerating into another dimension. Physical functions become anesthetized. Metabolism and heart rates slow down to near death-like levels, (very similar to the altered states achieved in higher astral travel). The blood coursing through my veins has a cold and tingly sensation, as body temperature lowers considerably. Many times I've actually died for a space of time that appeared much longer than the tarry of moments that elapsed in reality. Hours can be spent in His realm while being gone from this life for but a moment.

There were many times before I fully grasped the importance of my life and purpose in general, when I tried, (thankfully in vain), to permanently flee this unwanted life and return home, to the "valley of the shadow". I've always been alien to this place anyway. Always attempting to rush the reason for my flesh existence. This is, no doubt, why I'm here again. Impatience got the better of me too often.

When I was younger, all that I understood was that I loved the Angel of Death and would do anything for my want to be with Him. Yea! My need to be with Him! I certainly didn't want LIFE standing in my way. It had no right to keep me where I didn't want to be. No right at all.

Days were spent inventing romantic ways to return to Him, plotting exact times and penning elaborate, explanatory farewells. I confess that I made a few genuine attempts, that were either staid by a stronger hand, or interrupted by the ever present "Voice of Wisdom". Actually, it was quite annoying. I'd even gone so far as to coerce an old compatriot (who you'll meet later on) into nearly performing an "act of mercy" by appointing him as a kind of sacred executioner. But happily, he was too smart for that. He knew even before I did that I had to continue on in this life so that this story could be told to you now. The impatience of youth didn't, however, allow me this same far vision. It only recognized the immediate and desired no knowledge of a "Greater Purpose". It understood want only, and it had to learn real need.

It's out of this early ignorance that a twisted madness emerged. I began to truthfully despise life and envy those on the brink of the ultimate journey. I'd do anything to be with my lover. Hence, I grew attached to the things that resembled, channeled, or reminded me of Death. Even the dead eventually became catalysts through which we could communicate our affections.

*Actually, astral travel and death are similar excursions. Both result in almost identical physical and spiritual symptoms.

AN ARIES IN THE AGE OF AQUARIUS

Perhaps it would be best, at this point, to pull some vivid examples of our courtship out of my younger days. They will help to show how we became reacquainted in the twentieth century.

Without wanting this chronicle to become solely a one-sided biography of my earthly life, I will therefore steer away from the usual background information, and instead, extract the most pertinent excerpts of time as they pertain to the broader purpose of "our" story.

I will offer you this much, however. I was slipped quietly into this world in the 1950's. (But I much prefer to consider myself a child of the '60's.) I couldn't have chosen a more perfect time if I had the choice myself. I was thirteen when Woodstock happened. A blooming "flower child" who wished she was just a bit older so that she could've participated more fully in the "revolution". I had an early love affair with acid rock that still remains a comfortable romance. I was particularly fond of Black Sabbath. The original Black Sabbath, with Ozzy Osbourne. Their songs conjured familiar images and haunting truths with a powerful melancholy that afforded me an uneasy peace. Maybe it's the fact that they were also grossly misunderstood souls. Too quickly condemned for the way they said things, rather than what they were saying. I don't think their critics ever really listened to what it was they were trying to say. Nor dared to perceive the truths veiled in these tortured, young voices. We had in common, the fact that our difference, and our "darkness" was too overwhelming for their ignorance. Too fearsome to be addressed openly. Their music was too much like the Grim Reaper's symphony, or how they thought the songs of Death would sound.

✠

Even as a very, young child, I was haunted by random images: Things that weren't completely erased from my memory before coming into this life. Because of this, I found myself truly afraid of the embodiment of my own, essential reflection. The familiar image of a personified Death wasn't retained in my mind, and when I first saw Him, His appearance genuinely frightened me. The idea that Death was able to have a form, was something quite incomprehensible to me in those days.

I think now just how that bad reaction must have shocked and grieved Him. Why had I been allowed to retain some visions, and not others?

Back then, I remember cowering beneath His descending blackness, and trembling at the thought of his impending touch. Covering my face with the bedclothes, and praying that the grotesque vision would just go away. How, I ask, could He expect a child's mind to reason without a memory from which to reference? I suppose that's the excuse I offer now as a belated apology to Him, and to justify to myself having to abide the ignorance of childhood. But I guess this wiping clean is necessary to the sanity of all souls who enter this life. If we were all just thrust from one incarnation into another as adults, we'd soon be a race of inconsolable lunatics! As a result, we'd be unable to fulfill the purpose of any particular embodiment.

Still, try to picture yourself as a four-year old child, alone in a dark bedroom, in the middle of the night. You have no recall of any other life except the immediate present. All of your knowledge up till now is drawn from the world around you. You hear a cold wind howling in the eaves. You imagine the sound of a laughing demon. A jaundiced streetlight peers in from the Venetian blind's rippled edge. I remember how it beamed up at the small, ceiling hatch that led to the attic crawlspace. As it rattled on its narrow track, the light was just enough to provide a spooky focal point.

The first time I heard the noise was on a windy September night. I couldn't really determine if the sound was coming from "up there", or from the tree limbs tapping on the eaves outside my window. I would literally fall asleep watching that hatch and wake up in the morning with a relieved sense of satisfaction for having survived another bedtime.

It didn't stop there, however. There was a second, third and fourth time when there was no wind. No logical reason for the thing to be chattering up and clown. No reason at all why I was always the only one awake long enough to hear this.

It took some doing, but finally, I did succeed in securing a small night-light, hoping it would draw attention away from the streetlamps pointed glare. Still, the blanket ended up over my head in a matter of minutes.

That was it. Enough, I thought to myself. Something had to be done. I couldn't play the "brave little girl" any longer. I had to get help if I was ever to sleep peacefully again.

"It's just your imagination, honey," my mother would tell me in a gentle and patronizing voice. "Just turn over and go to sleep," she'd suggest, dismissing my sincerity as a plea for attention.

My mother was an affectionate yet haunted woman. And even though she made light of my childhood visions, she did have that inherently maternal way of easing my fears. She also had the ability to word even the most fantastic explanations in a manner that would satisfy an overly precocious child's curiosity. She was intelligent, gentle and loving. As time would later show, even she would be touched by past life visions. So much so, that she'd "disappear" into them for hours.

"Please!" I'd then appeal to my father, "You gotta believe me!" He'd yawn and then smile, causally announcing that he'd "see what could be done". I could tell, even then, that he didn't believe me. It didn't matter so much though as long as he'd simply allay my tantrum in some visible fashion.

My father was a staunch realist. (Note that I use the past tense.) In those days, anything that couldn't be put neatly into established categories just didn't exist, no matter how true their realities. He refused to find a place for them in his life. My dad's love was expressed differently from moms. While she was openly affectionate and serene in her reasoning, my Dad's affection was cautious and contingent on surrounding elements. He was often too busy "killing himself to live" to share in the early unfolding of my romance with Death.

"It might be mice," I recall him reasoning logically under the intensity of my protest. "I'll put some traps up there tomorrow and that should be the end of that." I could tell he was tiring of my "tantrum".

But - there weren't any "mice" up there. Nothing was ever caught in the traps. The tremor stopped for a while - but never for very long.

It was a couple of days before Christmas, as I lay in bed and listened, and waited... and it started again. This time I felt oddly more frightened than ever.

It began to rattle and chatter with such a frenzy that it flung itself open just enough to really scare the hell out of me. I may've been only four years old, still I knew enough to figure out that no "mouse" I'd ever seen could hoist a 2'x3' piece of wood. I tried to scream but only a faint shriek reached my lips. No one else heard a thing. I couldn't understand this. My parents' bedroom was just outside mine. How come they never heard this? Why didn't anyone ever come to comfort me?

"Help me!" I began to cry in a low whimper. I could see a slice of that black void opening up and the white-washed door disappearing into it. The blanket was already up around my mouth. Terror had frozen any further movement. I tried again to call out, but hadn't the strength to project any sound.

The semblance of a hand became visible clutching the molding of the attic entrance, and then another grasped onto the ceiling lamp. The shapes were long and thin like grey skeletons gloved tightly in a glowing, gossamer "skin". I closed my eyes but some thing opened them again, forcing me to watch the eerie apparition! I struggled to catch a breath beneath the shaking blanket. Suddenly, the door lunged fully open. A black form began to descend head first, defying gravity and simply floating downward while turning gracefully in mid-air into an erect position. Its feet never touched the carpet as it glided toward my doorway. Still too panicked to move or speak, I quietly and slowly managed to yank the covers over my face and turn gradually away from It towards the wall. I could feel It coming into the room; feel my tiny heart exploding in my chest! I was certain that at any moment The Thing would descend on me like some hideous monster straight out of childhood nightmares! Something touched the blanket… and my mind exploded into darkness.

I remember nothing more except waking the next morning. I could discern nothing past the point of my bed being touched, and the sensation of something sitting down beside me.

I was, however, never afraid of that doorway again. Still to this day, I don't know what transpired that night to quell my fears, but they were washed from my mind as if they never existed.

Even though that image is still vivid, as I think about it now, my views are ambivalent regarding the event's purpose at such an early stage in my life. On one hand, I feel that I should be sort of repentant for my lack (no matter how innocent) of basic recognition of one who is so close to me. I kept this guilt inside me for a long time. Why must it be that so much memory needs to be taken from spirits incarnating into this world? With that part of my recollection intact, I'd never have reacted the way I did. On the other hand, as I've said, no soul could truly survive here with complete recall of the astral world. We'd all go insane with the simple knowing of things. A world of haunted souls whose curse would be in knowing their length of incarceration in the physical realm. We'd be able to see the "way out" yet unable to pursue it because of the paradox this creates. The spiritual world can't be penetrated in a physical body. And one who has lived beyond the barriers of death couldn't easily survive here plagued by visions that haven't any truth in this world. Therefore, we each must return with a "clean slate", so to speak.

Maybe He just wanted to see for Himself the effect of being washed in His river, or simply to confirm that its supernal waters did a good job in keeping me from being too haunted, too early.

☩

As I got older, more and more visions of other worlds and other lives began to invade my psyche. More and more I was finding pleasure and comfort in things that repelled other people. I felt welcomed in places that others only frequented either out of disparate need, or grievous duty. I started to explore graveyards or any similar locale where I could feel close to the dark spectre that flirted with my sanity. I still had no idea who or what this being was. I was only learning where to find him. The concept of "death" was still inconceivable, and abstract to my young mind.

My early love for poetry came to be very useful in the keeping of a versified record of my encounters and visions, specifically instances of an intimately symbolic nature.

From that earliest contact to the next, seven years would elapse. Even though I hadn't seen His figure during that time, I knew that He came to me, veiled in disguises of a less imposing sort.

I can remember spending hours in the woods adjacent to my house in the company of a mysterious old man dressed in a shining black and purple robe. I vaguely recall his face, framed in a profusion of white hair that had a wild, windblown appearance. We would walk hand in hand, deep into the trees and he'd talk of things above my understanding with a patient affection. We'd sit together on a fallen oak behind the ruins of an abandoned house and just talk about things I can't even recall. With his long fingers, he'd trace strange designs in the sand, occasionally pointing up to the sky, and then referring back to the ground.

Everywhere I looked I saw apparitions of things that were, and shadowy glimpses of those yet to be. Everything and every time did, indeed, exist simultaneously. Eventually, I found that I could pick out specific scenes as easily as choosing a book from a library shelf. Pictures flash in my mind even now, and then transmute themselves instantly into something else. My concentration is spread between many images at once as if I'm sharing the thoughts and dreams of a small multitude. My life is played out in the fashion of this telling, jumbled and frenetic.

The first real indication of His affections for me came rather bizarrely when I was eleven years old. What began as an innocent flight of imagination, progressed into my first conscious astral projection.

One afternoon, I was lying prone on the carpet in my sunlit bedroom. Pen and paper in hand, I was pursuing my new-found love of writing poetry. My youthful imagination mentally conjuring a fantasy with which to delve into this harmless pursuit. As I began to write, my mind went deeper and deeper into a lucid trance state. My innocent imagination was suddenly taking me on an unsuspecting voyage. The yellow bedroom walls dissolved around me into a summer landscape of grassy knolls and shallow valleys. I found myself lying on a hill-top grave. Pen and paper still before me, I remained curiously at ease with my new surroundings and casually continued penning my awkward rhyme. There was a strange serenity that seemed to inspire me with peculiar emotions. I was moved into a level of feeling that was pleasant, yet sad. I didn't understand the emotions, nor the poem unfolding before me. My inspired ballad of young love had unwittingly digressed into an elegy for a dead lover. A Romeo and Juliet type of tale, but with a macabre twist. If my memory serves - in its final lines, the remaining lover placed "a bough of daisies" on the other's grave and lay down upon it. The dead paramour would "kiss" her by "making the daisies grow into a blanket" that would "wrap around her with a sleep so deep".

These words from an 11 year old child.

When the last word was written, the scene slowly reverted back into the familiar trappings of my room.

My affection for the power of verse grew tremendously from this weird experience. Somehow I believed (at times, still do) that there was a magic in the creation of poetry that could literally transport the writer into the scene at hand. And not simply into an inspired fantasy, but an often tangible type of parallel reality. I could actually touch some of the things I created. This was one of the first things the angels would later teach me about the power of thought, and how easily its energy can generate things.

After that incident, more and more of my literary excursions reflected similar themes. I hadn't any idea where all these images were coming from. I didn't really think anything unusual of them. I felt no need to share nor discuss them with others, believing that these feelings were just another, natural part of growing up. How was I to think any different? From what could I reference?

Even an early "normal " romantic infatuation manifested itself in a necrophilic fantasy.

At the interesting age of thirteen, I fell into a school-girl crush with a much older acquaintance, someone as "old," I believe, as 21. Every time I'd fantasize or daydream, the imaginary romance would display itself through an involuntary vision of his body lying dead inside a coffin beside my bed. In my dreams I'd climb into the narrow, wooden box and lie there contented by his side. Just lie there, nothing "else".

At this age, I still thought virtually nothing of these desires. I didn't lead a very outgoing life where I'd be surrounded by many others of my age who'd share such personal thoughts openly. I was a loner, and my passions were private - as I believed everyone's should be. Not the sort of thing for public discussion. Especially considering the unrelenting grapevine that teenagers are constantly weaving into a web on which they often "hang" their peers. Even those with so-called "normal" feelings soon discovered that keeping silence got you through the "brutal years".

Because I never got close enough with my familiars at this age, I still maintained the belief that everyone, at one time or another, experienced the things that I experienced, and like me, just didn't talk about them. Therefore, I didn't give their deeper meanings much thought then. I never knew there were any deeper meanings. They felt good! They were pleasant feelings, and their images were a comforting part of my life for as "long" as I could remember. I didn't require outside friends. I had my own "friends" and I could identify more with their world, rather than this one.

Little by little, everything I did, everywhere I went, and especially, in my moments of solitude, I was constantly shadowed by an imposing darkness. I could literally feel a protective overcast hovering around me like a gigantic black cloak. At times I got the distinct impression that this darkness would swallow any who'd try to harm me. This entity didn't "converse" with me, not on the level we'd grow to achieve in later years. He'd merely observe, dropping sporadic clues and eldritch messages of love. Now and then He'd draw me into a formless embrace

But even stranger things were beginning to occur. Things that defied the most abstract logic. Bits and pieces of which I slowly started to give away - trying to find out, if indeed, others did have similar happenings. I had witnessed enough of other people's lives to begin to seriously wonder why mine seemed so different.

I wondered even more about the identity of my "protector". All I had to go on thus far was what I'd seen, and what I'd felt. Sharing my experiences with others in a piece meal fashion, led me to embark on a research project that seemed endless - and impossible. Where would I begin? All I had to work with was either too ancient to be verified, or the conjecture of others who've never had similar experiences! Was He what the "books of knowledge" told me He was? And if so, which book was correct? About the only thing they could agree on, was the general description I saw when I was younger. But that still didn't tell me all I wanted to know.

✠

Early one Saturday morning, at the age of fifteen, I was suddenly awakened by the sensation of something being poured into my mouth. It was like I was drowning in a sweet and salty ocean. Blood was spilling down from an invisible source in the ceiling!

I couldn't swallow it fast enough, and it began to overflow onto the bed-sheets, and then onto the grass-coloured carpet. Soon, the whole bed was drenched in blood! I sat up with a start. The sweet liquid gathered in glowing puddles in the creases of the bed-sheets. It had a peculiar, phosphorescent quality that when touched, felt like quicksilver, cold and dry! Its red colour began fading into a pearlescent ectoplasm. It looked like liquid light as it streamed down the sides of the bed, onto the floor - and finally dissipated into a fragile scintilla that sunk into the thick shag nap.

I felt refreshed! As if I'd been infused with dynamic energy. The taste of blood still lingered, but no evidence of its stain remained on the sheets, nor anywhere on my body. I felt electrified. My spirit felt like a white, hot flame. Like a vampire after drinking the blood of the gods! I believe now, that I drank the Life-force of an angel. With this spiritual liquid, I was washed, as if in His river. Washed with visions and memories that were carried on its cool current as their emotions flooded into my body and soul like a fierce tidal wave. So many images filled my mind. So many questions found an answer in this bath of knowledge. I'd spent my first "moment in eternity" and for that time, my mind could access all universal thought. "I am the Angel of Death!" a voice echoed loudly in my mind. "I have not come to complicate your life. I have come to show you who you are!" In some way, I was baptized with His divine purpose and had partaken of an enlightened strength that served to more or less formalize my spiritual attainment. A ceremonial initiation for the stranger times yet to come.

One evening, later that same year, I felt His dark spirit hovering over me. I recall lying still, anticipating His touch. Then He'd come closer. I'd feel the fan of His wings as He'd reach down and lift me into His electric embrace, pressing what felt like cold lips to my throat. He'd drink deeply of my life-force with a gentle fury that brought me to the very brink of death. More visions and images would confirm to support the assertion of identity.

These visits grew more impassioned each time. His vampire thirst would leave me drained for days. My life balanced precariously on the edge of some divinely sensual abyss. The encounters would leave me with a kind of high that had me teetering on the edge of sanity with macabre pleasure.

When next He'd return, He'd replenish my well with twice the energy He took from me. These intimate exchanges were important to renewing our love in this life. Vital infusions of each other's soul that reconnected us to our past lives. Re-establishing who and what we were to each other. We'd soar from the mountains of the Moon to the seas of infinity each time our spirits' would intermingle in this dark romance. I didn't need any books to tell me who He was. I could learn this directly from the "source", directly from our combined memory.

Sometimes my psyche would be so overwhelmed by the things I'd see in His vision, the rapid-fire images flashing in my mind would overlap and distort their significance. Once, I woke up with the sensation of a hand clenched around my heart. I knew Death was trying to still its beat by squeezing the life from it.

"Ever shall the song of Life be silent in my presence," I'd hear Him articulate with solemnity. And the beating would stop... and I'd look down and envision His bony hand as a large black spider with its legs embedded in my chest, as if it was reaching for my heart. Then the queer spell would be shaken from my body, and the scene would again dissolve into something completely different.

My ability to reason was compromised more than once. Little by little, regaining memory of my past lives with Him made me even more disturbed. His way of loving me was not at all like what I saw in the outside world. I slowly began to realize that our passions were certainly not normal. Other folks couldn't feel what I felt, and couldn't grasp the range of emotion trapped in this teenage heart.

At this point, I really needed to share these overflowing images with someone, anyone, just so that I wouldn't be drowned in their delirium. I couldn't keep this inside any longer. I had to have a witness to the madness. An outside mediator, or someone who could help me to know, for certain, if it was all real or simply some kind of elaborate illusion.

The more hints I threw out, the less others seemed to understand. To the outside world my visions were cast off all too easily as the ramblings of some troubled teenager, a "phase" that would pass away as quickly as a summer storm when the difficult years were over.

The world tried to pull me away from Him. Tried to tell me that what I felt was "wrong, unnatural, imaginary". Some even tried to convince me that my "imaginary" lover was "evil", and that I was prey to some hellish incubus that came to me in the night for the purpose of "stealing my soul".

I grew confused, sad, and deeply troubled. My dark angel would call to me, and I'd hold back. His summons grew more intense, and I'd break down in tears.

"I do love you," I'd whisper in the darkness.

"Then come to me," He'd implore wistfully.

I must now admit, in those days my love for Him was stronger than my faith in any "Godsoul". After so many years of listening to unenlightened people tell me He was "evil" just because of His darkness. It came to a point where I said to myself, I don't care anymore. Then I shall be by His side in Hell!

So, I chose midnight and solitude for my "friends" and listened only to them. Through this pure and quiet catalyst, I began to hear the voices of other angels speaking to me directly! Telling me the truth about the Angel of Death and how the world would often cast off things they didn't understand as "evil". Or judge a being by its personification.

"Look in your own world," they instructed me. "Even in the physical realm, souls that are misunderstood are cast off as "evil". It is often the most divine spirits that are called "evil" simply because they lead a lifestyle contrary to the "norm". Even such petty things as physical differences can influence the thinkings of a spiritually primitive mind. Pay no heed to their ignorance, yet do try to allay it with what you know is true," they stressed. "Remember your first reaction to His personified form."

"But I was just a child," I reasoned.

"And humanity is in its childhood," the voices countered.

My search for answers turned me more and more away from the outside world. I began to discover that knowledge filtered through many minds was often extremely distorted, and that THE TRUTH could only be found by going directly to its source! I would confront my lover straight on then. I knew enough now to test His honesty. I trust Him implicitly. For He had never harmed, nor deceived me.

✠

About a year had passed and my soul was finding temperance through the counsel of angels that instructed in my silence. I could feel Azrael's oppressive shadow in the air that night. He was very near. I felt His love reaching out for me, and could hear Him calling on the wind. I peeled back my blanket and a cool tempest ran its hands over my body. The blackness hovered above my bed seeming to expand and contract in time with my own heartbeat. I saw no definitive form, yet I knew He was there. Something very cold touched my neck and traveled down my body like a frozen flame. Reaching down with His mighty wings, He lifted me from the sheets as if I was a feather. It felt like being wrapped in chilled satin as He drew me into a cold and eerie kiss.

Nothing this divine and pure of spirit could ever be "evil". In my heart, I knew this.

When He Comes

He comes not like a thief in the night,
nor descends on flailing bladed wings.
No malice has He toward the fearing soul.
No anger spits from His still, cold lips.
He comes as the gentle whisper of winter wind,
or the quick ecstasy of the lightning bolt
immediate yet lingering as if embraced
by a darkling shadow or a twilight shade.
He is not the wielder of the killing blade.

The River of Death teems not with blood,
nor the tears of selfish grief.
No lost souls are there adrift upon the current,
only lich-lights remain to mark each journey,
silent ripples on the deep, dark waters
that gently kiss indivisible shores.

He is not the barrenness of bones,
nor the stagnance of a winter pool.
He is the fullness of an autumn bouquet
and that which runs rife in the misty bog.
He is the free acceptance of primordial change
where no conditions stem the cycle,
where no tears float like heavy oils
on the surface of such crystal waters.

He is the twilight forever bounded
by the two extremes of day and night.
He is the moment wherein all things do change-
The stoppage of time and elimination of space
between all that was and all that is,
and all that shall be, is a stationary point
that contains all times at once
and all space on a narrow bridge,
where everything culminates in a "winking out"-
A moment of darkness
wherein all reality is contained
and all illusion cast aside.

Death is the dream come to flesh
only to shed the veil of sleep
and reveal the naked form of Truth
reclining peaceably and shaded by Life's afterglow-

When He comes, all of man's truths shall shatter.
And the thin icy skin afloat on His waters
shall crack from the weight of a single soul.

Part 4

Sailing The Sea of Time

There is only half-light now where legends once were cast. Where two shores overlapped, and time lay interbracing many folds revealing facets, each from futures passing!

After leaving Earth we flew across your universe through the North Gate and into another, older universe.

Michael bid us a gesture of departing, turned and vanished into an adjoining stargate.

Raziel and I were traveling together when we spotted an ancient and abandoned planet just below our flight. As we came closer, I could see the remnants of destruction scattered on its surface. The empty towers of its cities jutting upward from the ruins like sharp horns. The relics of a broken civilization gleamed in the stark, blue light, their crystal edges casting rainbows on the rubble.

We landed on the planet's bright side where the brilliance of a distant starwheel was spinning over the far horizon.

"Azrael." My brother's voice cut into the heavy silence like a thunderclap. "It doth appear that you bethinks of things on the innermost level. I cannot translate these thoughts. They are shielded from me?" He ended in question.

It was as if His words were being pulled down through a tunnel. The harder I strained to listen, the more muffled the sounds became. The immediate moment was fading, and my thoughts were being pulled back, into an even older life! Back to a place rife with disquieting memories. I began to feel so much less imposing on this lifeless orb. The atmosphere was thick with a sorrow that pierced any who came here. I was somehow especially sensitive to its loss. There are many memories stored in the sterile soil, and secret tears hidden in its devastation.

"Do you remember?" a disembodied echo hailed out of the ancient shadows.

"Yes. Very, much," I uttered pensively, with my wings dragging in the ashes and mud.

I could feel Raziel probing my thoughts from a mental distance. He was able to see what I was seeing, and sense the emotions that I felt. Our psychic link was very strong, particularly when it came to this place!

"Indeed! These things do tear and strain even an angel's heart," He answered telepathically.

This planet was called Esteris. The first world (in another, older galaxy, than yours) to form from the dusts gathered behind the gates.

Once, it was a place of glory, with cities forged out of stone and crystal. Where light and colour bowed to pure thought and gentle spirit. It was a land of legends, that became a legend throughout the cosmos.

The Ancient Ones favoured this magical realm, and came frequently to teach, rest, and inspire its citizens. Some of the Ancients even chose to reside on Esteris, drawn by the perfect harmony of its energy and the fact that it virtually became "the best of both worlds", combining the malleability of the astral, with the visible product of the physical. The winged ones founded a paradise previously alikened only in the imaginings of the Divine Consciousness.

The ether was so fine and pure that a casual thought could radically transform it. Anything desired could easily be procured from virtual nothingness. It was truthfully, the closest thing to the spiritual realm there ever was in the physical dimension. It was unfortunate that this very fact would contribute greatly to its eventual downfall.

Being the first material world, it was modeled after what we knew... but what we didn't know at that point in time, was that the things that worked in "our" dimension, didn't always work the same in the physical world. Some astral practices even ended up with opposite results in the material realm! This is something we hadn't counted on happening when we procured such an obviously perfect place.

OF MEN AND ANGELS

It was here that I had come, long ago, briefly dwelling among its people as one of them. For a short time, I wasn't Azrael, the "foreboding Angel of Death", I was simply a traveler through the galaxy, (as many were at that time) seeking solace and companionship on simpler shores. Remember - These were the early days when Michael still assumed much of my station. There weren't so many places to be at once, nor so many lost souls requiring navigation. Even I wasn't yet fully cognizant of the overwhelming power that I'd later become. We were all growing and evolving slowly along with the young cosmos.

Esteris was a melting pot of many life-forms. Some were angelic brethren, desirous as I was, of spiritual renewal through meditation and counsel with other life-forms, as well as our own. Others were familiar, yet lesser powers. And there was also a balancing of strangers that came from places in the outer voids, beyond the North Gate, of which I knew little then. (Uriel never spoke freely of those who dwelt beyond His keep.)

Their appearance was awkward, and their ways even more bizarre. They took tool to stone to create form. They laboured to turn thought into visible things! Completely sealed in physical bodies, they appeared to be sylphs: beings without a spiritual essence. Very peculiar life-forms, indeed. It was at a point in time where we had never seen humans before. To us, they were a curious race. So much the antithesis of what we knew.

My problem with chronology, I'm afraid, is going to make an epochal reference here nearly impossible. Although I sense that it's necessary to offer some sort of feel for the oldness of this world. Therefore, drawing on my translator, we can ascertain that the birth of the Esterisian galaxy predates the creation of Earth by some two hundred, thirty-seven millennia.

The oddest thing about humans was that they had no wings! No means to get about the universe, yet they somehow did manage to travel.

Israfel's music didn't even seem to move them. On the surface, they appeared to be some kind of very primitive incarnate life-form, similar to those who are a part of the collective Spirit of Animal. Their sole mission seemed to be either to build things, or to destroy them. We had no way of then knowing just how much unrest this half-animal, half-god would later cause in the universe. If we did, we may not have allowed them to cohabit with the angelic race. We could not foresee their cruelty of dominance, nor how much they'd try to change that which must never be changed!

I seem to recall one particular occasion when Michael, upon noting their unusual ways, challenged them to open their souls to Him so that we all might discover the truth of their purpose.

When they surprisingly refused, He descended upon the planet, seized one of them and took her to an empty planet where no other influence might disturb them.

"Now that it's just you and I," He said, "show to me your soul so that I know who and what you are."

I could see no light shining from her glance, nor was this odd being haloed measurably in the Divine Light. The dust formed around her in a dense personification that seemed too cumbersome for the lithe spirit it covered. Her embodiment was delicately sculpted, and as pale as Earth's own alabaster. Her eyes were as dark as obsidian, yet as piercing as Michael's sword. She seemed to look right through Him, rather than at Him. There was something about this being that felt unnervingly familiar. As if I was standing outside of myself looking in. Most disturbing.

"What are you?" Michael inquired with great curiosity.

Her torn white garment flailed wildly in the brisk draft of the wintry planet. A braided crown of jasmine flower sat tilted atop her tangled hair. What sort of queen was she, I wondered?

"I am what I am," she replied with calm sarcasm unaware that I was watching from a nearby threshold. Michael was obviously unsatisfied with her answer.

"Why do your people refuse to show their souls?"

"We don't 'refuse'," she boldly corrected, "but it is our way not to bare our true identities in front of others of our kind." Michael seemed honestly perplexed.

"Will you show me... here... and now?" He politely prodded her.

"Perhaps," she answered mysteriously. "Why is it so important?"

"Your people..." He contended, "they do things strangely. Build things using their hands. Communicate with alien noises! Travel in shining beasts."

"I don't understand," she said with a bewildered gaze.

"You haven't any wings!" He noted, "Are you then - animal?"

"Animal? What is 'animal'?" she questioned Him back, but Michael didn't elaborate, choosing instead to change His approach.

"Why do you labour in the physical to do what is best done in the spiritual?"

"I really don't understand you." She sharply confessed.

"Your soul is asleep," Michael fired back while probing her telepathically. "Almost dead!" His expression contorted with apparent surprise. "Surely you aren't an empty vessel?"

"No! I'm not," she declared with firm certainty, startling Him with her grasp of His metaphor. "If you look very deeply, you'll see that my soul is very much alive."

Michael then approached her. She stood amazingly stoic as He wrapped His brilliant wings around her, and began to search her dark eyes with the penetration of His gaze. In the span of a few moments His curiosity melted into sadness, the depth of which I've rarely seen on His radiant face. He backed away from the tattered figure, nodding his head lowly, as His auric light faltered into a dim haze.

"I do understand." He then nodded solemnly, "Your people are in great need of our counsel and guidance. Your soul, and the souls of the others like you, must be renewed. It's unnatural that this thing has happened." He stormed in anger as His aura re-ignited around Him like a ring of fire. "It must be rectified!"

She stared at Him, puzzled by His concern as He pulled back His flaming wings and bowed His head in meditation.

Even on this distant threshold, I could hear a chorus of "voices" become audible enough to sweep through the hollow emptiness of this outer world like a splendiferous refrain. In its echo, I could hear Michael's voice holding brief and private council with the Many. I could discern only part of the rapid interplay. Many influences spoke at once, some familiar, some not. Their messages brought on the sweet songs of the Hyads. It has been said that their melodies are filled with rapture, and to discover their wisdoms, one must surrender to their ecstasy. Michael was doing just that as a cloud of energies enfolded His fiery form.

"Come here." His voice reached out of the haze as she walked meekly toward Him. "By what title are you summoned?" He inquired like a father would of his daughter.

"I am Na'Haliel," she divulged with a strange uncertainty.

Michael offered a soft, radiant smile.

"I observe within you a great desire, Na'Haliel," He repeated the name with a more fluent pronunciation. "You've a yearning to relearn the ancient knowledge, and to teach it to others."

"No!" she shrieked and pulled away. "The ancient ways destroyed my world, and most of its people! Those of us on Esteris are the last of our race..." she paused to collect herself. "We can never go back."

"I don't understand..." Michael said, again proceeding to "read" her. "What is it you fear?" He asked, confused by His inability to more deeply penetrate her psyche.

"The past..." her voice faltered, "It must never happen again! We purposely imprison our spirits," she blurted out.

"Purposely?" Michael repeated.

"We want no memories. No chance for it to happen again. We want to cleanse our children of it by starving it... by not feeding it any energy on which to survive! Fully made of flesh, we cannot so easily harm one another," she confessed with guilt.

"Who has hurt you?" Michael asked with compassion. "Who has done this thing as to corrupt the very soul of an entire world?"

She tried to speak, but seemed unable to form the words. Her tenacity turned to pain, and He again drew her vulnerable form into His golden wings.

"This foul thing was the work of one?" He pressed, after picking up parts of her past visions. It appeared that she was opening up to Him, but still I could not shake that queer spell her presence was casting upon me.

"At the beginning..." she sobbed, "but then it spread. It was terrible!" she cried. "The souls of our race were slowly being consumed by its growing power! Every time It took another soul, It grew stronger. Some used It..." she continued in obvious pain, "...to change our world into an awful place, and to change us in a way where we could never again be what we once were... like you!" she divulged. "We could never again show our spirits without the fear of them being snatched and devoured."

Michael put His arms around her in a heartfelt effort at consolation.

"There weren't many of us left," she continued, staring out soulfully. "Those of us that came here, I mean to Esteris, we're the last... You see," she explained trying to choose her words in a way where the least would be most effective, "they fed on the spirit as we do on the fruits of our planet. They'd drain the life-force from souls that were weak, and leave them to be empty shells, catalysts for the incarnation of their additional energy. This is how they grew to become so strong. They'd devour the soul and use the accumulated energy to animate an army of sylphs! Zombies that would do the bidding of the collective consciousness'."

"It is a terrible wrong to assume the soul of another!" Michael flared with anger. His revulsion evidenced by the quickening of His Divine Flame. "How did you and the others come to be on Esteris?" He asked.

"One night, near the end-time of our world, one like you fell from the sky. His wing was torn and his light was fading. My brother and I found him in a cave just outside the city. We befriended him, and in exchange, he taught us how to use our minds to heal. Well, after that..." she recounted, "we gathered some of our most trusted people together. Using his instruction, with our combined energy, we restored his life! We vowed that it'd be the last time we'd ever use such powers. Unfortunately, he wasn't strong enough to save our planet," she lamented openly to Michael. "Yet he did want so much to help us! He offered to take as many of us as he could to another world. He couldn't bear to see us die off as a race. And we desperately wanted a chance to live in peace again. He was our only chance! The only way our people could continue."

Michael was profoundly moved by her tale. So much that He gave her some of His strength with which to continue.

"Tell me more about the one who helped you?" He asked. "What was he called?"

"He said he had many names. The one he gave us was something like... Tadkel?" she seemed unsure, "Tzadkiel! Yes that's it!" she exclaimed. "He brought us to Esteris!"

A cold gale was beginning to sweep across the planet's surface. Na'Haliel's form was shivering in the chill wind as the orb was turning toward the darkness of heaven.

"Can I go back to my people now?" she pleaded impatiently.

Again, Michael was deeply in thought and her words bounced off Him without absorption.

Neither of them noticed as I quietly spread my wings and held the wind back behind them, easing the bitterness of this outer world. Tzadkiel was an angel of justice. I knew of Him from a few earlier encounters. Like my brother Israfel, he had problems traversing through the frequently volatile storms between worlds. However, unlike Israfel, he didn't always have me to carry him on my wings. Some of the lesser angels had great difficulty maneuvering through the stargates. It does take some practice. I'm afraid that this was the cause of Tzadkiel's "downfall".

"Na'Haliel..." Michael began with His glowing hands cupped around hers. "There's a darkness in your soul that I cannot penetrate. I am told that you are the Dark Star in Heaven's Crown. Does this mean anything to you?" He asked. She shook her head, no. "I know there's no definitive purpose in your life on Esteris. There seems to be something within your spirit, that is as of yet, unborn. Something familiar... but without peace."

She regarded Him only with a confused grin.

"That is..." Michael began to articulate His impressions, "your true purpose is concealed from me and I don't understand why. You've come to Esteris, the world of exiles, simply by chance but do not belong. Nor, for that matter, do your people."

"But, we like it there," she insisted.

"It is not a place humans are ready for." He said bluntly. "Besides, most Esterisians are also fully of the spirit." He reminded her, "and are capable of the same powers, some tenfold, that consumed your world."

"I understand that. But to them it's a natural thing. They all have this ability, and they don't comprehend subservience to it. They don't consider it a special gift anymore," she pointed out. "On our planet, only some were able to tap the power, not everyone. Those that did, waged a war by dividing us up into the "good" soldiers and the "evil" soldiers, and they'd force us to kill each other in the name of these imaginary gods.

"One thing Na'Haliel," Michael backtracked, "The Power is always special. One day you'll be made to understand why. Why such a great desire to remain on a planet where you can't share in the shaping of the fragile ether?" He wondered.

"I guess it's just that we feel safe there," she said. "Protected by those like you. Why is it that you didn't salvage my world?" she asked of Him tearfully - but drew no reply.

Michael sighed. I could feel His tension. He wanted to explain it all to her, but of course, He couldn't. He wanted to explain the complexities regarding angelic involvement, but would she understand? Would she be able to see, with the same far vision, in the way we were able? Or would she mistake His explanation as being cold and unfeeling, as so many of those who are incarnate, do. They, nor she, couldn't possibly be expected to comprehend the greater complexities of the universe. Not in their present state of being.

"You and your people require challenge to reanimate your souls into using the ancient powers again..."

"We don..."

"Please listen to me," He quelled her protest. "You mustn't let them fade. They're part of the Divine Gift given to all living beings. Even those in the flesh! Humans too!" He said vociferously.

"All I want to know is why it's so important that we build things with thought rather than hands?" she actually began to challenge Michael's authority. "I can't really see the difference, in the long run."

"You will!" He assured her. "Besides, it isn't merely that," He cautioned with an upward gesture of His hand. "It's what cometh after."

"Now you speak in riddles," she complained.

"The elements out of which your body is formed cannot ascend into the higher realms," He attempted to explain. "It's only spirit that can pass through the fold of space and time. Even through a stargate," he emphasized, "flesh devoid of the ability to transmute can never pass. Even your shining beasts cannot thrust your spirits into the higher realms. You can never become One with the Divine unless you're completely evolved in the spirit. Your people are of the flesh, alone, consequently separated from their true selves. And the more that you suppress the "power" the further away you will grow from the Godsoul. You need to suffer the flesh for the rebirthing of your spirits. Do you understand?" He asked.

She nodded blankly.

"You cannot take your achievements into the next life, if they be made solely of matter - without the spirit to reanimate their purpose. For this reason, among others, your people will be taken to a place in the Western galaxy where they can evolve at their own pace and learn to embrace each, their own, unique purpose."

"Leave Esteris?" she asked nervously.

"It is for the best," Michael consoled. I have in mind a place for you where others will openly share their spiritual knowledge. Together, you will all relearn the ancient ways. You will build a world of balances, between what we are and what you are. I will help you." Michael gave His solemn promise. "I will always help your people."

✠

And so it came to pass that Na'Haliel and the other humans were destined to be resettled on a young planet Earth.

Between the time of His confrontation with her, and the latter creation of Earth, she and her people were meanwhile transferred to a timeless space. It was more like a waiting station where souls tarry oblivious to either the passing of time or space. Here, they remain in a preparatory suspension until new meanings can be forged for their existence. It is a type of "sleep" where spirits are replenished.

Such was the case with the early human race. Even though all timeframes co-exist, certain spirits must be conditioned before entering the future, lest they upset the delicate balances of the more natural progression of Life. We wouldn't want to send a being into the future without "reprogramming" the life-form, both psychically, and physically to function and sustain its life in a very different atmosphere. Certainly we couldn't send a spiritual being into the physical world without first skrying as to what incarnate form looks like in that particular timeframe. However, there have been a few exceptions where, in one particular case, human life-forms were sent into dimensions that weren't ready to receive them, or where their forms stood out as being "unique" to that period. This is the kind of thing that contributed to the early sightings of humanoid form on Earth. Your people call this legend, GENESIS.

Na'Haliel's people came with most previous memories intact. They weren't passing from one incarnation to another. They were simply being "relocated" within the same lifetime. In this way they could keep their past intact, and they'd be able to recognize any early signs of a similar disease in the new world, like that which condemned their first world. It was decided that all future worlds would contain one or more of these "original" humans as they'd always be sensitive to the "true evil" that lives in the hearts of men. This was permitted only by special exception, and solely at the discretion of the Godsoul. Sometimes we were able to provide just cause, as in this case, for the intervention of the Universal Soul.

Humans brought with them many skills in the working of the land, and the planting of seeds. But they also brought with them a brutality and a harshness that offended the fragile senses of more ethereal beings. The cruelty of dominance could be easily seen within them. They were different than other animals. They had individual spirits! And unlike other lesser life-forms, did not immediately return to a collective spirit upon the passing of their flesh. We soon discovered that humans were more of a hybrid life-form with the attributes of both angels, and animals. We tried to deal with them by always keeping this in mind. We would watch to see which "side" was prominent.

✠

The planet Earth was carefully cultivated like a rare and fragile flower in those early days. Michael upheld His promise, and attended there regularly to the needs and teachings of its multiplying inhabitants. At all times, He watched and observed how the human race interacted with the other races that then dominated the planet.

"Go slowly!" He would caution them. "And remember to keep the balances even. For each form of flesh you create, a spirit must be summoned to dwell within it. For each advance you make in the physical, must be made two-fold in the spiritual. This is the Law of the Balance."

It wasn't long thereafter, that Esteris, the angel's shining gem of a world, began to show signs of its own end-time.

Little by little, the seas and rivers had begun to swell. The light of the dual, scarlet suns eventually grew so hot that being exposed to them for more than a few moments would sere the skin and blind the naked eye. The Esterisian twin suns had been edging closer and closer to each other for many years. There was nothing we could do to separate them. Their heat was combining into a deadly brilliance that was setting the planet on fire. When the orbs finally did collide the singular fireball went nova. Its violent energy hurled the shards of the exploding star down upon the small planet.

Some life-forms stood frozen below, agape with shock. Astonished that this grand display was not foreseen by such an "advanced" people. What went wrong to cause such a drastic reaction in nature? They wondered. So did we, I must confess! It was a time when even the mighty seven could not foresee certain things. The Godsoul didn't want us tampering with the grand design, even if Its plan included the scrapping of whole worlds. For everything there was a purpose, even if we didn't know it yet.

I watched as a shower of flaming meteors began setting the dry planet ablaze. Huge chunks of glowing rock, some the size of small moons were hurtled into the seas creating monstrous tidal waves that swallowed total continents.

What evidence of life that remained, soon had no choice but to surrender to the ensuing cold that fell upon the lightless planet like a dark and icy casing. Even the most mighty combination among us couldn't save this world. And we did try! We learned much of sadness here, and how even we were not "almighty". It's only now that I realize why we were unable to save Esteris. It was simple, really. We were blind to its cause, and therefore couldn't heal a sickness we knew not existed. We realized then that unless we "believed" in something, we could not be influenced by it... nor could we effectuate any changes upon what we didn't acknowledge to exist. This was the lesson found in the death of Esteris.

✠

Thankfully, at least, the end came quickly and for the most part, painlessly. I remember carrying millions through the West Gate just before the twin suns exploded in a violent orgasm of light and sound whose echoes can still be heard reaching as far away as 20th century Earth.

After that event, it came to be that my thoughts magnified their burden. My consciousness was continually spinning with ghosts of Esteris, and visions of the mysterious Na'Haliel. I was starting to extract scenes of our future together from the deepest recesses of my spirit. I needed to "know" her. To discover why she seemed so detached and solitary; so far removed from many worlds... so much like me! She didn't even waver in the presence of one so beautiful as Michael as other incarnates did.

I began having trouble sustaining my station. I was obsessed with the notion that some part of me was "missing." The council of angels refused to advise me. Instead they kept telling me that I "wasn't ready" to receive this "gift". That both our souls needed to "blossom much further before seeds could be extracted from them". Their mysterious words failed to allay my enchantment. I knew that I had to make contact with her, even if I just approached her as a simple "man". I don't like unfinished things, and being in Na'Haliel's presence, albeit briefly, led me to believe that much was unfinished between us. I'd no wish to startle her, nor forfeit the potential honesty of such a fragile moment, when in but one, first glance, both of our "futures" could be dramatically altered. I had to touch her spirit in a way where she might acknowledge knowing me, yet still be able to choose from the many paths at hand. (We angels aren't permitted to directly influence the choices of either the Many, nor the One!) We mustn't interfere, even if we are ultimately destined to be together. That's the law. This had to be her choice, alone. Interjecting our own personal desires would severely upset the natural order of things, and the "balances" that Michael seems singularly obsessed with.

Would she recognize me in some strange way? And if so, what would she recognize me as? I wondered if this familiarity would answer my questions as well? Would we both be overwhelmed by instantly recalling some lifetime yet to come? There was a reason Michael could not see beneath her spiritual veil. A reason that I entertained privately - but dared not speak!

✠

"You be thinking of Na'Haliel, my dark brother." A distant voice seemed to hearken from across the forgotten void of time. "Yea," He rambled on summoning my consciousness back into the present. The scene around me came into focus. The ruined architecture, the desolation of the memory of Esteris... My brother Raziel's steadying hand.

"I, too, scan these sorrowed things. But she and her kind are fairing well on the new world." He offered some minor comfort. "Be not so distressed. Soon, we may visit there again."

Sometimes He was too perceptive! I knew that He was aware of the strange emotions I felt for Na'Haliel and that I'd tried to shield them from the others. He'd often warn me regarding such "perilous" secrets.

"A dangerous thought that be, the one you entertain. Such things may cause even a mighty angel to fall."

I was on the verge of reply.

"Don't you even give thought to the sacrifice?" He pre-empted my response. "Such a great forgoing, don't you think, to be thrust upon such a fragile life-form, that if she were to reciprocate, then like thee, she too be limited to darkling regions? Never to unite with the Godsoul!"

His perceptive reasonings saddened me with their truth. He understood more than I thought. Was He right? Would I be making her choose between the Ultimate Completion and an existence where she may never taste this rapture?

"I cannot help to feel this odd thing," I expressed to Him painfully. "Inside, I do believe that something intended need be revealed."

"Thou art an angel of the highest realm," He reminded me in a serious tone. "If such were preordained, would you not with certain Knowledge be assured? And wouldn't her soul be tethered to yours?"

"How do I know it isn't? How can I truly know something that I've never felt before?" I answered His question with another. "It's not at all the same as what I feel for you... or for the Great Spirit. It's as if I should know more," I said with determination. "Like something obscures this part of my knowledge, and it's a deliberate overcasting. As if the part of me that should know this, is missing, or as if..."

"She is that part of you that is lacking?" Raziel interceded prophetically.

"Can this be? Can this be what Michael was unable to penetrate?" I anxiously beseeched His wisdom.

"There are shielded things, even from us my dark brother. Or things we may stumble upon that haven't yet been entered into the "Great Plan". Time is very young. And we do have free will." He coyly reminded me. "As to what lengths go this freedom..." He shrugged His draped shoulders. "Trouble thee not with this," He then appealed to me. "Time is all telling."

"And what do I do with these troubling desires meanwhile?" I asked Him.

"Channel them, dear brother! Channel their energy in appropriate directions of revelation."

I tried this, it didn't help. Her spirit still haunted me. I was literally, being torn apart by this new flood of emotions. This painfully, pleasant sensation was something that I had to explore, regardless of the "consequences". My soul was at stake! And if there was discord in my spirit, the universe as a whole would pay the price. I couldn't allow this to happen. The fate of too many souls depends on my vigilance. I had to discover what the future held for us.

I believed that the reasons for the way that I felt superseded any potential "risks". "After all," as Raziel often inferred, "the Divine Book is constantly being written to include new chapters everyday."

Against the advice of my familiar, my mind became singularly obsessed. I took a last look around at the ghost-laden planet. A decision had to be made.

"You are leaving now," Raziel observed in His all-knowing fashion. "Be sure!" He pointed at me with admonition. "Before you interfere."

"How do you know that I'm not meant to 'interfere'? Couldn't it be that this is why I feel as I do? Don't you believe at all that this emotion has significance?"

He shrugged uncommitedly.

"I did see something in her eyes that day on the ruined planet." I said. "Something disturbingly familiar."

"Your own reflection, perhaps." He blurted out without thinking, only to then quickly realize the deeper meaning of His droll insight. "This could prove most interesting!"

"The stargates," I whispered to Him.

"Dangerous thoughts!" Raziel intercepted my idea before I could articulate it. I was thinking to myself, why not just simply use the stargates, and access the future? Or even return to the "before time" in order to learn just who, or what she is to me? I would simply peer through the window of time and space and espy our future life.

"But you will not simply look, I know you," Raziel remarked.

"What harm is there?" I asked, "I can easily erase an ill prepared entry."

"And in what form will you make contact? How will you mask who you are and at the same time reveal enough of yourself to evoke a response?"

"I will use my imagination," I told Him with a smile. "You'll see."

I would go then, being careful to veil my identity in a form less imposing. For various reasons, this rare masking was important. For if she had no immediate recollection of me, I certainly didn't want to startle her with my "true" appearance! And if she did discern my spirit, no mask could quell that recognition. Besides, I didn't want her committing herself to decisions that would change the natural course of things for us, or worse yet, awaken her total recall of any earlier life we might have had together! I was taking a great risk, as Raziel reminded me. But I deemed it important enough for us both to take the chance.

With that thought in mind, I bid Him farewell and climbed into the sky, making fast for the nearest stargate.

INTO THE FUTURE TO FIND THE PAST

It was 2:43 in the morning when my father and I were awakened by a soft knocking at the front door. Staggering to the window, I peered through the coloured glass but saw no one.

"There is someone there," my father insisted, and went over to open the door.

On the single platform, stood a tall figure dressed in non-reflective black. From his wide-brimmed hat to his soot coloured boots, he was costumed in the garb of a bygone age.

His face was hidden in the dark shadow of his large chapeau, and the only glint of light, reflected off the silver buckles on his pointed boots. His complete image looked as if it were derelict from the 17th century. A wayward pilgrim, perhaps, who'd just landed on foreign soils.

"I've come from a long journey," the figure spoke through the screen door in a deep, soothing voice. He looked uncomfortably cold standing there in the late autumn fog. "Have you any brandy for a weary traveler?" he beseeched politely.

"Who are you?" my father questioned him uneasily from behind the half opened door. His voice was shaking with understandable surprise at the strange nocturnal visitor.

"I've sailed a long way," he appealed, ignoring my father's inquiry. "I willn't stay long – my ship awaits me."

"Your ship? Where is your ship?" I pried with keen interest, eking the door fully ajar.

"There, on the river," he motioned behind him, in a Southerly direction.

✠

Now, you must understand that our house was situated between the railroad tracks to the South, and the rural, country road to the North. There wasn't any water for at least two miles. There weren't any waterways, anywhere near us. It was preposterous to believe that anything was out there other than woods, and more woods.

✠

Nevertheless, I approached the screen and strained to look beyond his imposing blackness.

At first, I saw nothing in the damp haze.

"It is there." He pointed just beyond the tall row of maples. Again we looked.

"Something's out there," my father said. "Can't tell just what." With that, the stranger waved his hand gracefully and the mist rolled back like a smoky carpet. I did see something now out there! Something quite impossible. It rose out of the foggy distance and stood high like the mizzenmast of a tall schooner. Torn sails hung from the uprights, some half furled, while others flapped in the wind like wet wings. The ghostly ship appeared to have been through a terrible storm. Gleaming icicles hung from its weather-beaten timbres, and hoarfrost coated its damaged hull. It was heavily festooned in webs, glazed in ice that gave them the appearance of a finely spun glass.

Wide eyed, we marveled at the unbelievable sight.

"Many voyages she has seen," the stranger remarked. He then put his hand on the doorknob. I don't recall unlocking the screen door - but somehow he was already inside the house.

His stature was commanding under the low ceilings of our old house. The top of his coal coloured hat brushing up against it forcing him to bow down just a bit as he walked.

The look on my father's face was one of astonishment and subtle alarm. As if entranced, he led the visitor into the quaint kitchen and automatically pulled out a chair from under the cluttered table. Even though dazed, my Dad maintained a respectable distance from the stranger as he slid to the opposite end of the table and sat down.

Meanwhile, I was busy fetching three glasses, and a bottle of Tawny Port from the cupboard.

"This is all I have," I said, showing him the bottle. He smiled slightly.

"That's fine."

I could still discern very little of his face as the three of us sat beneath the dingy chandelier like we were each on a bed of nails. Under the sallow light, his smooth complexion looked dry and colourless, and his thin lips had a pronounced cyanosis, from exposure to the cold, I surmised.

When he spoke he didn't raise his eyes, but kept his dark glance hidden down beneath his hat rim.

I proceeded to pour out three small glasses of the heavy, red wine. He obliged me with a shallow nod and curbed his elongated fingers stiffly around the crystal goblet. His hands were surprisingly gaunt and weathered, like that of an old field tiller's.

"Thank you for your kindness," said the stranger as he lifted the warm liquid to his lips and drank.

"Where did you sail from?" my father inquired with a firmer leash on his initial reactions.

"From a land far away," he replied with an archaic diction.

"Where exactly?" my father chided him. The visitor then looked up at him. Immediately, my father reeled back aghast! The man's eyes were like two, glowing amethysts set in an abysmal darkness. His full face in the light had a translucent, cadaverous appearance. The skin being pale and emaciated, easily revealed the outlines of his skeleton.

His glance then turned to me. The flame in his eyes raged like two stars the colour of sunset. A sense of something ancient stirred uneasily within me and I could feel a tingling sensation running up my spine.

"Be at ease Na'Haliel," the unspoken words filtered directly into my mind, "for I've no wish to complicate your life."

I looked straight at him. I knew him. Of course, I knew him! I wanted then to reach out for him... but hesitated. Had to be sure of too many things, my mind was reeling. He felt this. He knew that I recognized him.

My father watched silently. Not surprisingly, I'm sure by this point, he was also aware of the true identity of the dark stranger. How could he not be. Listening to me for so many years. My many, vivid descriptions of Azrael's (numerous) personifications. This was yet another one.

I thought to myself; it's good that he has seen my beloved first in this more "milder" of embodiments. Even though my dad was well acquainted with things supernal, I do not believe it would be wise for Death to meet him straight on in His more "spectacular" mien! Not yet anyway.

"Have you come to take her?" his forthright question took me by surprise.

"Not in the way you ask. Only for a while." He calmly assured him with a pervading regret. "I do wish it was forever," He openly lamented, returning His gaze to me. "I shall see to her swift return by dawn."

My father looked understandably relieved, as Death rose from the table.

"Will you take my hand?" He asked, and offered it to me. "There's something I'd like to show you."

Yes, I signaled with a nod, as He slid His cold hand into mine and drew me in so closely that I didn't at first notice His frayed garment spreading into half-formed wings.

"There's no need to be afraid," He gently assured me, wrapping His darkness around me.

"I'm not afraid at all," I said truthfully, "just a bit faint... and wonderfully cold." I spoke while steadying myself from a momentary black out.

He drew me in even closer until He completely covered me.

"Better?" He whispered. To which I smiled warmly. "Hold tight, my Love! It is a swift journey!"

Before I could acknowledge, the immediate "present" collapsed in His gaze, and I was now suddenly standing on the bow of His spectral ship. His skeletal hands gripped my shoulders from behind and drew me again into His deathly embrace. I glanced down and saw the Lich-Light dancing on the still water, and could vaguely perceive faces looking up from under the ripples. Hollow eyes watched us as we drifted without sound through some of the most desolate scenery anyone will ever see. Stark and barren forests, forgotten rivers that wound through grey lands filled with moving shadows.

As the wind picked up, I could feel His black garment swirling around me. Gently, He spun me around in His arms and I looked straight into His eyes that were now like two eclipsed stars! His face was decaying into a skull, and then rapidly reforming into an image beyond the most fantastic or descriptive eloquence. Like a Phoenix, His wings fully emerged from the decaying figure and wrapped around me with a loud swoosh! The scenery collapsed a second time, as He held me tightly in His rapture and drew me into a ghostly kiss that seemed to last forever...

AN ANAGRAM OF REALITY

Passing through the Stargate was a particularly disorienting experience. The laws of Earthly physics definitely do not apply here. In this weightless zone, our "bodies" dissolved into amorphous energies that were wafted through a wind tunnel where Time and Space held their breath as we passed. The narrow passageway then emptied into a swirling void where our blended spirits spilled out into space like liquid light and reformed into our original shapes.

We were moving through the universe so fast, that time stood still. And, as our flight slowed, I could see stars and planets in ranges of colour so bright and vivid that they were breathtaking in their beauty. I could reach out and almost touch the stars as we sailed from one galaxy into another - from one planet to the next.

We flew over an ancient battlefield where dead monarchs, still on their thrones, presided like macabre eidolons peering over the destruction with hollow-eyed astonishment. Veiled in cobweb filament, they were permanently enthroned in gargoyled seats that were carved out of mountains of precious stone. The horror so vividly preserved in their mummified expressions, it looked as if their bodies were instantaneously petrified by whatever catastrophe befell them. Their decayed faces contorted by the shock of some sudden end.

Great armies of the dead stood mounted on skeletal steeds as if time had halted them in their tracks. Their alien weapons poised to strike down a long dead enemy. They were clothed in tattered shrouds, caked in the dust of many centuries, making the cloth feel like brittle paper-mache. Such an eerie landscape, I have never seen. Glared at through empty eye-sockets, we were brushed by the whitewashed bone covered with a tissue-paper skin, stained by the weathering of age. Dust swirled wildly in the arid climate and formed around the cadavers like a phantastic sculpture that left them forever postured in their final stance.

"You are standing on many souls," He said to me. "Thousands lay beneath here..." He pointed downward, "...under the dust and ash of a million years. Do you remember this place?" He asked.

I shook my head sadly. "Should I?"

"No. Perhaps it's best that you don't. Come." He motioned, hurriedly grasping my hand as we resumed flight and headed back into the stargate.

We re-emerged where a brilliant sunrise was just beginning to break from behind a small planet. Oddly, it seemed to grow colder the closer we came to it. I shielded myself in His protective darkness as we brushed passed the frigid orb. I could feel the ice crystals forming on my "skin" as we swung around to the planets bright side.

"Do you remember this place?" He pointed down at the blue planet below us.

From where we were, it looked like Earth. Except that the landmass configurations were different! I couldn't recognize any of their outlines. Nonetheless, it did grow more familiar as we closed in upon a specific locale.

"This, I know!" I declared, "I'd wondered just where it was."

There was a definite sense of warm nostalgia here. Something "homey" and pleasant welled up inside of me as we gracefully landed on a deserted dirt road just outside a gateway. I recognized it immediately! I'd spent a good number of years searching, on Earth, for this phantom location. In my dreams I would be repeatedly drawn into its Elysium - my spirit pulled, as if by a spectral magnet into this waking vision. It often used to seem like I was living in two dimensions simultaneously. A kind of bi-location that divided my time between two different lives, in similar dimensions. While my physical, waking hours were spent in 20th century Earth, my hours in the "sleep of dreams" would often be spent haunting this parallel existence. I remember every detail of the scene that stood before me.

We approached the small gateway where tangled vines wound through the ornate wrought iron. Its design culminated in a low arch just above my head; ST. AGNES, its filigree seemed to quickly read. Although somehow my eyes saw an alternate spelling in the intricate metalwork - as if its real name was an anagram of what my mind read. The harder I strained to look, the more my vision blurred, until all that I could distinguish was AGNI SOMETHING, SOMETHING...

My glance then lowered upon a very small structure to the right, no larger than an old fashioned out-house. Years of alien overgrowth had all but claimed the modest hovel. I remember that long ago, it served as the "gatehouse" for this humble glen, and the name of its elderly gate-keeper was Phillip. When I was a "child", he introduced me to this realm's wonders. But he was gone now - or more likely, a permanent resident somewhere "inside".

"Go ahead. Look around," my guide suggested, letting go of my hand. "This is all a part of our courtship."

Somehow... that comment... here and now... required no further explanation. He gently withdrew His grip, and I began to walk the dirt path that wound its way through the hilly landscape in a serpentine fashion.

By far, this had to be one of the two most beautiful graveyards I'd ever known, in waking, or in dream.

To the far left were rolling green hills, picturesque and serene as they dipped gently into pastel valleys. On a distant elevation, stood a curious statue of a young female nymph, albeit diminutive, yet still imposing on its perch, all alone on the peak of the incline like an exiled fairie. Her arms were crossed over her heart and her face was enigmatic and expressionless. She appeared charged with subtle urgency as if hushing everything in her keep. Her "secret" was whispering on the wind. Yet I could not hear it.

Closer to the front of the left arch, was a grand, stone memorial. Equally as florid as Earth's own Victorian, cemetery splendour. It was a life-sized effigy of a bearded old man seated at a beautifully sculpted, grand piano. He had one hand on the carved keys, and the other in flamboyant gesture, while the expressive face was turned towards the other road as if to say, "Come and hear the music". It was this festive welcome that first greeted any who entered. "I play the songs of angels," his gaiety would seem to imply.

Further along, and to my immediate right, were many gravestones. Uprights and gothics, typical to Earth designs. Some in rows, others dotted like jagged teeth across the idyllic landscape.

I felt like a carefree child in a magic wonderland. Strolling through a familiar haunt where the ignorance of time and space preserved the scene as if pressed in cellophane like a rare and fragile shamrock. Within this remote silence lurked a host of images, spreading their wings in the open wind, and the sound was that of many different noises. I could hear music and voices, as well as other sounds that hadn't yet been heard on Earth.

Suddenly, the place came alive. The echoes in my mind began to clear and yield to the muffled tolling of a lugubrious bell. It counted out a rhythm of hours until it marked nine.

Just beyond the Gothic stones and wild rows of cypress, the land sloped downward and ended abruptly on a hidden, curved path. Concealed in the brush was a small, unobtrusive mausoleum. Its weathered, wooden door faced outward, towards the path, and another, even smaller door, faced into the back of the hillside. Obviously, it hadn't been tended to in years. The dilapidated tomb was literally being torn apart by the probing vines, and wandering overgrowth.

In my astral journeys, I had been inside there many times. Flashes of earlier visits invaded my vision. This is where I had come on my first excursion. I remembered the daisies, and the sunny incline, and the name on the grave! "The Key! The Key!" A voice in my psyche urgently repeated. "You know where it is!"

As if intuitively guided, I made my way around the structure and gave a quick yank to both of the doors. They were surprisingly, sturdy! Neither one would yield.

"Find the key!" the voice insisted, sounding now as if it was externalized.

I ran my hands along its splintered eaves, under the rotted molding, and around the door- jambs. I strained to feel the upper ledge, then down around its broken sills. All the time I was trying to remember just where I'd placed it at the end of my last "visit", which must have been at least a decade ago! I kept feeling blindly for the cold metal - until I found it.

Making my way to the larger portal, I inserted the old fashioned key into the simple lock. It was so badly rusted, it barely budged.

But after forcing it a bit, the iron bolt scraped against the chamber and the door sank on its loose hinges, and squealed open.

A gust of stale wind pushed me back. I could swear that something passed through my soul!

The inner chamber was magnificent, and impossible. It looked enormous. Certainly too large a space to fit inside the small tomb. It was definitely not an optical illusion. Perhaps more like a tangible hologram that one could walk into. How could this be? This isn't how I remembered it. In my dreams, it had a disarrayed and humble interior, and contained only, flaccid catalysts of my lover's affection. Not the lavishness that sprawled out before me. "Impossible. Impossible," I kept repeating to myself as I glared dumbfounded from the narrow threshold. The chamber looked to be at least 30'x30' square, and perhaps 15' high. It was all made of shining black marble from ceiling to floor, and illuminated by a recessed firelight that made a perfect circle around the central platform. The centerpiece was graduated like an Aztec temple, leading one step at a time, on all four sides, up to a marble sarcophagus. The heavy casket was set on an elevated platform, atop an ornate pedestal. A radiance seemed to be issuing upward from is opened lid.

I was drawn toward it. Had to see what, or who was up there. Every step I took drained my strength, yet I kept climbing until there were no more steps. I stood over the bier and glanced down at the form that slept within it...

A hand caressed my arm from behind.

"We must go back now," the Angel of Death said. "I've had you away longer than promised already."

"That's me!" I pointed with amazement into the open casket at the figure dressed in reflective white satin. "Is it real?"

"Everything is 'real'," He commented philosophically.

"What does it mean?"

"It is simply another life that you have had," He replied quite casually. "One that your memory has forsaken."

"But, why show it to me now?"

"I wanted to confirm your inner thoughts," He said. "To show you that our love stretches beyond your current world. You're always to be joined to me, I wanted to show you that you needn't wait for this, that we are already One Life, with one purpose - that is served in two different worlds. Look." He waved His ghostly hand over the reposing body. "She is already a bride. And she is promised to me. Isaro El. My Promised One."

I watched as her gown flared like a white fire. The sparkling light shooting out in colourful beams that played like a laser show through a diamond. A haze began to rise from the marble floor, and soon the whole crypt was filled with a diffused halo.

I felt my Host enfold me from behind as the scene began to crumble around us. I could actually see the atoms and molecules of atmosphere coming apart, their images disintegrating into an amorphous flow of particles that were being drawn toward an open stargate. Suddenly I could feel nothing under my feet! Nothing supporting my weight except His firm embrace. It was the only thing keeping me from being sucked through the stargate as well.

Again, I was growing light-headed. I could feel my consciousness slipping away into a black-spotted void. My senses were quickly overwhelmed by the opposing polarities of an invisible magnet that was drawing my psyche into its bosom.

I remember swimming upward through a viscous sea of lampblack. My eyes slowly opening to survey its surface. The free sound of the wind replaced the howling echo of the time tunnel, and the gentle splash of water was the first crystalline noise to restore "reality".

We were once again standing on the bow of Azrael's spectral ship! Laggardly, we glided over the liquid darkness. Our voyage left no ripples with which to retrace our path. No evidence of our passage reached back to the shores of Earth. Only the angels, and a host of attending shadows saw us come and go.

Again, He spread His massive wings and pushed back the heath-haze. Through the swirling vapor, I could vaguely see the lamp on my porch still burning bright.

AN OBSERVATION FROM HIS VIEWPOINT

Going that far into the future of Na'Haliel's last life was worthwhile indeed! Touching her soul lifted the veil from my memory, as well. Raziel's concerns proved benign, and for that small blessing, I was glad. By the writing of this book, that voyage will not yet have happened, using Earthly definitions of time, that is. This is very difficult to explain to you - She knows the journey will happen. Very soon, as a matter of fact. Because even though it's technically in her future, she's already experienced it through me.

I'd hoped that by showing her the desolation of Esteris, her mind would reawaken into memory, subtleties from our meeting there. Alas, that life would not return to her memory. I had also hoped that in this way, I would prove to her the reality of the past lives that cause her to be haunted. Even if those other lives occurred in "dream-state"!

Taking her to the alien cemetery also attempted to confirm her suspicions about the tangibility of the parallel world, and the truths revealed in their symbols. I was able to answer her questions only by becoming aware of their truths moments before her. Going into the future not only brought my truth into her mind, but brought her truth into mine. The future told me who she was. Her simple asking of the questions, filled my soul with their replied realities. She is my bride! At last, I know why I feel as I do. And I could impart her this certainty only now. Only now, that our spirits were able to unite and answer each other's inquiries with the completeness of their truth, can we come to know the reasons for the emotions that plague us both. I saw why her identity was shielded from Michael that day on Esteris. If He had known that "we" were one, this might have affected His decision to send her to Earth, thus altering all of history.

Realizing that even I was a duality, forced me to evolve a whole new way of dealing with the new sensations I felt when I was near her. I became more attentive of their "larger" implications and savoured each emotion like a perfect nectar one sips slowly, and sparingly. It was too easy to get drunk on this ecstasy.

Just the thought that her consciousness may well be the result of my own inner need for a soulmate is astounding, even to an angel. This duality is projected out of me! Her existence grew from a powerful thought. A perfect practicality, of the Certain Knowledge that THOUGHT CREATES! A seed that the Godsoul planted in my consciousness, as if IT knew that when the time came, I would call forth its blossom. And that I would nurture it over many lives, letting it evolve slowly, and gestate into a life-form that would eventually be my eternal consort. One that would return to me at the end of its last incarnate purpose, and in doing so, we would complete each other, as well as the will of the Great Spirit.

She is literally, the product of my imagination. This is the true paradox of our existence. We are both resultant from the energy of thought, powered by love. The question is, who made whom?

In that future visit, even her Earthly father recognized me through my disguise. This was good. I had lent to it just enough of my true identity, yet not too much. Certainly it was best to temper my traditional appearance so as to not frighten him, or worse! Besides which, in a less imposing mien, it's easier to cultivate communication, rather than just leaving my host, shall we say, "awe-struck"?

✠

But that life was still very far down the road for her. Many other lives would pass between now and then. I wondered if any of the future visions of our voyage would filter down into those earlier lives. There was only one way to know, and that was to return to the young planet Earth where Michael had taken her and the other humans.

While she was allowed to retain much of her memory of Esteris and of the horrors on her first world, certain things were "extracted" to enable Na'Haliel to adapt more quickly and easily, to her new surroundings. At first, we had blocked out much of the fear and pain of her original world in order to allow the more fluent emergence of her innate natural abilities. When their development was attained to a certain level, we'd then return these visions to her, so that she could finally put the horror behind her by drawing upon the newfound understanding of its root.

✠

The humans had been on Earth already for the equivalent of one cosmic cycle, (appx. seven Earth years).

We, of the higher realms, had increasingly more lives to oversee all across many galaxies. Respites became even more brief, as additional incarnate lives complicated the Great Work of angels. Even though we had awakened many sleeping familiars from their celestial wombs to assist us, incarnate lives soon outnumbered our available legions. Some angels had taken corporeal bodies to help in a more "hands on" fashion. It began to seem that the more time was passing, the further the tangible life-forms grew from the Divine Way. We came less frequently to each, individual world, as so many places needed tending. Even the stargates could not shuttle us back and forth fast enough to meet the needs of all worlds. The dwellers in the flesh began losing touch with us, and the vital simplicities of our teachings.

Eventually, their children grew to know of us angels only through legend and the fading memories of those old enough have shared in the earlier days.

Some even began to fear us! Still, others came to doubt our very existence. This was the most distressing!

Our plans for Earth rested with those who were the last descendants of the union between humans and angels. We had hoped, that in our absence, they would struggle to keep the flame of Truth burning. But even the most powerful one among them; the one called Kaela whom Michael had touched with His fire, could not resurrect the Divine Spirit. Part of the planet was dying. Na'haliel recognized the signs of this cancer; remembered its symptoms from her first world.

"I will not let it happen again." she said to me, "Not here!"

But I couldn't tell her that she was powerless to stop it, again.

And Nothing of Time

And when He touched me, my heart became a shadow,
My life, an overcasting of my soul.
An elongated image of a very small design
that the twilight somehow lengthened
into imaginary strides.

But, when He touched me, and I regained perspective,
my life was so much smaller than it seemed,
so much less imposing than the shadow it had cast-
So much more a part of memory.

Then He touched me, and I forgot all I once was,
for all I am, where the view from the bridge
has no perspective other than the immediate moment
in which is contained all of eternity
and nothing of time.

Part 5

Two Ancient Lives

*The silent winds enchanted isles
teem with ghosts of elder days
assembled in the madrigal glare
of paling pinks and iron greys.*

A LIFE TOO LATE?

The benevolent yet impotent queen surveyed her world in its final days. The great, blue sea, thick with blood and shattered crystal began to swallow the city more and more each day.

There were no quiet places left to go where the screaming and weeping did not echo. Soon, all the good that had been done was being washed away by one thought held by many minds. One desire burdensome enough to tilt the fragile balance of all things; the desire to Dominate! That inherently human quality that affords them a false sense of power. Humans purposefully distort the Truth and try to mold it around the image they have of themselves as demigods. They do not understand the concept of universality, therefore they shape their logic by eliminating particular realities that don't conform to narrow interpretations.

Those of us who witnessed the final days of this once proud and sovereign land, beheld a tragedy so disparate that many of the lessons of our race would forever be lost in its whirlwind fall. Many truths, never to be recovered.

My having seen all of this before, in "another" life, was of little help. It was already too late to make any real difference here. I was simply reliving another end-time on a "newer" world and couldn't then see the reason for this repetition.

✠

In more pleasant days, this antediluvian land was a glorious kingdom, a shining testament to the achievements of psychic alchemy. The angel's glittering jewel in a system of many worlds that had already succumbed to untimely ends. The winged ones tried so hard not to allow that to happen here. Tried hard to make a "better" Esteris!

In the earliest years, the Esterisians dominated by sheer number and an advanced understanding of the nature of things. These primary inhabitants, along with other interstellar influences, had procured for their children, a bountiful land of order through peace. Very much like Esteris was, in its heyday. The ways of the Great Spirit were taught to all who came, and to all who were born into this world. The natural laws were sacred, and all things could be measured and achieved by utilizing their subtle mysteries. All life-forms were instructed in the importance of the Universal Nervous System and how its network energies ran through the planet itself, as well as through each life thereupon. We were shown how to locate and mark earthgates, which are similar to stargates in principle, but serve a more tellurian function. The angels used to teach us how specific minerals amplified the power of the gates for various purposes, from the most practical to the most uncanny. It always amazed me how the simplest of nature's riddles revealed keys to the most complex formulas of the universe; like the parable of the solar system and the atom.

Our "god" was the law of the relationship between the microcosm and the macrocosm. This was the supreme deity of all beliefs. The key to the universe itself! The perfect science of truth. The importance of such basic things as colour, light, sound, and pattern was stressed regarding their influence upon matter, as well as spirit.

I became a reluctant participant in the approaching demise of this once fair land. I felt as if I'd been awakened from a long, peaceful sleep just to behold an awful nightmare.

✠

I vaguely remember coming into the city, and seeing it for the first time. Its magnificence compounded by precision mathematics in everything from the dowsing of a well, to the planting of a single seed. My first sight was a fabulous, stone fountain cascading with the clearest water I'd ever seen. I had heard that it had special healing properties, and that many once came from great distances to partake of its cool clarity.

In the center of the circular fountain, an imposing likeness of Michael stood scowling down at passers by like a fierce sentinel. His crystal sword brandished and ready to strike at an unseen adversary. An inspiring effigy, I thought, but it gave me the uneasy feeling that it was intended more as a memorial to something that was no longer alive. Overall, the crumbling stone left me with a chilling impression... and a sadness that I could not define.

Something down here was going awry. Something terrible was hiding beneath the lush facade of fragrant gardens. A hideous ghost was veiled under the wisteria that hung like a heavy carpet in the curling mist. A weeping phantom of a land about to die, unnaturally still, like just before a storm.

I looked down again at the water, and noticed that it wasn't as clear as I thought. It no longer flowed like liquid diamonds, but barely trickled out enough to sustain the flow. Few in those last days, made the long pilgrimage to be healed in its mystery. Most had to be turned away because there just wasn't enough anymore for all who needed it. Its power was growing weaker and weaker by the malignancy that was rapidly consuming many souls, human and angelic.

I could see a procession beginning to pour into the walled courtyard. Several white robed figures with heads bowed encircled the silent fountain. Their forms bathed in a cool, green pearlescense. Three, older females stood opposite them, sobbing lowly into their multi-coloured garments.

"It is no more," the eldest of them lamented. "This is all that's left."

"Come, and make a circle with us Druesa!" One of the robed men hailed to her. "We will try again to tap the marker stone. "

"No!" a stern voice warned. "All the energies are corrupt. They mustn't be summoned."

The one that spoke was called Kaela. We would become very close friends in those last days. Even though we hadn't known each other for very long (only since I came to the city). We seemed to have an understanding that had little need of verbal explanations. I knew what she was thinking, even before she did! In a matter of weeks, we'd grown as close as sisters. We'd spend hours in serious discussion on things of a spiritual nature, especially the afterlife. She grew to implicitly trust my counsel, yet oddly could never bring herself to accept a sisterly embrace. Whenever I'd get close to her, she'd cunningly shrink way. Strange, I thought, although I never pressed the issue.

She was what the modern world would term a classic figure. Her body looked as if it was carved from stone; a careful sculpture by a Michaelangelo or a Rodin brought to life by the strike of a lightning bolt. The last spark of its power evidenced in her menacing glance. Her skin appeared opalescent against the foreboding grey sky, and her face was as pale as moonstone and accentuated by a sleek brunette crown that afforded her a stern, yet feminine mien. She preferred the wearing of a turquoise-green garment that had the shine of a fine silk as it billowed from her shoulders to her feet. Trimmed with emeralds, and belted with a golden serpent, its colours changed and shimmered in the half-light as if it were a flowing rainbow, able to reflect the mood of the wearer.

Kaela was an acutely adept clairvoyant. Owing, no doubt, to her strong angelic blood-line. She repeatedly suffered from persistent visions of other lives. We had this much in common. Many times she'd tell me fantastic tales of a land where "perfectly pointed mountains rise up out of sandalwood deserts". And places where, "a wide dark river divides through the total length of the continent". She was particularly obsessed with visions of "a man with the head of a dog who stands guard in fire-lit temples of gold and sandstone".

"He speaks to me through my dreams," she would say. "Tells me that I'm safe with you."

"Where is he from?" I'd ask her.

"From a land where the dead are masked in gold." This is what he told her.

✠

But here and now, those visions didn't matter. No lessons could be extracted from their images. Kaela was convinced that she had failed her proud, angelic heritage by not using her "vision" to foresee the events that would unfold, and subsequently lead to the end of her short, yet valiant rule. She realized now that she'd placed too much faith on "outside" influences to save the land. Her not wanting to disrupt the natural order had also blinded her to the sickness that grew within it. Like a spider's web, invisible, yet enveloping.

"How do we know what is meant to be - and what is not?" she would ask.

She despised the feeling of helplessness. It was never drummed into her nature. She'd never been helpless before, and didn't know how to cope with this handicap now. Kaela was always a valorous leader. An exhibitor of enormous strength tempered with a truly Divine compassion. Under her guidance, the city had once flourished in ways unimagined by her predecessors. She was one of the last direct descendants of the original race line. The remaining daughter of one of the early unions between humankind, and the incarnate winged ones. Her ability to "tap into" the Universal Mind gifted her with a special insight that brought the already "advanced" society into a future that, unfortunately, many were still not prepared to handle, much less understand.

She truly loved the people and wanted everyone to touch the Godsoul. She had hoped that all could share in such perfect visions. If Kaela is guilty of anything, her only crime would be her obsession with teaching all life-forms how to tap into this great force in order that each might use it to effect benevolent changes both personally, and for the common good. However, some failed to stop there. The more power they took in, the greater their thirst for it became. The human symptom of the dwellers in the flesh began to grow stronger, and in too many cases, overtook their fading, angelic lineage.

It was the old world all over again. And I was as powerless as she. Why was I summoned to the city if it was too late to do anything that mattered? I didn't understand my point for being here. Kaela would often sense my frustration.

"I only know that you're not here to save the land," she would say to me in a semi-trance state. "I don't know why you're here... yet."

As the ancient lifeline grew more indistinct, so did mankind's consciousness of his universal link. Human thought was becoming more withdrawn, with the Self taking precedence over all else. Many were no longer even aware of anything other than their own, individual survival.

Incarnate beings began viewing themselves as "separate" entities. The original teaching that each individual was a universe became grossly distorted. Its interpretation so twisted that more and more people grew confused. Individual souls were tearing away from the Greater Whole. They turned inward with a perverted fascination, and explored this "new" world with a shield and a sword, rather than an open hand. They went so deeply within themselves that they eventually set themselves completely apart from all else, becoming cells existing independent of the total body. The more each cell disconnected from the "body" as a whole, the more the body, itself, began to wither and die.

✠

On the eve of the end, I was walking toward a glistening dampness that gathered at the bottom of a long, sloping corridor. Two towering obelisks bordered a wide, stone stairway of just eight steps that led up to a private terrace. As my glance ascended, I noticed Kaela standing alone in the gloom, deep in thought. Her slender arms caressed a dry spray of orchids and wild fern. She was staring off into infinity with her eyes looking moist and soulful. A stray tear marred her pale cheek, and pierced my heart like a dull dagger as I went to try to offer some minor comfort.

We stood together for the longest time in silence, silhouetted in the cool, amber corona on the terrace that overlooked a sea of blood. All things were stained with its scarlet glow, even the smudge of sunlight looked like a paling ruby.

"What have I done?" Kaela lamented. "This is my doing!"

"You're not at fault." I tried to console her. "Humanity complicates the quest for perfection," I uttered from past experience.

"It was a good place, wasn't it?" she reflected nostalgically while seeking affirmation.

I nodded in agreement.

"To see so many spirits cast upon the waters," she whispered to herself, and then turned sharply towards me. "I've never felt so helpless." She confessed in great pain adding, "I should've known when you returned to the city that the end-time was inevitable. I should have known this!"

I wasn't really sure if I understood what she meant.

"Even I didn't know." I blurted out involuntarily, wondering if she somehow knew who I was, when at this time, even I was still consciously unsure.

For a while there was a silence. Her expression even began to mellow into a strange kind of peacefulness.

"We'll be washed clean... as if we never existed," she spoke with forced complacency.

"That's not completely true," I reminded her. "Some have already made their way to other shores."

"But this thing will rip through many lands before it subsides. Like a ripple from a stone cast into a lake, it'll be felt in many places, all the way to the future."

She bent over the terrace rail and aimlessly tossed bits of the broken walkway into the sea below.

"You know the time, don't you?" she turned to me and asked. I didn't know how to answer her, so instead I offered a sympathetic look and an open hand. At first she pulled away, but I just came closer until she acquiesced into accepting my comforting embrace.

"All right," she sighed with the sound of a final surrender, "I'm as ready as I'll ever be. I'll at least get to see Him, won't I?"

"I don't know." I answered, somewhat startled at her perceptiveness.

"What will it be like?"

"All I can tell you is not to be afraid. It's a journey you've taken before." Someone else was speaking through me! These were not my thoughts.

"In my dreams. Yes."

"You're going home," I assured her. "Here, take my hand."

She flinched briefly.

"Why do you do that?" I asked her. "Why do you always pull away from me?"

"I'm sorry," she said piquishly. "I didn't know it hurt you."

"It does when I don't understand your reluctance."

With that, she proffered me her hand, as if to apologize.

Her skin felt clammy, and her grip, stiff and tense.

"There's nothing to be afraid of," I repeated. "The time is near."

"It's amazing how sometimes you know things, and sometimes you don't," she observed. "It is that you know more than you tell? Or don't you really know?"

"What is it that you think I know... or should know?"

"I don't claim to see everything," she said, "but sometimes when I look at you, I see the face of the Ferryman. The man with the head of a jackal. The one that takes me to the afterlife in my dreams!" That statement made me reel a bit.

"Do you remember when I told you about the Guardian in the temple?" she asked.

"Yes."

"He told me who you really are..." she hesitated. "I asked him why you came to the city, but this, he couldn't answer. Can you?"

I really didn't know, and I told her this. Not at that point in time, anyway. This was to be something that we'd both discover in the afterlife.

"Give me both hands," I said to her, as chunks of the terrace began to break away beneath us.

"Don't let go. You know I can't swim," she joked uneasily. I smiled and held firmly onto her hands. "I won't let go," I assured her. "I promise."

The ocean of blood rose up around us. The tall waves grabbing hold of the terrace like cold hands and trying to force us down into its swirling vortex.

"I'm afraid!" Kaela cried.

"Of what?" I asked rather callously.

She regarded me with a puzzled expression. "I don't know!" she said, as if her words caused her a personal revelation. "You're right!" she exclaimed. "I'm afraid... and I don't even know what I'm afraid of."

"Considering all the times we spent talking about the "afterlife," you, of all people Kaela, should have more anticipation than most for this journey. And, if you claim to really know who I am (even when I'm unsure), certainly your fear is unjustified," I attempted to reason with her.

"You're doing it again," she nervously blared.

"Doing what?" I snapped defensively.

"Pretending not to know who you are."

"I DON'T KNOW. Why don't you tell me?" I threw one hand up in frustration.

"You're the Ferryman's consort!" she said to my face, very seriously. "That's who you are!"

Suddenly, the scaffolding below us gave way. Kaela flung her bare arms around me as the landing broke away from the hillside and fell into the sea like an avalanche.

Together, we took a deep breath, and held it as the sea pulled us under its darkness until we were so deep inside the Earth that we could no longer hear the weeping.

THE VIEW FROM THE BRIDGE

Hand in hand, we resurfaced on a silent river, and exhaled our old lives. We could see Death's phantom stretching across the still water as He lifted her soul from my keeping.

✠

The planet as a whole had been spared. Only the seat of its corruption was plucked out, like a weed among so many daffodils.

It was a psychic bomb that destroyed this place you call "Atlantis." One no less destructive than the force of a modern nuclear war. The only difference is that the former weapon is the kind that destroys from the inside, out. First by corrupting the spirit of one, and then like a carrier, he in turn spreads it to the many, until all spirits turn inward, convinced that they're not part of anything larger.

Humans were not ready then to have Kaela's divine power. We're still not ready.

My memory was returning again. I began to realize that that incarnation had come to an end. Kaela was gone, but her wisdoms now made sense. Of course I know who I am. It's just that being in the flesh doesn't always afford me the luxury of retaining this knowledge.

I ask again: Why do you take so much recollection? Why do you fill others with the knowledge that I should know? Why do you have others tell me these things? And why do I continually cast them off? This, I'll never fully understand. No matter how many lives I'm given.

✠

I returned with the Angel of Death to the astral plane, and retook my place beside Him in the valley. Every time I'd come home, I'd bring with me a fresh understanding of who I was and what my life, as His "consort" signified. Each time growing closer to becoming "One" with Him again.

With every life exchange, I'd begin to retain greater portions of my times with Him between incarnations. Each new life allowed me to keep in consciousness, certain facets of our romance; specific scenes from which I could extract meaning and love. The emotions and experiences that I'd absorbed and witnessed on the physical plane served to broaden "our" unified understanding of the flesh experience. Through me, He is able to feel what it's like to be human.

As an extension of His spirit, I could teach Him about things that He couldn't possibly comprehend dwelling in the astral realm. He was too detached from the "human condition". If we were to help mankind, He had to know what mankind needed most. He had to understand things like fear and love.

"Eventually..." He would explain, "you will come full circle, from complete unity with me, through purposeful separations, and then back again to the singularity of our spirit. Love is the bond most necessary to fulfill the Divine Purpose where each soulmate finds its "other half", and in so doing, completes the cycle in a perfect and powerful union that transcends its origins."

I gradually began to realize that the objective of my incarnating was more than to simply be a messenger, constantly shuttling back and forth between worlds. I could do something that He couldn't. My half of our duality was able to dwell in the flesh for periods of time long enough to effectuate His station. I could in fact, educate Him in the ways of the world, so to speak. This participation couldn't be attempted without me, not for any real amount of time! Least of all, the lengthy years and decades it often takes to make vital teachings and messages stick in the flesh realms. But through me He is able to live in this world.

In this way, He could serve His station, both in the spirit realm, and in the material world. A form of "bi-location" similar in many ways to the experience in the alien graveyard that He extracted from my "future" life.

Would any of these wonderful, new memories survive my next birth? I pleaded with Him to allow me this time, to just retain the simple knowledge of our love to help allay the terrible isolation I feel in the physical dimension.

THE ANGEL ISLE

"Take these seeds and return." Michael gave what looked like a handful of fireflies to another angel. "Take them back to the soil from which they were grown. They are good seeds and will yield a perennial harvest."

The smaller angel cupped them gently in her hand and headed back toward Earth, through the North Gate.

I was standing on a nearby threshold where a thousand of your Earth years passed by as I watched the angel's mission. She seemed momentarily uncertain as to where to sow her precious crop. Looking below, she took count of the land. Seven possibilities remained beneath. Carefully opening her hand, she counted the seeds. There were also seven.

"I will give one to each land," she thought aloud, making a straight run towards the planet.

When all seven seeds were planted, the angel sped off behind the West Gate.

Little by little, the balance of the land was being re-established. What was left of the ancient world was nurtured like a wounded lamb. The seed that the angel had sown in the land of gloom and darkness was the first to bring forth new life. It grew mightier than all others even though precious little sunlight fell upon it. Eventually it blossomed into the most beautiful rarity of nature. An emerald land sparkled in a setting of golden blue.

"Come and see." The angels hailed to all the gates. Michael burst forth like a javelin of light. The gate rumbled from the speed of His passage. He landed as a pillar of fire that burnt a twisting tunnel through the heath-haze. Other angels soon followed Him down through the mile high opening, until many hovered wing to wing around the small continent.

"Sweet homeland that is tended to with gentle rains, I recognize your visions," Michael proclaimed to His resplendent army. "You are the Angel Isle, remnant of the most ancient land on Earth."

It was here, that many came who fled the drowning of "Atlantis." It was the last remaining part of the antediluvian continent, and one of the few places where the cosmic network was still somewhat intact.

Michael regarded this place with a special fondness and took great interest in its reconstruction.

"This land will always remain, even while others might fall. This place, though unassuming in its size, shall be invincible!" He said to the Hordes of Light. "One that I shall protect forever. Tender to the hearts of all angels, as well as their consorts."

✠

In the last days of the Old World, I ferried many to this guarded place. Even through the failing of "Atlantis", we still maintained hope that one day the dwellers in the flesh would live peaceably along side those from other worlds, and dimensions.

But there's also something else about this land that haunts me as I speak. Perhaps I feel this way because in places, its Stygian beauty is similar to the likes of my realm. There's a special familiarity that goes beyond Michael's vigilant affections, into the joint memory of other lives I've shared with my beloved. Something great happened, or will happen, here between us. A thing that could only occur in a land blessed by mighty angels.

I will let her tell you of one life, for I am woefully unable to formulate these images in a way that you would understand, and we do want you to understand.

✠

Mostly, I remember the special places. Doorways through which ancient spirits would mingle with Earth souls.

At certain times of the year, the gates in the sky would align with the gates on Earth. The terrestrial ones were more like wells of energy that comprise the planet's "nerve center" Here, at these natural thresholds, those of us with recollection of earlier lives (or just other lives), would gather, almost instinctively and try to touch our old memories by interacting with the transient souls that passed between adjoining dimensions. We would reach out our hands lovingly, in the hope that something, or someone familiar would accept our outstretched welcome.

As life here progressed, stately monuments were set on these reactivated gateways. Impressive sentinels marked the way so that other travelers might come and share in our fair land. Even some spirits wayward from the first world found long lost families waiting to greet them in the ancient manner. Our legends then told us that many others of our race were taken to the outer worlds by rescuing angels during the fall of the old cities. We were trying to re-establish those ties. Trying to locate lost friends and lovers.

The winged ones, most now fully immersed in their spiritual forms, regularly instructed and otherwise aided us in the measuring and dowsing for exact locations where the monoliths would most effectively draw and amplify the sacred energies. These were powers from within the Earth, itself, as well as those pulled down from the cosmos. Everything had to be precise. Better than Esteris. More fail-safe than Atlantis! Calculations had to be refigured allowing for the loss of a large chunk of the original continent. The whole system required much restructuring. Many things needed to be shifted to compensate for the loss and rebalance the forces.

You must understand, that at this point in history, we had neither the tools nor enough knowledge yet of our own planet to have so accurately built such an intricate and powerful network without divine assistance. The pillars were made of a special stone, brought by the winged ones from remote and uncharted corners of the planet. Stone with high specific mineral content which, we were told, aided in "conducting and refining" the graceful ballet of energies. We found that they could literally be "tuned", more or less, for a variety of supernal purposes. These huge monoliths were actually levitated into place, as if they were feathers wafting to and fro between positions. The scene looked like a floating chess game. Each move made with the utmost intensity, and countered with a rival strategy until each pillar was meticulously positioned. They glided overhead like heavy grey storm clouds, pushed along with ease by nothing more than the subtle wave of a hand.

When the network was finally rebuilt, the planet seemed to "hum" with an ethereal quality that only those with memory of the first world could appreciate. The harmony between all elements was nearly re-established. We could feel it in our souls. We were once again able to freely converse with other dimensions, and have access to the wisdoms of the "Old Ones". This was virtually impossible for a very long time after the destruction, and the Earth suffered terribly for this imbalance! Some wounds were too deep to mend and had to be compensated for in other ways.

For a time, artificial bridges were used to take the place of the "lost" continent. But they didn't hold for very long, and eventually had to be replaced by a completely new pattern. One that would eliminate the need for "temporary" stations. Because the stones had such high contents of specific ores, they also served as energy storehouses, not just for collective uses, but also for individual purposes. Sometimes this aspect worried me. But I knew that Michael was watching, and wouldn't allow "THE SELF" to exploit this power.

Having physical contact with these "charged" stones could influence the levels of life-force energy by actually invigorating the spirit, or "auric field". In this manner, natural bodily healing properties were also effectively stimulated. We were working with "live" energy! Raw, life-force! We soon began to realize that it might take years to learn how to fine-tune such an incredible power. And it seemed it would take even longer to fully complete the linking of these "stations".

✠

"Stonehenge" was such a place - once! As was Avebury, and numerous others, all across the globe. These are names you recognize. Modern names of ancient earthgates guarded by steadfast sentinels of proud solemnity. "A brooding nobility that stands no more like the towering kings of yore", to quote a phrase translated from the angelic tongue.

I have had two lifetimes in this land. The one that I'd seen through "His" eyes... and the one into which I would yet incarnate. The closer this story comes into the "present", the easier it is for me to personify time with an immediacy that you can relate to. I had incarnated into the "Land of the Angels" approximately 800 Earth years after the gates were repositioned. Using current measurements of time, this would equivocate to be approximately the year 7012 B.C., give or take a century. It was already my third, physical manifestation - twice, on earth.

✠

I remember walking with an unnamed companion, among the monoliths, and being seized by their strange sadness. Their imposing shadows fell upon us like a troubled pall. I didn't understand this feeling.

"They say the stones have souls," my consort told me as I touched one, and felt its energy run through me like a mild electrical charge. "It is said that they were once living beings...in the time before. Their bodies petrified by the Old Ones in the last days for the evils they committed against the land."

"Do you believe this?" I asked him.

"I've lived all my life among the stones. I hear the echoes of many worlds that bounce between them. I've no reason to doubt that inside, they are alive. I can hear the ancient summoning," he would whisper. "The spells that brought Atlantis to its knees. Can't you hear it?"

I listened intently to the silence until the sounds grew in my mind like a subtle madness. But these were tongues twisted in anguish, and they caused me to weep with despair. I always knew the stones were special. "Alive". But I believed that their life came from the charged ore. That the planet was the source of their energy, not the struggling of imprisoned souls.

I came down with a terrible feeling in the pit of my stomach. Not all had escaped. Not all had been taken to new worlds, or found exile in the after-life. Some of the old ones became trapped by their own spells. Their souls paying the ultimate price by being sealed in the stone forever.

I looked at the troubled young face of my companion and noted a palpable empathy in his iron-grey eyes. His shoulder-length hair, the colour of burnt umber, twirled about his head with a windblown curl that looked like so many wriggling snakes.

"Can anyone free them?" he asked of me. "Can you?" Even the whiteness of his robe couldn't reflect light beneath the stones deep shadow.

I had no answer for him. No answer that he'd want to hear.

"Is this why I'm always drawn here? Are they waiting for us to free them?" he wondered aloud.

"Even if we could, what would happen to the balance of things?" I reasoned with him, although I don't think he quite understood.

"The stones would still stand," he said.

"But the stone isn't the power in itself, is it. It's the energy contained within the stone."

"I understand," he said with sorrow, "though, it was better when I didn't."

This was an observation that I could easily identify with. Part of the torment of knowing "things", is living with that knowledge. And also knowing that you can't always change the sad and painful things that are certain, necessary realities.

✠

I can only recall brief excerpts from that particular incarnation. I was allowed no further recall - I'm afraid - to be brought even into this current life. Therefore, even I cannot readily "decode" for you, this esoteric passage.

Moreover it may be that I had failed that life's end. Maybe I should have heeded my young companion's plea to release the souls from the stone. This, still, I do not know.

Musings

No wings have I
Save for those thoughts
Aloft in memory

How easily then
Were visions
Given to pinion
Far above this dream

From which I shall awaken
Yesterday into tomorrow
And cast off this heavy cloak
That imprisons the moment

Part 6

The Current Incarnation

*Out beneath the open night, a wanderer lies weeping
in some unspoken sadness while his dream is oversleeping.*

THE OTHER SON OF ARATHORN

Some there are who pass unseen. Who blend so perfectly in appearance with men that they really begin to believe that they're one of them. I once knew such a creature. He had been a compatriot of mine in two lives, I believe. Once, as my nameless companion in the last life and then again, in this current time.

His name in the latter is Carle, and he can weave a spell on the silver strings likened only to that of Israfel. Each borrowed melody, a unique translation of some mysterious intent.

We met when we were both in our late teens. I was his "Black Poet", and he was my Sage in Regal Blue". Two intense souls in a stoic world. Diametrically opposed yet drawn to the same shores like stars into a black hole. Our curiosity led us to embark on an intense quest. A quest for the things most hidden, most dark and most deadly. Together, we had an unrefined power that if controlled, could have been devastating.

As if he was exiled from "Middle Earth", he could have as easily been a high necromancer who somehow got caught in a faulty stargate and accidentally ended up in the 20th century. (A nightmare vision no matter how you look at it.)

In the best of times, we didn't want to change the world. We wanted to create a whole new alternative. At the height of our friendship, our energies were fused like a supernal flame. A powerful psychic light that we used to illuminate many overcast doorways to other worlds. We had an uncanny knack for locating natural earthgates. If we'd only had the time to hone our combined powers, who knows what fantastic things we could have done together.

Bearing nothing more than a candle, a flask of Burgundy, a couple of goblets, and a fragrant spiral, we would pass through the darkest realms where our spirits were forged into a formidable key that eventually opened the gates to the houses of Death.

The "outside" world didn't understand our special friendship. Impassioned, yet not passionate. Each, the other's testing demi-god. Two totally opposing forces coming together, partaking of each other's energy, exchanging polarities, and eventually... sadly, repelling one another in the process. He was LIFE, and I was DEATH, and this revelation cut through our alliance like an axe. I would not share in his Living, nor would he partake of my Dying! The more he became aware of who I was, the less appealing to him was the prospect of being alone with me, in the darkness... in a tomb. All the things he'd learned about the after-life seemed to fly out the window in the face of this new enlightenment.

"I need to conquer the here and the now, first" was one of the last things he told me before he left.

But I know something else. Another truth, less told. Carle had deeper feelings for me than I ever realized. At that time I couldn't hear the hinting in his music. Neither did I understand the torn look in his eyes when he'd be an unwitting catalyst for Azrael's affections. I didn't know there was a war raging in his psyche. A battle he could never win. Perhaps I should have never invited him into my twilit life. Maybe then he would now be spared that touch of melancholy that afflicts only those who've shared consciousness with Death.

It pains me still, after all these years, how the stuff of legend can be emptied with such a bittersweet sorrow.

✠

I prefer to remember the good times, when we'd choose our friends from the cairns of an old graveyard, and charm them with our daring and our youthful innocence. They, in turn, would entreat us with magical mysteries beyond our wildest dreams! These were friends that would be with us forever. We needed no special spells, or tools to call them forth, only love, and a guarded reverence... and a sincerity of spirit that could rise above its physical bounds.

We had all this, and much more!

> *"To a place of ancient splendor,*
> *I returned to moments nigh*
> *to catch the lightning in your eye*
> *and tame it with a lullaby."*

IN THE VALLEY OF THE SHADOW

It was a particularly cold and brutal New York February when I first came upon the "Promised Land."

The snow was knee deep, which made each step an adventure in discovery. This place was by far, the finest cemetery I'd ever seen on Earth, and the most secluded. As if something had brought me to its gates, I was lured in with the same affectionate whisper that drew me into the alien graveyard.

The graves lay quietly behind the quaint shops, hidden from view by hundred-year-old timbers and untamed brambles. I had lived here for most of my life, and never saw this place until then.

It has an astounding beauty that went beyond the visual. And it seemed to loudly welcome me as if all those who slept below had opened their arms to greet me. I could feel the love as I strolled with surprising ease through the deep drifts and hidden stones. Within its intensity, I could sense a powerful earthgate coming into alignment. Something was happening here - there was a pervading excitement to the landscape - an inexplicable anticipation.

In the far south corner, a most unusual tomb caught my eye. Heading to investigate, I was followed by a faint humming which sounded remarkably like a child's singing. As I neared the grave, I noticed the faint tracings of a name and date crudely etched into the weatherworn stone; BERENICE-, 189?-1904. It was styled as an underground vault, and topped with a massive, cement globe that perched precariously on a thin slab of granite. An obviously awkward arrangement, as the weight of the heavy ball was cracking the lid. Poison ivy grew in the cracks and fissures, resembling tiny veins stretching across its entire, mottled surface. Strangest of all, however, was the fact that no snow covered its lid. Not even a flake adhered to the low stone crypt. Glancing around quickly, I noticed that all the other graves were more than totally immersed in the undisturbed blanket. I reached down and touched my hand to the slab. It was as cold as an iceberg. I couldn't understand why no snow stuck to its flat surface.

The carefree singing began to sound more like muffled sobbing, and seemed to be coming from the woods directly behind the unusual grave.

"Is someone there?" I called into the woods. "Are you all right?"

No answer.

The thicket wasn't very deep, so I decided to have a closer look. Wrapping my black midi-coat around me, I headed into the brambles, but could still see no one in the sparse expanse around me. The trees were barren, so I was able to see a good distance ahead.

"Over here," a small voice startled me. "I'm here!"

I turned toward the sound, and caught only a glimpse of the fleeting form.

"I can't see you," I said. "Where are you?" It seemed to be playing a weird sort of hide and seek. I walked deeper into the woods, so caught up in my search for the playful phantom that I failed to notice that I'd been treading in ankle-deep swampland.

"Oh, great," I complained aloud. A subdued tittering came from just up ahead.

"Oh? You think it's funny?" I yelled crossly toward the sound.

A girl appeared out of nowhere! She stood barefoot in the freezing water, dressed in nothing more than a red and white cotton night-gown.

"I'm sorry," she said meekly. She couldn't have been more that 13 or 14 years old, and even that may have been stretching it. Her tawny, brown hair hung limply about her narrow shoulders, as her sad eyes entreated me with an apologetic look.

"Will you sing with me?" she asked, oblivious to the cold.

"Who are you?" I countered with astonishment. "What are you doing here?"

"Berenice!" she called out her name. "But I like to be called Beth. I live here… sometimes. I was hoping you'd come," she added mysteriously.

"You knew I was coming?"

She smiled impishly. "If you go up there you'll find what you're looking for," she pointed toward a small rise in the treeline, as my eyes followed her finger into what appeared to be simply more woods. I wasn't consciously "looking" for anything.

When I turned my glance back to face her, her thin body grew translucent. I realized just then, that neither her mousy hair, nor her clothes seemed to be affected at all by the brisk gusts of wind that blew through the branches.

"Up there! Up there!" she repeatedly urged. I could see the outline of her skeleton as if it were traced in smoke! "Then come back and we'll sing together. Go ahead now," she egged me on as a wind came up behind me and literally pushed me up and over the incline. When I looked back, she was gone.

From here, I could see the narrows of a dying stream. Its stillness revealed unspeakable things lying on its shallow bottom: sweet things, cold things, abandoned things.

✠

Across the dark water, lay a second cemetery. Its beauty sprawled out before me like a Friedrich landscape painting, overflowing with accumulated gloom and bound up in ivy like a bride that had never been touched. Somehow, I knew that "she" would yield her love, and her secrets, only to the one who'd free her from bondage.

I had come home... or at least, as close to it as I could get in this world.

Walking along the river's edge, I could swear that I saw faces hiding in the shadows of the evergreens. This was a fine place indeed! It would be the last earthgate I'd ever see. The final threshold between incarnation and eternity. Here, I'd forge the last piece in the jigsaw puzzle of PURPOSE.

✠

Carle and I had frequented the Promised Land almost every weekend diligently for the next year or so. During that time, Beth entreated us both with her ghostly friendship. She helped us to see things we wouldn't normally notice unless they were pointed out to us by her spectral hand. In turn, we'd ease her loneliness with our company, and join her in song, and teach her some newer ones.

She helped me in particular to realize that not all those who pass over are automatically happy and content. She was trapped between the worlds, I never knew by what, but somehow I had to eventually release her, if not only to allay her strange sorrow, then to some how "make up" for not releasing the souls from the stone in an earlier lifetime. Hers was a very dismal existence. As if she was unable to cross the River of Forgetfulness, yet unwilling to try. Something was holding her here. And I had to find out what.

In that time, Beth and Carle had grown extremely close. Many nights she would summon him to her tomb. With each visit, I could see that she was beginning to fall in love with him. The spiritual interaction between them was no longer platonic, no longer the company of a comforting friend. More and more he began to entreat that she manifest herself to him. (He had never seen the figure that I saw in that snowy February afternoon. But I did tell him, many times, of her appearance.)

"She has the body of a child, the soul of a woman, and the quiet wisdom of an angel," I'd tell him. "A ghost in exile from the spirit world searching for love and companionship in the land of the living."

"And this we give her," he would say.

But her sleep beneath the Earth was a restless one. Carle could feel her touching his dreams, stretching her innocent "body" across his bed, and weaving her phantom's caress through his sleeping spirit.

One night, Carle entreated her to appear to him so that he might know the face of the phantom child. And when she did show herself, he pulled back in horror from her waiting embrace! In an attempt to please him with tangible form, she had tried to weave a body from the cobwebs and crinoline inside tier narrow coffin and fit it around her pale apparition. She endured a kind of half-life standing in front of him, decaying hands outstretched as if to say, "Please! Please, love me!" But her appearance repulsed him, and he spurned her affections.

For many nights thereafter, she haunted his dreams and played upon his mind until he could stand it no more. "I don't love you!" he'd cry out.

"But you told me that you did," she sobbed.

"Please leave me alone," he begged.

"You summoned me! You called me from my rest! Now, you would cast me away?"

What he did to her, I can never forgive. For many months I had to comfort her. Had to explain to this young girl why love was often so painful, and not to take too much stock in the things that come out of the mouths of mortals. "They often say things they don't mean, not because they intentionally want to hurt you, simply because they don't understand their own emotions."

"It's because of being washed in the River of Forgetfulness," she would tell me. "He doesn't remember that we were lovers in another life:"

"He wants to conquer the here and the now," I said to her.

"Will he ever remember me?" she began to cry.

"One day," I told her. "I promise I'll do this for you. I'll make sure that he at least knows who you are."

As time went on, Carle became engaged in more "earthly" romances, and Beth began to strangely fade away. Each time her singing and sobbing grew more distant, until I could hear it no more.

I remember seeing her crossing the River of Forgetfulness. I knew, she would weep no more.

It wasn't long thereafter, when someone I know very well, gave birth to a very haunted child... called Beth.

There in gloom-choked shallows, I come search for you once more
And in the foggy mid-night, I stand weeping at your door.

GUARDIANS AT THE GATE

Another year had passed. In that time Carle and I had made partial amends and decided to get together and pick up where we left off on our road to discovery.

On a cool November evening, we returned to our nocturnal haunt and headed for the point where we felt closest to revelation; a small golgotha that I found in his absence, hidden behind a cloak of ivy. It wasn't stately or grand by any means. It was rather a humble structure, simple, grey stucco facade, rusted sheet metal roof and white, wood door. Part of it was underground as evidenced by a second cement roof that protruded from the ground like a low semi-circle. It was covered with moss and hundreds of tiny, strange red flowers. The part that was above ground looked small. Having no windows, we couldn't see inside other than through two, small air ports which couldn't accommodate a hand, and emitted a heady aroma of wet earth and bitter flowers.

For the next eight months, we'd be drawn to this place as if we were in the grip of a great and pleasant magnet. Each Saturday Vespers we'd come and dutifully "keep watch" for some promised sign of attainment. And as if it were part of the ritual, we would instinctively reach for the iron ring and give the door a cursory, yet hopeful tug.

Carle tried it first. Nonchalantly slipping his spidery hand into the ring and pulling. This time, it yielded!! Astonished, he stared. First at me, and then into the yawning blackness that crept outward, over the rotted threshold and lunged out at us like a dark hand offering an ancient welcome.

The tomb exhaled a sweet scent that enticed us into its recessed antechamber.

"After you," Carle gestured, and pulled the planked door fully open. Gently, I stepped one foot onto the brittle, wood staircase that led to the underground. Our eyes peered with wonder and curiosity at the scene below.

"Victory!" I thought aloud. We'd waited long and patient for this hidden gate to yield us its mysteries. And we knew it had many. With our combined psychic energies, we had clairvoyantly espied certain aspects of its interior long before now. For instance, we knew that the lower inner chamber was partitioned with an iron gate. This, I had seen in my mind almost a year ago. We knew that it harboured more than decaying bodies. We knew that it was the core of this place. The "heart" of the cemetery.

To us, the opening of this door was a symbol. A sign of some deserved achievement, afforded us by who ever dwelt behind the "gate". (Gate, having a double meaning here. The visible one, and the invisible one.)

We were just about to step down into the tomb when we heard the sound of cars coming toward us. Just then, a funerary motorcade entered the cemetery gates. We stood half in, and half out. Soon they'd pass right in front of the mausoleum, and our "secret" would be in full view. We certainly didn't want our portal discovered. The outside world wouldn't understand our need to be here. To them, graves should remain locked and uncovered, their secrets consigned forever within their darkness.

We eyed each other with disappointment and frustration. Reluctantly stepping out and hastily shutting the door, we took cover behind a nearby row of yews. From there, we watched as the procession came to a stop about a hundred feet from us, across the wide avenue. The hearse pulling up in front of a covered grave, where four men waited to hoist a gleaming, metal box onto the catafalque. More cars were piling in through the narrow gate like an unbroken chain of bumpers. Our prospects for a swift resumption of the quest dimmed.

"Why don't we come back tonight?" Carle suggested. "This place is beginning to look like Grand Central Station."

Our destinies thwarted, we scurried back down to the river's edge and followed its narrow shoreline to a hidden exit that deposited us back out into the world of the living.

NECROMANTIC

Later that night, I returned to the cemetery by myself. Carle remembered he had other, "inescapable" commitments. He promised to join me later, if he could get away.

Not wanting anyone else to know I was there, I left my car in the supermarket parking lot on the main street (aptly named "Grand Union") and came in through the secret entrance, tumbling down the steep incline, and landing rudely in the swamp.

The place was pitch black. The only light was that provided by the distant corona of the village streetlamps. Their pallor backlit the tall stones through a pink haze that looked positively eerie. It seemed that every creature held its breath. There was no sound here. There never was. No birds chirping. No insects buzzing. No leaves crackling beneath my stride. No echo of muffled engines from the distance. It was as if this world was soundproofed from the world "outside".

I saw the whiteness of the painted, tomb door glowing up ahead. As I made my way towards it, the moon peered out from behind a dark cloud, and glared down at the door like a spotlight. Quickly, I opened the door, slipped in, and closed it tightly behind me.

Once inside, I pulled a small candle from my pocket and lit it. Making my way down the shaky staircase, I opened the rusted gate and entered the lower level. It was roomier than I thought. The cracked ceiling was high enough to easily accommodate an upright stance. Even though it was mid summer, a delightful chill seemed to permeate the moldy air. Three coffins were stacked against the wall to my right. Wedged in on all three sides, they could not be budged. To my left, was an unnaturally large sarcophagus. Large in length, not width. Its top was torn open as if it somehow erupted from within! The rusted metal looking like it was pushed outward with a tremendous force. With a bit of effort, I bent the sharp edges back to get a better look inside. Then I lifted the hollyberry candle and set it on a small cement ledge beside the old box. Exaggerated shadows of its low flame danced on the moss-covered walls. The glow falling dimly over the supine figure that laid lifeless on a damp bed of straw and cool earth.

I reached down into the ravaged casket and began to peel the sheet from the dead form. Gently unwrapping the brittle cloth from the decaying body, I had to reach underneath the corpse to untie the twine that held the withered arms folded across the chest. As I bent over him, one of the skeletal hands slowly reached up and caressed my body, and then another clasped me in a cold embrace!

"Here as well," I whispered to myself, as he pulled me down into the coffin until my lips pressed against his cool decay. The taste of his ancient love was like the bitter harvest of a dying bloom, and as sweet as an exotic nectar. I could feel the outline of his bones pressing up against my body - as I pulled the sheet away from his face and saw how magnificent and beautiful he was.

"Let me sleep beside you," I whispered as I gently parted the veil of cobwebs that covered him and climbed into the open casket and lay down beside him. Drawing the fragile corpse into my embrace, I could feel my heartbeat pounding against the hollow chest. For the first time in a long time, I felt close again to my beloved Death. Somehow, the dead were able to serve as direct catalysts between Death and myself. This was something I'd recently discovered the more and more I had such contacts. Being near "them" somehow brought me closer to "Him", and made me more fully love all aspects of what He is. After all, the dead were empty catalysts, tenantable houses that could be occupied by passing spirits - In this case, the Angel of Death.

Lying beside him, I suddenly began to feel more intentful movement. The attempting of a definite embrace sent shivers through my soul. The arms that pulled me down were tightening around me!

"Come through. Come through, my love," I appealed silently to His attentive spirit. "I call to you my most beloved," I said as I surrendered to His approaching gloom. The skeletal embrace became even more distinct, as the stirrings in my soul intensified. A soft wind swept through the tomb, extinguished the candle, and then billowed over our tangled forms like a cold breath. Some light was still visible, but from no apparent source. The grey mausoleum was ever so faintly bathed in a familiar, amber afterglow that seemed to originate from within the walls themselves!

The straw and dry leaves rustled beneath us as I turned my glance back toward my withered lover and saw the most awful glimmer deep within His lampblack gaze. The dim spark grew into a flaming amethyst that flared as Death's touch became more pronounced, and more loving.

Everything around me was changing! The chamber. The light. The air itself! Everything within my immediate vision and sensation transformed in the macabre sensuality that washed over us like a gentle waterfall. Watching out of clouded eyes, I saw the outline of two huge black wings slowly emerge from the changeling in my arms. They extended upward and then came down and folded around me like a heavy cloak, enwrapping me completely in His thrilling embrace. His darkness was framed in a ghostly light and glistened with traces of sticky web. The figure in my embrace was no longer a human remnant. The dust and decay had somehow reformed... into something way beyond explanation! Something too incredible to describe. Something without form, yet totally corporeal... Still, I knew It was my beloved Azrael. I could feel His soul. By some magical means, He was able to alter the molecular structure of the decomposing elements and form them into a tangible chrysalis. A truly personified embodiment of Himself. A genuine, animated catalyst! I lay my soul in His electric embrace and could again feel His eerie kiss set softly on my waiting lips. But this time, His touch was made of something other than decay.

In the distance, I could vaguely discern the hum of the outside world. As if we were moving away from this dimension, it seemed to grow more and more distant until its whisper was completely gone. I closed my eyes and felt our souls unite. Ours is an eternal, unconditional love that has no need of words. No longer could I differentiate our "separate selves". We were One spirit as we left our 'bodies' anchored on the shores of the Borderland and transcended the need of this flaccid catalyst...

✠

THE MORNING AFTER

I was awakened by the vibration of the churchbells. Their muted songs played like a panegyric in the early morning silence. No sounds of life invaded my sleep, just church bells... the rustling leaves... and the wind whispering through the rotted door-jambs and vent holes.

Still pinned by Death's firm embrace, He wouldn't allow me a full breath. I was so content and complete in His arms, I had no desire to move at all. I wanted to stay forever in this place. Forever as a comfort to His loneliness.

But... I knew that I had to return to the outside world. If not now, then tomorrow, and the longer I stayed, the harder it would be to leave. Besides, my car would soon be spotted in the daylight, and those who knew me well enough, could easily discern my whereabouts.

That reality quickly cleared my head.

"I must go," I said sadly to my lover. "They mustn't find us like this. They most definitely wouldn't understand!"

So I gifted Him with one final and passionate kiss that left the taste of dust and sweet earth on my lips. He didn't respond. I didn't expect him to, yet I knew that He felt it. I knew my affection would be carried across the river on this empty vessel. The Angel of Death had vacated the ravaged corpse, leaving him as he was when I found him, so still in his seduction and ever so silent. It was time for me to steal away into the half-light, and knowing this, he released his grip.

AN OBSERVATION FROM HER VIEWPOINT

Obviously, Carle never did return that night. But there were to be many more nights! And many things that he did get to share in. Experiences that eventually grew to weigh too heavily on his mind. Things that could see through him, and discern his inner motives.

Not long after the incident in the tomb, I was fortunate enough to gain employment in the mortuary trade. In this business, you meet a lot of "interesting" people. It's the kind of work you either love, regardless of public reaction, or hate, and are in it either because of family, or business obligations, or the belief that there's money to be made in death. "People are just dying to get in" and other such corny clichés. The fact is, only those who either own, or inherit into the business live up to this image. And even this is not always the case. Discussion of the funeral trade, however, is a totally different subject, for another book altogether.

Although, once at a trade convention, I recall an unusually jolly gentlemen who offered me his business card. It was cleverly shaped like a casket with a paper "lid" that popped open to reveal his name and address.

"I'm in the coffin trade," he informed me with an upbeat bounce, and proceeded to shove under my nose, a posh, colour catalogue of "recent models", complete with photos of buxom females stroking the smooth mahogany as if it was a new Mercedes Benz. What next? Will they be sprawled out over them, legs straddling the lids in some obscene manner? Or better yet, reposing on their inner-springed interiors, clad in flimsy nighties, lips parted in a way that would suggestively anticipate the kiss of Death?

I know the beauty of Death better than anyone else. I don't need sex to sell me on the sensuality of Death. The flesh shouldn't even come into play. It's the soul that is seduced by Death, and the body, simply cast aside like a tattered shroud. The American way of death has contributed greatly to the remainder of death as a "taboo". By trying so hard to make the dead look alive, they're implying that the real face of Death is ugly, and shouldn't be looked upon. How unfortunate.

When I first began working with the dead, I had an intense desire to know and experience everything to do with death and dying. The growing realization of who I was and what that meant made me into an obsessive thanatologist. I wanted to know death from every angle, stage and description. It was a necessary part of my "retraining", so to speak, so that when I resume my place beside Azrael, I would be able to be a more complete soulmate to Death. It was just as important that I understand "spirit" as it was for Him to gain human affiliation through me. Catalysts were not really necessary, but sometimes 'they' were the only viable way for us to touch.

The more intense our spiritual romance became, the more conspicuous were its repercussions in the physical world. More of the dead were becoming willing catalysts through which He could love me. Spiritual contact exclusively, was becoming more difficult the closer we came to returning into One. The lesser astral encounters we were able to have, the greater the reactions through His material channels. These bizarre encounters were at times so intense that the tremendous power of His being welled up within them, making them do the impossible.

The earlier encounter in the mausoleum paled against what He was now able to do in both dimensions.

However, these things must remain unspoken lest they take this story way too far out of the realms of plausibility, if that's even possible, at this stage. Even in the light of their truth, I can understand that they might seem too fantastic. Too macabre to be easily believed by even the most open minded seeker. It is suffice to say, that I soon discovered that even the best catalyst could not fill that part of the soul that yearns the most, and yawns the deepest. Only His pure being can do this! Eventually, I would transcend the need of any catalyst.

Forget Me Not

I can never forget the nights,
out beneath Orion's watch
in some dark place
not of this Earth -
as if we'd crossed between
two worlds
on an unseen bridge.
All was quiet, suddenly –
No sounds familiar,
no sound at all –
that I could recognize.
The only living things were
stars
that somehow seemed much
closer then.

I cannot forget the fragrance
of Autumn's bittersweet,
the scent of dying blossoms,
jasmine spirals, and memories
exhumed from moldy crypts
and damp straw ... and brittle
leaves.

I cannot forget the touch
of Death, like Winter's sigh.
A cool breeze caressed
by shadows and ivy
entangled and draped
in this gloomy vale.
I have become a part of it,
therefore I am invisible
to the outside world
as anything else
but a silhouette.
Simply just a shadow,
like so many others
leaning and hovering beneath
the trees,
shading ancient monuments –
keeping the sleepers
out of the Sunlight,
safe in their dark catacombs
that I protect
with my overcasting,
and my love.
I cannot forget
how your darkness filled my
doorway
that cool, October dawn
when Time held its breath
and the Sun blinked
long enough for us
to say goodbye.

Part 7

Prelude to The Seventh Age

A Silent Sound;
(Eros Writes of Thanatos)

A silent sound
is the one my lover makes
when He comes alive.
A yearning expressed
but not heard
falls from His image
in tears that dissipate into fragile light.
His touch is like an electric wind
charging the edges of my soul.
His kiss is a breathless cold
that inhales life
and exhales the perfume of the crypt.
I am the living part of Death,
a delicate balancing of two worlds.
A precarious entity
with a foothold in many dimensions
and a wingspan that stretches
from shore to shore.

A silent sound
is all that most will hear
of our cry.
An uneasiness
will be the only remnant of our madness.
The only evidence of our love
be found in trails of nightmare
few will chase.
My lover is a gentle fury
who embraces with a storm
and slays souls with a touch of His hand
that pierces like a lightning bolt!
His truth is absolute.
His kiss, irrevocable.

A silent sound speaks
of a love expressed
so beyond human understanding
it cannot be heard.
So difficult a language
that it cannot be translated.
So veiled in melancholy

that it cannot be recognized
by any but the Great Spirit
and certain guardians of the Gates.
I am the living part of Death,
and though I haven't His power,
I do have His understanding-
and sometimes...His vision
And I can hear the sound
that falls from silent lips,
and I answer with a kiss.

The memories rekindled in daylight's last foray,
I stand alone and solemn in my field of hooded grey
with nothing, and yet with everything balanced in the fold.
Wrapped in PURPOSE, I am sacrifice, slowly growing cold!

It was on the twenty-second of the eighth month, ten years ago, that I would last "see" Azrael in His true form for what was to be an endless age of traumatic change.

Somehow, the reflective and complex time that followed was what all the preludes were leading up to. All the previous visits and manifestations. Every temptation and testing. Every shred of faith, love and purpose would shortly become the constricted lifelines of my very existence.

Memories became a vital sustenance that fed the fires of future happiness. I was a candle in the wind, and the wind was winning.

But my world needed time to expand its narrow interpretations. Time to understand the events of my complete life thus far, and put them into a perspective that would yield their consequent meanings. I required time to draw wisdom from their enigmas, and strength from their obvious certainties. Time to condense the millennia into a workable formula with which to execute our present purpose.

This ultimate goal required that I see everything. Not simply the things of beauty, but the horror as well. I saw these things through Him. His vision contained some of the most terrible images from this world, as well as others. Although what startled me even more, was the content of beauty and gentility also preserved in His gaze.

Even in the most apocalyptic scenes, a thing of love was found and emphasized. For example, when the first world collapsed and such a frightful tragedy descended upon the people of Esteris, the Angel of Death would select those who suffered most from the fear of dying and proffer them His gentle hand saying, "There is peace in my darkness. Do not fear me! For I will take you to a place where you can rest and find reprieve from all the destruction."

The most painful thing about this excerpted image was not the wasting of the planet, but rather watching those about to die pull away from His open hand. Even then denying His compassion, and actually preferring to perish alive, so to speak, instead of trusting their souls into His protective embrace. Even when Kaela went down with her world, even she pulled away at first when Azrael came to bear us away. This is how deep-rooted the fear of dying is in human society. And why it will take much more than even my words to eradicate it. Even though we're speaking to you directly, you will still weigh these words against your fear. I can only hope that this telling will make the balances come up more even. The dream is that "my" truth will eventually weigh-in heavier than your fear.

Watching souls pull away, over and over again, hurts me very deeply. To see how far humanity would stray from their angelic roots, and how this unfamiliarity with their own spirituality blinds them with ill found fears. Even today! Here, in the twentieth century, things are still unchanged.

☦

I love Him, and always want Him to be aware of that. Every time He'd come to me and reach out His spectral hand, I'd take it with affection, remembering those images, and somehow attempt to make up for human insensitivity by loving Him more each time.

There are a few, occasionally, who do accept my lover's release. Most, however, do so out of despair, pain, disillusionment, or simply because they think they have no other options. They think they can escape their incarnation by stealing away across His river. They fail to acknowledge the dilemma of repetition such a fool act creates. Ultimately, they will have to complete the goal of that lifetime, if not by reincarnating on Earth, then somewhere else.

I accept His hand because I want to, and not for any other reason. And if it were that easy to flee the prison of the flesh, I would be the first to do so immediately. Fortunately, I now understand the consequences of such impatience. It would simply mean that I'd have to endure yet another physical lifetime until my original purpose was fulfilled. And this is a nightmare vision I refuse to entertain.

Our last night together began with a prophetic dream that would herald the coming of our own, personal "new age". As I lay my head on the pillow that warm, autumn night, I was unaware that a strange dream would also signal the end of an age as well.

A DREAM WITHIN A DREAM

"Men tell lies for two reasons only," a soothing voice echoed through the ancient corridors. "Because they're either ignorant of the Truth, or because the Truth simply doesn't suit them."

"I see." I said to my faceless guide, as our footsteps sounded like dull thunder in the long and stately foyer.

In the dream, we were walking through what appeared to be an old yet well maintained library. I'd never seen so many books. Neatly shelved in gargoyled bookcases as high as the eye could see. White and gold pillars of stone interspersed between the ornate shelving served to support a palatial structure.

"Rather than changing to conform to the Truth, they manipulate the Truth to conform to them. Twisting the "Divine Word" and passing the iniquitous doctrine down through the generations, where it continues to be altered until no one knows the Truth at all!" the flaming figure explained dramatically.

At the foyer's end, two large golden doors swung open and we entered a spectacular room, richly paneled in a warm cherry-wood. The fire-lit chamber was circular in shape. The bleached alabaster walls were almost completely covered with even more books. A musty scent, made bittersweet with sandalwood permeated the heavy drapings with its potent spice. In the center of the room, was a large, elaborately carved round table. Carved out of either mahogany or rosewood, it was oversized to say the least, and an impressive feat of detailed artistry.

Seated around it, was a flaming council of twelve white robed figures humanoid in shape, yet just as faceless as my host. Looking at them directly for more than but a few seconds was like looking into a white-hot sun! Their bodies appeared to be made out of pure starlight!

"Come. Sit." My host pulled out an empty, Queen Ann style chair, opposite the others.

"Do want the Truth?" another of them asked, very earnestly.

I'm sure it was obvious to them that I was made somewhat uncomfortable by their intensity. The fact that I was seated facing them led me to deduce that this was either some type of symbolic "test", or a probing inquiry. I felt as if I was on the stand and that they were some kind of divine jury waiting to determine my guilt or innocence of purpose. I felt it best to go along, as the general tone was one of serious intent.

"Yes, of course I do!" I answered with enthusiasm.

"Good!" he appeared pleased.

"The individual mind is the infinite universe," one of the others blurted out impulsively.

"Feel free to ask any question," my host spoke in a more cordial tone as he took a seat beside me. At least I had one "friend", I thought to myself. "Anything at all!" he loudly urged.

"I hear a question," a low voice from the right side of the table broke in. The sound of many voices could be heard coming out of his mouth. All in unison like a perfect chorus. "I see hands flailing up at a desolate planet. You want to know more about who you are," he announced. "So you implore the heavens to speak and threaten an unseen god with your fists raised with impatience."

He was alarmingly perceptive. He could pick up even fleeting thoughts in my mind. I was impatient with the Godsoul for keeping me from my beloved.

"Yes!" I said. "I'd like to know why I'm here? Why we're all here for that matter?"

"Do you not ask your own reflection this very question each morning in the mirror?" a softer voice interceded.

"I suppose… but I'll look anywhere for answers."

"In essence Na'Haliel, we are all the Many and the One," the same voice continued, addressing me by an ancient name. "Cells in the Universal body. Each with its own function, power and capability. Why I am "here" or you are "there", is simply to help the cosmic body grow and flourish."

It sounded all too easy, and it wasn't really the kind of answer I was looking for. I needed something more practical, more geared towards my immediate life.

"What for? What is the ultimate goal of LIFE?" My bold query drew a few strange looks from around the table.

"To achieve the completion of both individual and cosmic purposes of course!" I was unsure of exactly who answered as the voices again seemed to be many.

"How can we achieve this?" I fired back politely.

"By teaching the principles of the Universal Mind and acting upon their lessons," the first voice said, to which my host attached:

"But only when you're certain that you truly and fully understand them and how to apply them to best suit your station. Knowledge without the wisdom to use it, is useless."

"And don't just listen to the ramblings of one source!" another added scoldingly.

"Or one book," said another.

"Listen only to direct and personal communications from the Godsoul," my host again spoke. "This is the ONLY TRUTH!"

"No catalysts." I mumbled under my breath.

"Not unless you can honestly discern who speaks through them."

"But I can, now."

"I know."

"Where did we all come from?" I pointedly addressed the resplendent council.

"We? You and I?" the soft voice returned by query.

"All life," I clarified. "Everything that is! Time, space, the Godsoul, the Universe!" I exclaimed with dramatic hand gestures.

"From the infinite womb of the space-time continuum," a different voice answered with contrived humor. A few low snickers followed, and were quickly silenced by my host's menacing stare.

That's no answer anyway, I thought to myself. Sounded more like something Carl Sagan might say. Didn't think he was hiding under that flaming robe. But, it was a dream, after all. So, I guess anything could be possible.

"You're right," my host unnerved me by his easy reading of my thoughts. "That isn't an answer."

"And you deserve more," someone else contended.

"Look around you." The figure next to him bolted up adamantly from Its chair. I had to turn away from the brilliance of Its full garment. "Everything that is, is simply a dream! And when the Godsoul awakens, everything will be no more." He shrugged, then added, "If, and when the Great Spirit does return to sleep, It may dream something completely different. Where would that leave us all then?"

After that outburst, he sat down. The others eyed him with embarrassed chagrin, shaking their heads as the meeting lapsed briefly into an uncomfortable silence.

I could tell that he said something he shouldn't have. (I discovered that even angels can be victims of "foot-in-mouth" disease.) I felt the mental adjectives being hurled around the table. Theirs was an argument to which I was not privy.

What he said made some sense to me, though. It seemed quite plausible. After all, this dream was creating its own unique reality for me. How do we know that we're all not simply the product of a dreaming deity? Hum?

"Dream is creation," my host resumed speaking in an attempt to relax the tension in the air. "Every time a mortal surrenders unto dream, I am born. Death is the dreamer's life. Do you understand that?" he calmly asked.

I nodded. I did understand, but I couldn't put my thoughts into words.

"Essentially, we're all "here" to learn why we are here."

The others concurred with a nod, but now he was losing me in riddles. He could see this and tried a different approach.

He got up from the chair and moved about the room like a tall dancing flame, the scintilla flying off His garment with each motion, leaving a trail of sparks as He glided across the floor.

"Do you see these books?" he pointed a fiery finger at the wall of volumes behind us. "They are all lives. Not individual, physical lives," he stressed each word slowly. "Rather, each is a complete accounting of one, individual soul through many, physical and spiritual lives." He searched my face for evidence of comprehension.

"Some books are small and unfinished." He picked one at random from the shelf. "Others are long and complete." He motioned toward a heftier tome on the shelf below.

"Yours, for instance," he reached for a large dusty volume the far corner, "is one of the lengthier ones." The book he pulled from its slot looked to be an antiquated text, marked in several places with frayed red bookmarks. Carefully, he opened the worn, black cover and thumbed to one of the marked pages. The paper crackled with a crisp brittleness. "Here," he pointed and began to read aloud with the echo of many tongues. "Coincidence is the divine element at work trying desperately to gain our attention by SIGNS IN SUCCESSION. Do you remember this?" he asked.

"Sure I do!" I replied with amazement. "It's something I found to be true in my life."

"It is a Truth!" said one of the council. "And eloquently expressed! Bits and pieces of the Ultimate Truth are scattered into all minds. Pity they can't share this enlightenment on the physical level."

"Divinity brings the Many and the One upon seemingly chance encounters for a very definite purpose." My host resumed quoting from the fragile pages.

"Is everything I've ever said in there?"

"Not everything," he answered, as he closed the book, "only those things that are expressions of the Perfect Truth… and a few, specific events of importance in your complete life."

"That includes all of your incarnations," another voice pointed out.

"Can I see it?" I asked with great curiosity.

My application drew a chortling reaction. Again the adjectives were flying. I gathered they didn't want me to see it. What was the big deal anyway? If it's a record of my own life, what was the problem?

"Why do you wish to see it?" my host inquired, a bit on the defensive. "You know everything that's in here."

"So, what's the problem?" I asked.

No reply. "Maybe by reading through it I can get a better understanding of some of the things that happened to me." I tried to give them some kind of valid reason for wanting a peek. "What about the events from my other lives that I've forgotten? Aren't their lessons important? Couldn't remembering more of them help me in this life?"

"You haven't forgotten anything important," a voice interrupted in a patronizing timbre, "It's just that you've not reached that point in this existence where you require that specific knowledge."

That made some sense, but I still wasn't convinced.

"I'd like to see the book anyway."

They engaged briefly in another psychic conference. I could tell that at least a few of them were on my side in this matter.

"Very well," my host reluctantly supplicated, and carefully handed me the heavy, bound volume. Its weight required both hands to steady. Its textured cover was made of an unusual material that looked like velvet, but felt like stone! It was damp and strange to the touch.

"Any particular life?" he casually inquired.

"No." I shook my head, as he reached over and peeled open the book in a random fashion.

"You'd best put it down," he said and guided the awkward volume out of my hands and onto the table in front of me. "This will be a very special time," he told me, pointing at a particular passage on the upper part of the left-hand page.

"Will be?" I repeated his words. "You mean, it hasn't happened yet?"

"All things have "happened". Or did you forget about the coexistence of all time, including your "future"? It's just that you've not reached this point yet."

Slowly my eyes surveyed the open page with anticipation.

"I can't read this!" I complained, noticing the unfamiliar hieroglyph it was written in.

"I'm sorry," my host seemed genuinely apologetic. "Here, close your eyes. Please!" he entreated.

I did as he asked for but a few seconds.

"Now you can read it," he told me as I opened them, and refocused on the glowing page. "If you speak aloud the words, you'll recreate their images," he warned. "If you summon names the entity associated with it will appear. For this is the language of angels. So take heed to only see the words, and not to conjure their images by lending them emotion!"

I took a deep breath and began to carefully read the scribed pages:

October 16 - Final Entry:

The climax of an unusually rainy Saturday where twilight seemed to explode with a prism rainbow of warm hues.
The familiar gravestones appeared to be washed in a gentle shower of blood.
A small assemblage of varied figures gathered anxiously beneath the scarlet and lavender, while a distant bell tolled a solemn nine count. Lilting off key and muffled by the heavy dampness, its sound was floating on an invisible sea of quicksilver.
Some came out of her past, almost instinctively taking their appropriate places. Places vacated years ago because they either didn't understand the importance of their stations, or were afraid of its implications. Some preferred to "conquer the here and the now" - although it mostly conquered them. Few, if any, really "knew" her. Most assumed things that were grossly untrue. Many knew more, but chose not to share their knowledge. Still others came from distant worlds. Places more fond within her memory; friends closer than any this world would allow. True friends, the ones who never abandoned her when they were most needed. Those who held council through many lives, and were not burdened by obligations to any one life in particular. And newer friends - the family she had gathered together during her final life.
I could see so many faces. Some seemed confused, others looked on with serenity and complete understanding. A couple nurtured sorrow: one or two, devoid of expression. A few wide-eyed with a childlike sense of anticipation... a few more hidden behind them with faces contorted with dread.
Carle was there, I saw him standing apart from the crowd. Dressed in a dark blue velvet robe. He carried a large, silver cross in one hand, and a crystal key in the other. He stood over the draped bier in reverent communion. His iron-gray stare fixed upon a distant time could impart but one tear for their times together. It streamed down his aging cheek and dropped loudly onto the casket lid.
Behind the few, stood the Many. Like a thousand-fold of gleaming orbs, their ghostly eyes glared from beneath the skirt of nightfall. I could see the spirits of so many lifetimes and places out of the halls of wild imagination. Their advancing forms stood as far as the eye could see. Even into bordering dimensions.

Some started to dance a macabre ballet of veils, their frayed shrouds winding frantically around their gaunt bodies in the chill wind. Other acolytes broke free of their spiritual boundaries and began to take partners among the living. Even those who couldn't see them began to sense the thrilling aura that swayed all of nature to and fro.

Beth was standing in the crowd, detached from the others. She looked oddly content. Still in her nightdress, she smiled timidly when she saw Carle. When he spotted her, his first reaction was to quickly turn away... and then slowly turn back and sheepishly acknowledge her glance. She floated towards him and extended her small, white hand. He looked down at her with an old sadness, realizing, just then, how beautiful she really was.

"I forgive you," she whispered to him softly, and he fell to his knees in tears and drew the petite ghost into his robed arms.

She didn't reciprocate his embrace. Instead, she melted away into a smoky nothingness, leaving him suddenly with emptied arms. He trembled... but struggled to feign composure. All was somehow even now between them, and both could perhaps continue on in peace. I really believe that he did love her, but was afraid to allow himself to accept this emotion because of the torment he'd known Na'Haliel to endure in a similar romance with one beyond the grave. In any event, it was too late for them both to change what was written.

A paean could be heard stretching from "gate" to "gate". An unearthly melody rang out from an unseen orchestra like it was being piped in from a remote dimension.

The Promised Land was cloaked in many shadows. Each overlapping the other until definitive form became blurred and indistinct, as if one world was superimposed upon the other. An earthgate was opening in the familiar sculpted garden of stone and shadow, festooned in a veil of mist. Every inch of the place was "alive" with that same, strange energy that first drew her into its romantic gloom. Every waiting soul quivered with excitement. All eyes were turned toward the Western horizon, as the dark angel came up the road, framed in the sunset. His shadow stretching out in many lengths before Him, receded as His awesome figure emerged fully at the top of the long, wide road. His blackness billowed in the cool, autumn wind as He floated toward the congregation and stopped about twenty feet in front of them. Sounds of alarm emanated from the crowd as they watched the dreadful Bridegroom manifest in full form. Death personified in all of

His macabre beauty. Just as she remembered Him from that very first encounter. His lampblack draping flowed gracefully from head to ground, secluding any visage of features. The gentle spreading of His huge blue-black wings shimmered like satin in the pale light, their full expanse easily measuring twice His prominent height. Shadowed against the pink haze, His spectacle, as always, brought many to their knees. Many more fainted away as He raised His head and His electric glance fell upon the crowd. Everyone pulled back from the gravesite, giving Him ample space to approach the shining coffin. Slowly, He extended a withered skeletal hand from beneath His undulating raiment. The long, bony fingers seemed almost gossamer and "gloved" in a transparent skin that gave off a weird luminescence. His whole, magnificent form was framed in this cool, lavender-blue halo. Any time He'd touch something, and then take His hand away, the "liquid light" would stretch between Him and the object like the glowing tentacles of a plasma sculpture. The further He went from the object, the more it would attenuate, just as it would thicken as he came user to touching it.

With his left hand, He made a sweeping upward gesture as the casket lid lifted open. A few of the spectators dared advance for closer look. The body of Na'Haliel lay inside, loosely wrapped in a soft black velvet shroud. She looked positively radiant. Her skin was as white and as smooth as moonflower, and as cold as statuary marble. On her head was a braiding of fresh jasmine flower, interspersed with smaller purple buds. Her blue lips were slightly parted in a serene smile, and her glowing eyes were deeply set like two, sparkling gems into the angular and colourless face. Their gaze fixed intently on some twilight world. Azrael reached down, inside the coffin, making a subtle gesture, as a spectral hand rose up to meet His own. With surprising case, He lifted her spirit right out of the lifeless body. Her essence appeared like a glistening mist, writhing into a humanoid shape. She turned in mid-air and their eyes met.

✠

He looked straight into me! His terrible gaze was like a bottomless black pool that reflected images of other places far removed from this green Earth. His stare was enchanting and breathtaking as His cold hand lovingly grasped my own. With one loud whooooosh, I was swept into His gigantic wings as He enfolded me in His ethereal form. The gentle fury of His love filled me with strange rapture. I looked up, and I was once again captive to His Fatal gaze. He spoke, but not with words. He spoke in my mind, through my knowledge of language, and in a telepathic code of transliteral pictures, and vibrant emotion. A rapid succession of symbols and feelings, combining the total experience of many lifetimes assaulted my soul with profound imagery. Endless ages of stored angelic passion pierced my being like a million volts of electric current. His love plunged into my heart, slaying my soul as if with a spear of lightning.

I could hear Him now more clearly and more succinctly than ever before. His love was flowing with an unspoken eloquence I'd never known Him to be capable of sharing. He continued relaying powerful images into my vision, telling me to "close my eyes and see through His". The things that I saw have no equivalent words, in any language. The emotions felt on this level cannot adequately be expressed from one to another in this retelling! The intense nature of what we were exchanging affords me now only one description: Extraordinary! Truly extraordinary.

There was a rush rising in my head as I lay against His silent breast. A dizzying anxiety that culminated in the Certain Knowledge I'd been waiting for all my life. Visions of His luxurious river snaked out before me as total recall of all other lifetimes flooded my mind like a brilliant light. I could see His crystal ship waiting at the narrow shore, all polished and fitted with silver sails. Soon, we would journey back over the River of Forgetfulness on an ocean of faith that returns us to our homeland. Returns our souls back into One.

The sunset began dividing itself into two separate scenes. Two bloodied orbs melting into crystal rivers. Delicate willows inlaid with silver blowing like tangled hair in the wind from an open stargate, its branches twisting around the stately oaks, tangling the two worlds together. The sound they made was like the frenzied strumming of a thousand mandolins.

I felt His divinity pour over me like a voluptuous waterfall, its purity washing away all the sorrows of many lifetimes and bathing my soul in a love long forgotten. My spirit seemed to pulse with an energy whose rhythm was gradually changing and slowing with each beat. Until...I could hear nothing more except the hollow sound of rushing air become a fading sigh...

My last conscious thought was that I was FREE. Free, at last of the flesh that held my soul captive for so many lives! Free forever of that solitary existence! And free to quell His loneliness in the twilit borderland, and to remain beside and as One with the Angel of Death forever. I felt like a butterfly struggling to emerge from its dead cocoon. I was no longer prisoner to the illusion of separation.

A pale aurora surrounded their floating forms. As He swept His wings upward, the trees shivered and the brittle leaves danced upright on the pavement. The sky darkened until all light was eclipsed momentarily while He climbed into the evening's halo. The final vestiges of day's end revealed their hovering spirits locked in a ghostly embrace - as they united into one form - and then dissolved into the shadows.

✠

The West Gate opened fully, and out shot a wild tentacle of light. It struck at the old mausoleum and hurled the planked door from its hinges. A glow emanated from inside the open crypt, glowing brighter and whiter until it became too intense for the naked eye to watch. Even I had to turn away.

After a while, the flames cooled and all that remained of the familiar old tomb was the metal ring. It lay half buried in the sand glowing like a neon circle.

Carle walked over to it, carefully picking it up and cradling it in his soft garment. He then moved to Na'Haliel's corpse and placed the cooled circlet on her wrist. Her eyes were now like dull onyx. No residual of light flickered within them. Her spirit had completely flown to that distant vale, and nothing of what she was remained in the elaborate box.

He stepped back, glancing out at the others, searching their varied faces for some final nod of completion.

"It's over," a voice pealed from behind him. Carle flinched as the cold breath touched the back of his neck.

"I was too late to tell her I loved her," he lamented with uncharacteristic openness to the stranger as he turned to face him. "She knew this," the other said with a notable, German accent. The stranger was an unusually tall man, dressed in a casual tan uniform whose military style was unfamiliar. Carle looked strangely at the soldiers' compassionate face. Somehow he thought he seemed vaguely familiar, but he couldn't quite place him.

"Do I know you?" he asked, to which the man's kind, blue eyes smiled back mysteriously. Disregarding Carle's question, he walked over to the coffin and placed a sprig of pine in Na'Haliel's still hand.

"We shared something once," he said while moving toward the empty space where the old mausoleum used to be. Pulling his khaki coloured trousers up by the knees, he bent down and ran his fingers through the cinders.

"Home sweet home, my friend. Yes?" he jested in a ghoulish timbre.

Carle did not connect.

The man sifted through the remains and discovered a small glass goblet, and plucked it from the sand. At first Carle appeared surprised at the find, but his expression quickly melted into a more maudlin demeanor.

"This is all that's left... An empty vessel," the man waxed poetic. "The wine is gone. Consumed by a thirst that could not be quenched by this life, nor by anyone in this life."

Carle nodded. Somehow he understood the strangers' veiled analogies.

"All is as it should be," he mumbled.

"Somewhat," said the tall German, plucking a second glass from the cinders. "But, it doesn't matter now," he quickly added as the tone of his voice dramatically lowered, "The 'Black Poet' no longer walks alone." He looked up at Carle ominously, and casually dropped the goblets back onto the sand. "You once told her that your lives were ever linked."

"I once told her a lot of things."

"I speak of only true things," the man stressed. "Do you still believe this?"

"Yes, I still believe that," Carle replied.

✠

"Please! You must stop!" A voice was hailing from inside my mind. The scene before me burst like a pricked balloon. "I warned you about lending emotion to the angelic tongue! Now, you must close the book," my host said as he drew my attention away from the open page.

"A moment to collect myself?"

"Of course," he nodded.

How wonderful! How absolutely marvelous that these fondest wishes can be played out so vividly before my eyes. So real, so positively real! So unnervingly personal. Where did these images come from? How did they get onto these pages? Moreover, who recorded their impressions and emotions so perceptively, so intimately?

"Who writes these books?" I addressed the council nervously. "These are quite intimate descriptions," I told them, noting their personal relevance, and highly "private" nature.

"Why, each soul dictates to its own personal scribe." my host casually replied.

"I don't understand," I shrugged. "Are these 'scribes' witnesses to even our most intimate moments?"

"These aren't external beings," the soft-spoken one emphasized. "You're writing your own book! This is the true power of the angelic language. To impress its image directly and permanently into the cosmic library."

"Are you telling me that the words write themselves?" I inquired with balking skepticism.

"You could put it that way," stated another.

"Perhaps, it'd be better to say that you write them indirectly. You participate in the events, both as an observer, and as the central character. This way, all their details are sure to be recorded. They don't "write" themselves. The images have no energy without the emotion a living soul puts into them," my host corrected.

"They're like a psychic diary," said yet another.

"Like the symbols in your mind," my host cut in. "The emotions that lack a word equivalent. These are transliterated like glyphs, and then entered into the archives of eternity for others to reference from. Do you understand?" he probed my face for evidence of perception.

"I think I'm beginning to," I said. "And you are all "Keepers" of these archives?"

The host entity leaned closer. His presence was an enormous drain on my energy. "It's like when you and Azrael communicate," he explained with a whisper. "It's how you're able to feel His "touch" when he doesn't actually touch you." I smiled a knowing smile.

"Yes!" someone else asserted. "And also how you are able to then explain the feeling to others! His thoughts become animated symbols in your mind which you translate into words."

"I do understand that," I assured them. "I guess it's just the metaphysics of the actual process that's a bit beyond my grasp."

"Perhaps," my host agreed insouciantly, "but we know that you comprehend much more than you let on. You're just seeking confirmation of things you already know. You always do that," he said as he rose from the chair and deposited the book back into its empty slot. "Come," he motioned from the doorway. I got up from the chair and tried once more to get a clear look at any of the faces around me. "Please, come." He seized me gently by the shoulder. His touch was charged with a tempered and pleasant electricity.

Together, we left the room and began to head back down the stately corridor.

"Being in this world doesn't change who and what you are," he said as he walked beside me. "You mustn't be afraid of letting this be prominent."

I looked at him as his veil of light parted slightly, revealing the face of a young man, who I recognized as Michael.

"But they don't understand," I tried to tell him, suddenly finding myself more at ease - more trusting of His words.

"Make them understand. You cannot be hushed by simple ignorance. You are consort to the Angel of Death. This is a troth that you willingly accepted. Would you change this now?"

"No, of course not. Never!" I answered him with conviction. "I just want to feel that I'm doing Him justice. That's not easy when everything you say and do gets turned around."

"Think back. Hasn't everything of Truth been twisted in the flesh world?"

"I guess." He was painfully right. "Sure it has!"

"You aren't expected to force your point, merely present it."

"Then what gives it real importance?" I asked, to which he stopped and looked straight at me.

"Time," he answered resolutely, "simple time. You can't force those things that must take their natural course. Even if that course is subject to Earth-bound laws. You cannot always apply the astral to the physical. Besides, humans are notorious for avoiding truths they dislike. I should know. Sometimes, you can only serve to set the wheels in motion. You're doing just fine," he assured me with open affection. "Just fine. You know that your rewards are not in the immediate. Your faith is your strength. Draw from it freely."

He led me down the corridor toward a place where its grandeur emptied out into open space!

"Do you still remember how to bridge the obstacle of the unknown?" he asked, pointing to the sea of stars that waited beyond the gilded threshold.

"To fly on wings of faith," I cited His previous teachings with confidence.

"Then fly!" he exclaimed, as he pushed me over the threshold.

THE LAST VISIT

In the early morning light, I was lifted from the dream. Barely awake, I saw the Angel of Death standing in the narrow doorway of my room. His magnificent form filled the space with a fluctuating darkness. Shaking my sleep, I tried reaching out to Him, but found that my body had barely enough strength to raise one arm. He turned in the entranceway and looked back at me. I saw His hollow eyes flickering with pale lich-light. For some reason, I was purposely being kept immobilized so that I couldn't follow after Him, nor try to prevent His leaving. I felt Him wanting to reach for me. Yearning to take me away with Him on His impending journey. I tried again to move, still unable. The sadness that emanated from His departing form was fighting to pull the soul from my body and send it leaping to His side. Something was terribly wrong! His leaving felt different, more ominous than ever before. Troubled and nervous. Too silent... too final. I had to stretch my spirit to its limits, had to touch Him. "Please, wait," I begged, as I probed His soul and painfully discovered the secret He was keeping from me. He was unable to bring Himself to tell me that this would be the last time we'd ever have "together" in this life... at least in the intimate and direct way we were accustomed to. The only way I knew then how to love him.

All too quickly, He turned away from my bedroom and vanished into the pink of dawn. His figure trailed by a dripping light that I'd come to recognize as a symbol of His tears.

If I knew then that this manifest visit would be His last, I'd never have let Him go. Never had released Him from my arms - and He knew this.

On My Deathbed

There is ecstasy in the cold bed of Death.
A splendour that could only be expressed
as Divine.
With a breathless kiss, He seals my fate
and stills my heart, and thrills my soul.
In His dark embrace, sweet dreams take wing
and fly in to His cool river
and wash away this prison of flesh
that I may awaken into His loving arms
like a fragile phoenix conjured from the flames –
and light the way for other souls to follow.

Such constant madness at my stead
Those spectres, I have always said,
would drown me in their promises
if but one tear was shed!

CATCHING UP WITH THE FUTURE

A decade had passed. During that time, many things came to bear. My mother would pass over the river, leaving my Dad and I behind. Our reasons for being had yet to fully surface. Hers, complete, she willingly let go of her life. She thought she had taken her deep-dark secret to the grave. The private sadness that she thought no one could see. Maybe if she would have trusted us enough to share it, she might have learned its cause. Might have been better able to deal with the flashes of past lives that plagued her final years. But instead, she closed up, hemming her soul in around her and closing her eyes to the impending journey, and dying alone.

☦

Greatly in need of a change, we decided to pick up and leave the house we had dwelt in for the past seventeen years. A new beginning on all fronts... Dad was recently retired, and I had quit my job during the time of my mother's illness in order to take care of her so that he could continue to work.

It was really the first chance my dad and I truly had to "get to know each other" in over twenty some odd years. Everything that was happening now in our lives seemed intent on bringing us closer together. Giving us both the opportunity to teach, and to learn from one another. The chance to make up for "lost" years. Our close alliance was very important to both our futures.

As he no longer needed to be within commuting distance of New York City, we scoured what was left of rural suburbia until we finally found a quaint and unassuming residence about eighty miles east of the city. It was an old house, buried in the woods between the railroad tracks and the rural highway. However it wasn't until we actually moved in that I was struck with a peculiar sense of future deja vu! Until the nighttime came, and I glanced out through the screen door... and saw the outline of the high, thin trees looking like the tall masts of an old schooner against the moonlight. And I remembered what would come... sometime in the days ahead. And how anticipating this future event ran chills up and down my spine!

Living here did afford us the opportunity to recapture many lost years between us. We started out like two strangers, and ended up as the closest of friends.

Before my mother had crossed over, my father had been, basically, a "non-believer" in things of a spiritual nature. However, he soon became both witness and confidant to the strange events unfolding before him. He could no longer doubt the things that touched his life, through me. The images were always there, he just needed someone to point them out. Gradually, his vehement skepticism began to melt into a peaceful acceptance that remarkably transformed his character. The war that was continually being waged within him - between the flesh and the spirit - began to cease and free his captive consciousness. Allowing it, for the first time, to see the "enemy" it fought wasn't real. All these years he had been simply fighting the product of his fear; the demon created by his own thought. Together, we buried that sucker! And soon, his apprehension about death became nothing more than a sweet surrender to the faith and certainties that opened in his mind.

If I do nothing else in this life, I often say, I made a true believer out of a once inflexible skeptic. Not by forcing my visions into his mind, nor seducing his spirit with pretty pictures. Not by the blatant casting of benign threats. But simply by allowing him to participate willingly, and at his own pace, in the uncanny events as they unfolded before us. Thereby replacing his fear with understanding.

"The next time He sees you He'll take you," my father surprised me with this latest revelation! "I don't know why, but this is something I feel."

The more he evolved, psychically, the more pronounced and evident his natural ability as a "receiver" became. I've come to trust and rely on many of his observations, simply because they're often born out of spontaneity, and not coloured by analysis.

When I think about the things that obsessed my past lives, and then return to this final physical life that is forced upon us, I get the feeling that it will soon prove to be the most important life "we've" ever come into! Though, what a task we are burdened with. Having to drastically alter the way the Many and the One view death. This means that we also have to change the pattern of collective thought as it pertains to the basic concepts of "life" and "death". Wipe out centuries of posterity. We have to literally revise history! Interject our legend, where need be, to illuminate certain "darknesses" that have been filled in with non-sense, fantasy, and lies. Quite a chore, wouldn't you agree?

✠

As Death's paramour, my life often seems to play before my eyes as though it is an abstract movie, spewing out a phantasmagoria of detached images. Pieces of time, unrelated to all else often viewed from outside of myself as if I'm merely a spectator in my own life, participating on an empathetic level only. Through this intertangling of lives and times, vagrant images pop out of memory. Every time an ancient emotion peels away the veil of forgetfulness, I can put old ghosts to rest. Put in place pieces of the puzzle that unfolded in our past lives. Like a revelation, I came to understand, for example, the significance of Kaela's archaic visions. Why it was that she saw the things she saw. Now that they are part of the "recognizable past"! It was that she would return later to Earth, in the land we know now as Egypt. And she would rule again, but this time her kingdom would flourish in legends that still enchant the minds of men. Her name, then, was Nefertari. And like Kaela, she once was a proud and elegant queen who now has a place in human legend - as well as remembrance by the angels. Kaela didn't fail them in "Atlantis". She simply required the experience of more lives to fulfill her purpose.

I live in a medley of time. That's the best way to describe how I see my life. This bizarre passion play unfolds before me, tempting me with its immediacy yet repelling me with its empty promise. I do not desire an Earthly kingdom. Therefore Kaela's lot would never satisfy me.

The more I yearned for Azrael's love, the less I received. I don't understand this. The more I require His touch, the deeper He comes within me, and ironically, the harder it becomes over time to feel Him as an "external" or separate entity. I know inside that we are truly returning back into One... and it troubles me! I know this is what we've wanted, but it isn't without its own kind of loss.

Even now, as "enlightened" as I (supposedly) am, I have a difficult task remaining inside this body. Preferring instead to watch from "above" as it were. The moments in my life that aren't filled with busy thoughts, loud music, or intentional, mental exercise often become infected with a barrage of intense and opposing emotions. Confusion! Impatience! Madness! Yes, visible, acute insanity. This feeling of being ancient torments me with its accumulated awareness. There is no outlet for such things on this level. Solitude by choice, and by default becomes an ironic necessity - a friendly demon that both taunts, and comforts.

"The next time He sees you He'll take you," these words plague my mind.

What do I do meanwhile? How can I heed Michael's advice and be "at ease with who and what I am", in front of the world, when I must sometimes strain to shield this essential "being" even from those closest to me. Even from my father at times. Even though he knows well who I am, he would secretly, prefer that I not be myself when I'm with Him, or that I'd at least try to mask my true identity.

I want to be who I am! I don't want to hide it any longer. I cannot do this, and serve my life's purpose at the same time. These two things are one. "We" are one! Life forces them into contradiction.

People are curious about my life, so they ask uncomfortable questions, and then balk at honest answers. How then, can I be the "Bride of Death" and grow hardened and deaf your complaints? Why do you pry into my secret world and then regret doing so? The way we "make love" repulses people. Well, what about the way humans "make love"? The superficial pressing of dust against dust... the lusting after a transient flesh... the blatant disregard for the soul... the utter abomination of spirituality.

I wonder how many Earthly romances could survive as ours has, over a decade of inability to touch, see or hold each other.

Who among you can claim to be able to "make love" in the spirit only, across indefinable distances, with only formless energy as a catalyst? We have grown to despise the flesh and what it is doing to our romance.

A MANY AND ONE MIND

"It is I who killed Ceasar!" he would boast and then laugh. "Do you know why? Because I am Mankind, and I kill all who are destined for greatness," his laugh grew more sinister. "Even if they are devils in disguise," he added.

It is only late in this last lifetime that an entity, who calls itself "Andros" began to personally intercede into the Divine courtship between the Dark Angel and myself.

There were times when my spirit called out so loudly in anguish that even the souls that dwelt behind the gates could hear my echo. But only Andros answered, often lending his sharp wisdoms to my troubled quest.

"I am the collective spirit of Mankind," he would tell me. "Mine, is the nearest place to the Valley."

I grew to understand that he was basically a verbal personification of humanity as a whole. And while he told me that he had incarnated with me in earlier lifetimes, I couldn't remember him. Nor the "characters" he claimed to be. My recollection of most of the earlier lives were of abstracted instances - not their totality.

"Oh, but I'd often play a devil's advocate and provoke you into action," he said as he tried to jar my memory... with little luck, I'm afraid.

Andros had a few unique abilities. One of them, his capacity to relay messages between the Angel of Death and myself when all other means appeared closed. He had his own special way of slipping tidbits of information through unsuspecting channels. He knew how to make Death's messages reach me when I didn't know where to look for them. Andros carried Azrael's love through a secret channel and planted its verbal expression in the most unlikely, yet practical vehicles! A song, fed through the radio waves would blare on every station of the dial, something with a lyric that would be fitting for the moment. A phrase that would be repeated many times in one day by unrelated speakers. Prophetic wisdoms dropping from the mouths of children, yet unable to speak! And other such marvels that took some getting used to. I learned to pay more attention to the subtle things, the "coincidences" of life.

But, Ande, (as I'd taken to calling him) could also be purposefully deceptive. Intentionally feeding me false or exaggerated information in an attempt to test my ability to discern fact from fiction. Sometimes he'd embellish on divine messages, even to the point of assuming credit for their wisdoms. Eventually, I learned to tell the difference between genuine Truth, and invented truth.

"This is the age of the Holy Spirit," I recall him commenting one New Year's eve. "When all that was embodied in flesh will be transferred into the soul. Earth is leaving the age of the 'Son', the 'New Testament', as they like to call it," he explained. "Many have transcended the need of the flesh, and in some ways have revived the age of the 'Father', 'Old Testament', in that some are once again able to converse freely between dimensions. You realize now, Na'Haliel that you needn't go through the flesh to reach the spirit. Merely transcend it." He finished with valiant enthusiasm - "This is the completion of the mystical Trinity. This is the Book that follows their book of 'Revelations'. This is The Book of the New Age!"

I was able to sit and talk to him in a way that I couldn't with most others. He was a friend who interceded for a while when I greatly needed some intervention from beyond the realm of the physical. He didn't stay long, just enough time to teach me where and how to look for Azrael's tidings of love.

✠

It is in this final incarnation on Earth when I, as Azrael, have become trapped between the here and hereafter, yet unable to touch Na'Haliel directly. Having to rely on intermediaries so as not to upset the delicate balancing of the forces by the potency of our love.

Meanwhile, I, as Na'Haliel, am dying, not only of Earthly mortality, but of spiritual starvation. In essence, The Angel of Death is experiencing what it feels like to die.

The only, true cognizance of life that we have, comes from the Divine Purpose for which all this suffering is wrought. Would you think me absolutely mad if I told you that even through all this, I love the Godsoul for making me suffer to comprehend the worth of my life? Even though the wait is consummate torment, I appreciate the need of it in order to earn understanding of the importance of PURPOSE. It is only when you come to love the reason for your agony, that you truly comprehend the glory of the Divine Soul.

Even so, for us to nourish our common spirit and make it strong enough to shatter the paper cage others have sealed us in, we must complete our own ultimate purpose, in order to thereby deliver mankind from his fear of death.

This is no simple task, even for angels. The folly of man continues to confound even an ancient spirit that has had privilege to dwell among you. If you really think about it, all of "my" incarnations have been near the end time of civilizations, or on the final frontiers of revelation. (They are frequently interchangeable!) I often wonder if I'd ever "made it on time" so to speak. I mean, did I achieve the purpose of my previous lives? Or, was I just floating around aimlessly in a kind of "time soup", lacking the knowledge to recognize purpose as many humans today still do? Time, there's that elusive concept again. You'd think by now that I'd at least have some grasp of its progression. Why is it so imperative to the fate of humankind yet so detrimental to the power of the human spirit? What spell does this "time" cast on the human psyche? And how is it that angels are immune from its power?

I know that "our" departure from this world will be a tragically spectacular event. No quiet passage for Lady Death. No sleeping through the glory of the journey. All of my passings have been tinged with either violence or melodrama. I accept this. It's familiar. Being drowned in blood in the age of "Atlantis" was nothing next to being speared by lightning in the "Land of the Angels"! Visions of that end returned to me only recently, bringing with them other, hideous images of another, second incarnation in that fair land that is now known as Great Britain.

I was with a very small and mysterious "order" that had to be cloistered away at a location in the country where no one could find us. I remember working in dark and damp chambers with old books that no one knew still existed. Somehow, it was the job of our small enclave to learn their "forbidden" knowledge. Preserving the text in our minds, in a place safe from the ignorant, whose habit in those days, was to destroy anything they didn't understand or didn't jibe with the current, theological tyranny. My life was short, interrupted by a violent and heinous murder that took the lives of all of us.

There were seven of us - one older man and six young women. We were a religious order of some type wearing heavy garments of deep green and brown velvet that resembled nun's habits. I can only approximate the year as being around the late 1500's. This is based solely on the trappings in my immediate view.

We were cloistered together in a dank basement cistern of what appeared to be an old abbey. We were nestled way out in the countryside, busy with a sacred task that was both clandestine and tedious. We were transcribing ancient texts and hand copying them into book format. The small musty chamber was thick with smoke from oily candles. It was cold and damp, very dark and extremely cluttered. We each sat at narrow, slanted wooden "desks". No one spoke, each toiled meticulously with quill and brush. The fragile parchments brittle in our hands, we were instructed to duplicate each and every detail. From the intricacy of the page illuminations, to the esoteric text, we were somehow time-pressed to copy from nearly illegible writings. Some showed evidence of being burned, others simply weathered with age.

Our task was to preserve the words of Truth from those who would come to destroy them out of fear. Somehow, the writings had power. Manuscripts deemed "heretical and blasphemous" by the ruling parties of that time.

And come they did, in the early morning light when we were weary at our stations. Come they did with fire and brimstone in their hearts and at their heels. I remember them bursting in from all portals, brandishing blades and torches. We tried to protect the "Truth" by feverishly tucking it under our cumbersome robes. We all scattered into shadowed corners and the dark niches of the small roost. But, there was no way to escape. They came at us like madmen with torches and blades flailing. There must have been 40 or 50 in all. Some garbed in long white robes that resembled tunics with bright red emblems. Others clad like rag-tag soldiers from some unholy army.

The attacks were brutal and vicious. Everything around us was being set ablaze. A group of them took our "protector", an aging white-haired man, and lashed him to a stone column. They proceeded to gather up what books and manuscripts they could and piled them at his feet, and set it all on fire. Others cut away at his flesh with blades heated in the flames until he could scream no more. Black smoke filled the chamber and it burned to draw a breath.

When they finished with him, they came at us, tearing away our robes, searching for the books and caring not whether they rent flesh or cloth. My friend to the left held some loose pages to her breast as they ran her through, impaling her hand to the pages, and then through her heart, the blade coming out her back, pinning her to the wall. Again, they committed her to the torch's flame. Another "sister" and I crawled our way through a narrow window, barely large enough to fit through. Once outside, we climbed up from a ditch and ran out onto the grassy plain choking and coughing. We could see nothing around us for miles. No place to run. No sanctuary.

A small army tore after us from all sides until we were trapped standing back to back between them. In fear, my friend bolted. A sword tripped her up. Her torn robes caught in the brambles as she was trampled under foot by a bucking horse until her flesh split open. Still, she managed to scream, as the brute on the horse laughed and drew the beast back and forth over her remains until she wailed no more. She lay there like a lump of bloody rags and thorns. Some that witnessed looked on in horror, but did nothing to express their distaste. Panicked, I tore between the horse and the one who had turned away from the spectacle. They quickly pursued, but I was fast! Unfortunately, I made the mistake of looking back and ran face first into a red cloak, falling down into the dirt under-foot. An arm hoisted me up and a dagger pushed into my chest. The manuscripts that I had concealed were abandoned in the fleeing. He cut away at my robes nonetheless until I stood almost naked in the cold wind. My head was burning! Those behind me couldn't figure out how to remove my headdress so they set it on fire and let it burn into my skin. Falling on my knees, I struggled to pull it off. They were urinating on me to put out the fire. The smell of burning hair and urine was making me sick. I was reeling, and slipping in and out of consciousness. I could still hear the cries and screams of the others, and the laughter of those around me. I could somehow "feel" as each one of my "sisters" was tortured and slain. Our tormentors called us things, like "witches, Satan's whores of the abbey of St. Agnes". Anger possessed me as I turned and stared into the eyes of my tormentor. Though, I could do.... nothing. I was growing weaker by the moment. I was being pinned to the ground by many dirty arms. There, I was repeatedly raped by both man and blade. I was fading away. I remember making no sounds. Oddly, I was numb to it all. I could feel very little of what was happening to my body. Almost as if I was detached from my flesh, though still bearing witness to the horror. Everyone was awash in blood. The sounds of this life were giving way to the roar of a wind tunnel. All was growing dark as my life was sinking into the cool earth. I fell into a deep, dark sleep, and awoke without this nightmare.

It was over one more time. One more memory to trail me. One less life, until the next. I can still only remember the End-Tymes.

✠

This death, I expect, will be no less intense.

When I am finally finished dying and have been reunited once and for all with my beloved angel, our union will noticeably begin to put an end to the fear of death, and will culminate in the true turning of your "New Age".

My death will afford a "different" light, a more complete and balanced diffusion of the Great Spirit. Our combined purpose is evident where Dark and Light merge. This, I will not explain, it is for you to learn to understand. Our "message" is in the simple silence of the twilight. In its beauty and its shadows, there is waiting Truth: Not all that is goodly and fair is a product of the

Light. I have shown you beauty where you've been told there is only ugliness.

What do you think of when you're standing on the edge of vespers? Or when you lay, facing the first glimmers of dawn? Dying is like passing from day into night, and then waking into a whole, new dawn. It is a glorious experience. This, I promise you.

Perhaps one of the reasons that it's so difficult for angels to comprehend time is because in their reality, they can't separate one moment from another. There is no difference between past, present, or future. They are all coexistent! It is souls that move forward through time, thereby leaving the "past" in another dimension of reality. Remember, the concept of reality depends on where you're "standing" when you make your assessment.

Time, itself, doesn't "die", but simply remains still as lives move through it. This is how I'm able to lay past and future side by side for you. The past always exists – as does the future. It's only the physical limitations of your immediate present that affords time the illusion of reality. Everything I have told you is true, it was all created from the energy of thought, and therefore - it is real. I am real. As real as you.

There's an identical principle at work when the flesh expires and the spirit reassumes its original form. Life continues in the form of an energy-embodied consciousness (soul). This is all that survives the body. And it's all you need. It's your "vital essence" - Life-force, if you prefer. There's no purpose in the flesh alone. The heart and mind simply couldn't operate without this spiritual quintessence. Consciousness is the purest energy of thought, and thought creates all things, including form. Thought can also create distortions of form, and perversions in the way we perceive certain things. For example, the power of thought can be used to invoke "demons" whose embodiment is formed by the energy of fear. It is better to use the power of thought to seek Truth, rather than alter it. There's been enough of that in your world for ten worlds.

The recognition of purpose is the key concept in the greater comprehension of death as a natural and beneficial part of spiritual attainment. You must all come to realize that when a person's purpose in divine service here on this Earth is completed, no force in the universe can or should detain that soul from moving on. Most dwellers in the flesh aren't aware of the ultimate purpose that an individual soul has here. Many purposes, although complete, aren't evident in their own lifetimes. Some may even seem insignificant at first but may measurably alter a future generation with nothing more than a simple word! It requires but a moment to change all things. Remember that.

Actually change is perhaps humanity's best "enemy". You should run out and embrace it. Tremendous advances can be made by learning to understand and apply the reluctant wisdoms offered in such shifting. Personal sorrow can be converted into universal joy simply by realizing that the rapture of a soul released from the confines of the flesh supersedes one person's selfish desire to imprison that individual in the flesh simply so that he or she remains physically nearby. It's like sealing a baby in the womb and not allowing it to be born. One cannot "save" a life that's destined for a more important, and necessary service on another plane of existence. We must each move on to where we're needed most. The individual spirit, and the collective spirit (or "Body of God") must continue to grow and evolve, and cannot do so if even one soul remains trapped in a stagnant existence. All destinies are remotely yet eventually entwined. They reach the ears of the Godsoul as One Voice, just as the voices of the angels are a chorus of many, the voices of mankind should ring out as one.

If you truly do love someone, you must let them go. This I've come to know all too well. These are human words, so you do understand. Now you have to begin to heed your own wisdoms even if they he couched in cliché. I am not human, although, I'm just as subject to such laws.

The whole of humanity is Earthbound for a very definite purpose. An ancient one, and a future one. Each entangled with the other. The past overlapping the present, and uniting the future - a Many and One Mind!

BREAKING OUT OF THE PAPER CAGE

"If there are angels, there must be also demons." This is what they will tell you, those souls that claim to be "enlightened". But theirs is an "artificial" light.

Don't believe them. Demons are not quite what you'd expect. You've come to learn that we angels aren't exactly what you've been misled to believe. Neither are "demons". My very existence dispels the belief that something visually unpleasant (to your eyes), is automatically evil. This ridiculous analogy doesn't even apply in the physical realm, so why then apply it to the spiritual just because you may not like the contours of someone's face, and may even deem them "ugly". In your eyes, does this make them unquestionably evil? And only the "beautiful" are envoys of good? Do you see how foolish it is to equate visible personification with overall intent?

You want to know about true evil? The real demons that mislead humanity and detour its collective spirit from the divine path? The only "devils" that plague souls are those created by fear. Fear, is the "demon-seed". I cannot put enough emphasis on the human obsession with fear! It's what holds your race back from the enlightened knowledge. What keeps the stargates closed in your face.

Talking to people with closed minds and dormant spirits is like talking to the proverbial stone wall. Everything bounces off of it, like words failing into dead ears. Until a crack develops, that is, and bits and pieces of the "light of truth" begin to get through to the captive soul waiting in the dark, on the "other" side. The more light that filters through these deepening fissures, the more the "prisoner" is able to muster enough strength to finally tear down that blinding boundary.

The only "demons" that exist are those harboured in the blindfolded fear of a closed mind. A mind that has been blackmailed by the lying bastards that threaten "fire and brimstone" be the fate of any soul that dares to stand up and look the Godsoul in the eyes. This pitiful "demon" feeds on fear and eventually becomes pregnant with paranoia and gives birth to a "brain child" that is not only blind, but deaf and dumb as well; a child called "Ignorance".

I have found, too often in too many worlds, that humans enjoy keeping other humans captured by ignorance. Some guise themselves as "spiritual envoys", and in this forged capacity, prevent the masses from being able to touch the Godsoul directly. They work their plot by convincing others that they aren't worthy or are not as "good" and "pure" as their leaders and therefore cannot commune with "higher" entities, other than through them. This strategy keeps people from knowing any other "truth" than what they tell them, a great controlling mechanism. The dwellers in the flesh are quite adept at it! Brainwashing and blackmail are their fortes. The people remain so convinced that the Great Spirit cannot speak to them directly, that if He or His angels were indeed to attempt communication (as I have) these poor deluded masses would believe themselves being entreated by "demons". After all, "average" human beings can't talk to "God" directly any more than they can love an angel. As a result of this lie, many turn away from the very source of Truth they claim to seek. The Godsoul is not the "God" of your holy books!

The Great Spirit Itself didn't pen your christian Bible. If this were the case, wouldn't He have made sure that it jibed other such "important" works, like the Torah, the Koran, The Books of Enoch, etal.? It's a good thing that the real Truth is still retained in the cosmic archives. Leaving history to humans is like putting matches in the hands of a child.

Gentle reader, I've not come to preach to you. Although certain things that are wrong need to be corrected. And if I can help do this, then perhaps you may come to fear me even less.

The point of all this being, don't just rely on one human source of information only. Nor the "one book" as the council of angels instructed. Its meanings have been filtered down through the translations and interpretations of many "editors", not to mention the personal whims of other pseudo-editors! Their definitions have lost even the vaguest essence of Universal Truth and this lost knowledge can only be found by seeking its direct source. This requires the opening of a closed mind. The death of the "demon" whose name is Fear, and the awakening and unshackling of the human spirit. The asking of the ultimate question that is poison to human ears - WHY?

There's a very specific and deafening "noise" in the silence of the human subconscious. Listen intently to it and heed its hearkening. It is the clamor of souls vying for your council. If you recognize the spiritual self, this new knowledge will bring hope. With this primal spark, you'll have enough light with which to search for your purpose. You must suffer for this knowledge, that is part of its glory, but you'll eventually find peace because of it.

Listen! Really listen to that faint inner calling and you will understand. I promise. If you respond to the "call" you'll be granted wisdoms beyond your wildest dreams. There's no such thing as "impossible", not in my world, nor in yours. It is only a word, and it is words that limit the fluency of my message. It is true that letting go of your fear of Me may mean some major alterations in the way you currently think. Allow them to occur. They're a necessary part of your spiritual growth. Open yourself to your purpose and you will know Truth like no man can impart from one to another. This Truth is called THE CERTAIN KNOWLEDGE, and is beyond mortal tampering. This gift is only afforded by becoming "one", even for an instant, with the Universal Soul: "A moment in eternity", as it were. A brief knowing of all things in all dimensions denotes touching of the Godsoul directly. Remember this, that I have told you!

The tools necessary to complete the Great Work of your race, and your individual spirit, are in your hands. When what you seek is not without look within. "The kingdom of heaven is within you" were the words of an enlightened human. Why don't you really try to understand them? The astral plane is not in some lofty location beyond the stars. Even a stargate can lead inward, rather than across the bridges of time. Take time in silent counsel with your soul. This is the primary catalyst of the Divine Voice. Its universal language is translated here, after which it filters down into the physical mind ready for application.

The blood and wine sweetly mingled
on cold, blue lips that kiss the dawn
with fury and gentility
that mortal men will only mourn.

OUR NAME IS MELANCHOLY

Humans are always asking me why, if I'm such a benevolent being, do I "take" so many lives through "unfair" means such as illness, tragedy, and so on.

In order for me to answer this, first of all, you have to understand that there must be things like this. They are imperative for maintaining the vital balances between all things, both Earthly and cosmic. Material, as well as spiritual. There is no "acceptable" way to relieve a spirit of its flesh, certainly not to those who dwell in the physical world.

My kiss is too often misjudged to be some sort of punishment, or poetic justice that the Great Spirit inflicts upon its people. I am not some sordid reaper of grim tidings. This is only what your fear has made me. On what are your fears based, the hearsay logic of the ignorant? The forceful lies of aspiring demigods? Not only is your historical view of me a grave misconception, it is also an elaborate support that aids in promulgating the apprehension of passing across my river. It is an offence to my gentle nature. I am not sent as a "punishment". Nor is the method facilitating the separation of body and soul to be construed as some kind of divine retribution. Specific people are not pursued by illness or disaster as if such were a sinister devil avenging itself by the "taking" of life. Have you ever actually seen me chasing anyone around with a scythe - flailing it about like a deranged apparition?

Here is yet, another dilemma. If I may break away from the point for a moment, Semantics! Another reason why I deplore your spoken language. I do not "take" life. I transfer it from one "body" into another. I give life back. I come to release the consciousness from its decaying flesh and afford it a strong and immortal body.

It's only a fool who would want to live forever in the flesh, in one, solitary life. Existing on a planet where no one would ever die. Where no one grows old, and no one grows at all. No evolution of life, spiritual or corporeal. A world so overrun by flesh that there be little room for anything else. Imagine the millions of bodies that would require a space in which to dwell. What about enough food to sustain this perpetual embodiment and other resources essential to eternal, physical survival? Where would they come from? Most importantly, what hope would anyone have of ever passing into a more evolved being? Everyone would remain a stagnant soul, suspended in time in one single dimension with no hope of escape from the personal and collective emptiness that would grow deeper with each year. There'd be no hope of ever returning "home"... no joy of completion. Prisoners of forever. Is this really what you want? I think not.

Having had consciousness for endless aeons, I can tell you, first hand, it's not something that a flesh being would, or should aspire to. In the spirit, it's different because your world is made limitless by simply being spiritual. There are no boundaries here.

Each one of us, whether angel, god or man, is a cosmic circle, a special messenger come to deliver, complete, and retrieve pieces of the "Great Plan".

However, divided in two as I am, part of me often feels as if it's been marooned on an alien planet. Devoid of the nourishment our spirit needs to survive here. We cannibalize memories of both worlds, until they become unrecognizable carcasses, stripped of any substance. Their brittle bones tossed with reverence into the cairn of time.

This is the longest life I've ever had, and by far the most tormented. Even the faintest contact between our isolated spirits stands out like a dim candle flame against the great blackness of midnight. The more lives I live, the more restless I become. The accumulated history I acquire becomes more of a curse, and less of a blessing with each new revelation. At times I even revert to believing that simple ignorance, albeit a shallow consciousness, might have indeed been better for the cause of my own sanity. That carefree careening fool still lives inside me, but I will not allow its escape. In any event, logic tells me that innocence, in this manner, would've just prolonged and increased my incarnations. Foolish thoughts ultimately melt away in the light of our promised eternity together. I would withstand anything to assure this. No sacrifice was too great.

Knowing who and what I am not only segregates us from everyone, else, but begins to feed my madness in the very way I alluded to earlier on - by the simple knowing of too many things. I have very vivid and horrible memories of being brutally wrenched from my beloved Death. I can still hear the echoes of angels wailing. The feeling tears at me like a taloned wraith. I experience this torture over and over again until my reasoning becomes twisted in a whole new direction, bringing me to the edge of the "forbidden" thought of "ending it all", one more time.

And whom in this world can I turn to? Who can I explain these feelings to that will understand enough to be able to advise me? Gentle reader, you must realize by now that I have no real friends in this dimension, none whom I could entrust with the delivery of my very soul. No one with which to share, openly these innermost emotions as I have with you. No one willing to catch our bitter tears. No one to save me when the Beast of Emptiness tries to swallow me whole.

When I'm totally alone, I pick up the pieces of melancholy and try to make them into a collage of joy... It is always temporary.

Gentle reader, you are a stranger to me, yet I can comfortably share with you my most intimate moments, maintaining this "safe" distance, divided by paper and pen. Your unconditional friendship is mine to keep. You know me at once, and are therefore not given time to judge me. You understand my life by viewing its totality, not by eking it out with me, moment by moment, stringing events like pearls onto a fine thread of sanity. You are privileged to see the whole picture at once, complete with detailed annotations. You are offered reasons with which to fathom even the most unbelievable scenario, even if the truth shocks your sensibilities. You know me too well now. And I am grateful for your friendship.

The dwellers in the flesh can't comprehend the depth of our sorrow. It's an anguish that pierces through ages, rather than years; through souls rather than hearts. I am constantly assimilating the grief of a million generations of mortals and immortals. When you grieve, it is often for the simple passing a life partner. Ours is not this kind of loss. It is the dying of the One, being reborn into two utterly separate entities - each having evolved its own consciousness, thereby becoming a permanent duality. Even when we are reunited, we will retain this dual mind. Only now, that I fully understand this do I completely feel its pain.

I am so far from home in this world. At times, so profoundly lonesome. Sometimes, I feel as if I'm the last person alive on Earth, and all the other forms are just ghosts in my imagination. Phantoms of what has been... or perhaps I am the spectre haunting your world.

We are in agony, and no one sees this. No one in the physical dimension, anyway. If they do, they turn away. Gentle reader, don't you see? Every single human and cosmic tragedy is part of our soul. Nevertheless, I know all too well that the most singular, personal loss is by far the most grievous.

All that has died, be it worlds, angels, gods or men, is reflected in my eyes. I am the Angel of Death. At all times, a legate of this personified expression. I've witnessed galaxies collapse in upon themselves. Whole planets made the victim of the fears of one soul. And even though time and space cannot enfold an "incomplete" world, many have tried to foolishly circumvent this eternal law with temporal means. The result of which is not only a rerunning of time, but an upset on the grandest scale whose ripples are felt from one end of this universe, to the far shores of another.

I've beheld tiny planets embattled for even smaller specks of land, or for other, equally trivial reasons. Do you know how easily your globe could fit on the head of a pin in the grand arena of infinity? Your battlegrounds would fit just as easily on its point. Such a waste! All this vital energy spent on hurrying those across my river who aren't ready to pass over. The human race is as guilty of this crime - if not more, than most. Even your smallest horrors and petty brutalities weigh heavily on the hearts of angels. Yea, even Michael, who has been washed in blood many times over, hides His tears behind a warrior's maile. You'd be shocked at how affected we are by what you consider the least of your cruelties.

I've witnessed the rape of purity itself. She screams ever so faintly, yet her pitiful cries echo from one end of eternity to the other. In such afflicted moments, all things Divine cover their ears and weep in secrecy, as the universe loses more than you could ever know. I've seen Faith slain a million times over and then rise again each time like an ancient Phoenix, stronger, yet more melancholy with each new rebirth... like me.

Do you think that I don't feel? I feel all of your emotions magnified a thousand-fold! I am capable of a love beyond any image the word invokes. I can teach you to feel a love that mortals do not even know exists! A love that angels don't even dare in their wildest dreams. Yes, even angels dream.

I know what true separation feels like, and the agony it inflicts on even the mightiest of souls. Why do you think the Universal Soul needs us, as much as we need it?

You experience on the level of but a few, brief lifetimes what I've suffered with since time began. I grieve for every tear you've shed in my presence. Not for the discarding of a worn flesh, but instead, at your misunderstanding of what dying means, and the pain this inflicts upon Me.

The kiss of Death is a sweet thing. It is a gentle and passionate gift bestowed on weary travelers. As if to bid a fond farewell, this parting gesture is shared between friends and lovers in all dimensions. But when a spirit is recalled for incarnation and bids a tearful adieu to its soulmate, even the kiss of the Great Spirit Itself cannot allay this kind of sorrow.

If everyone would just stop trying to improve upon what is already "perfect" in the eyes of the Godsoul, the balances that were in effect at the dawn of your world may be realigned. Stop trying to shape that which is without form. Don't attempt to artificially change that which changes itself, when necessary. Learn to understand that the more souls you prolong in the flesh, the more I am forced to release to maintain the balance for your own good, not for mine.

When I take a soul from your world... from your house... from your arms, I give it true freedom. Something it can never have in the physical world. And I offer each soul a choice, also something essentially unavailable in the Earthly domain. The ability to know all there is to know! To travel through time, as you have done with me, and find each soul its own, true homeland. Whether you wish to retrace ancient memories, or to choose a new path that's an extension of your soul's unique purpose, I am the one you will come to need most... and the one you desire least. I hope my story will change that.

If you saw things from where I stand, you wouldn't accuse me of "taking" life, but rather you'd thank me for giving life back. The body isn't meant to be eternal. Physical life is analogous to the changing seasons, a perfect example of the micro and macrocosm. When summer comes on your planet, you shed your heavy overcoats and head for the waters to wash the winter away. When you die, you abandon your flesh in a similar fashion, and wade into the cool river where I wash away the shield of forgetfulness that served as your protection from madness in the flesh.

Gentle reader, I need your help. When you see a widow weeping, tell her what I have told you. When a new mother holds her lifeless child, fill her with my story. When it comes your time to pass over, remember my gentleness... When I kiss you, it is the kiss of my Bride that tenderly frees your sleeping spirit. I am both Fury and Gentility. And we come to you as one. I have touched all phases of life, and have seen things "inside out". I've held opposites in the same hand, and I absorb human suffering every moment. Your humanity drains me more than you'll ever know.

My hand is there. It is opened to you in a loving gesture. Please, let me comfort you. It is part of what I do.

> *Blue angel smiles.*
> *I can sense the half-life that has become him,*
> *and touch the walls of time that hold him*
> *captive between both worlds.*
> *His back to the light, and face in the shadows.*
> *His songs seem to come from everywhere.*

SONG OF THE BLUE ANGEL

One time, when I had come to free a human soul from its withered flesh, I brought the angel Tzadkiel with me. He had never seen a spirit being released from the body and wanted to see what it was that inspired such trepidation in the hearts of mortals by the mere thought of dying. Tears began to well up in his eyes as he watched the suffering spirit pull away from me.

"They will not take your hand," he observed with surprise. "Perhaps if you came as a gentler god," he reasoned. "Less imposing."

"There is nothing harsh in my approach, and they do not all see me as you do," I explained to him. "Often I appear to them as they envision me to be."

"But isn't it a collective vision rather than a personal one?" he asked. "Humans fear the countenance to which it's attached. They can still sense who you are."

"They refuse to know me during their lifetimes," I lamented as I pulled back from the woman's cowering spectre. "But didn't Na'Haliel fall in love with this "collective" vision? Even though the veil of remembrance was not yet lifted from her face?"

"Surely, my brother, her memories can by no means be compared to any other mortal. Not pertaining to such matters. You know her love for you relies not upon any specific personification."

"She's always preferred my 'darker' image," I found myself defending against his reasoning.

"That's because she loves you for who and what you are. Full knowing of both! She, too, has chosen to share this lot," he reminded.

"How is it you've come to grow so wise?"

"The brief times we've shared consciousness were most enlightening. I'd never before experienced such profound depth of emotion... ever... anywhere," he emphasized strongly.

With that, Death reached down a second time and lifted the woman's frail spirit out of the trembling flesh.

"She still fights you," Tzadkiel commented, as I swept the flailing ghost into my arms. "Will her fight not cease?" he asked.

"It will," I assured him. "As soon as she realizes that she's already in my embrace and there's nothing else to fear. She'll look up at me and begin to understand what I've done for her."

✠

I have put much of who and what I am into this world as the woman called Na'Haliel. She has melancholy at her stead, and doesn't always understand why. She weeps at things others will not see, and smiles when others cry. Her emotions are drawn more from my realm, than from the physical world. Certain differences between both dimensions may, at times, beguile her reasoning. This is caused only by the illusions created by dwelling in the flesh. Over this, I have little control. I'd love to flood her soul with certain, ancient memories. But I dare not risk the consequences.

Nevertheless, she knows that she must eventually strip the veil from her soul. She must become a "naked spirit" so that mankind may learn to recognize his own spirit. There isn't much time. There's a weird sense of deadline at work here that even I can't fathom.

Somehow, all of our lifetimes have led up to this moment. All experience culminates here, on the tail end of Earth's 20th century into the beginning of the next. We'll never be closer to the collective soul of humanity than we are right now.

I will not be tamed! I will no longer be bound by these narrow bones, nor tied to this planet by threads of silver sinew. "We" will be who and what we are whether it pleases you or not. I've no reason to be afraid of you, nor you, of me. Tell me, what "awful" revelations does my life really bring? Simply that I exist as a living spirit? Surely I am entitled to Life as much as you are.

Does the fact that I'm able to love, or better yet, be loved repel you? Perhaps it's the fact that I've a consort walking among you, and that she loves me for what I am, in all of my many forms, from my cobwebbed embrace, to my winged majesty. She can love me as easily in the grave as she can in the stars.

I will no more remain silent. I've too much to say, and precious little of your "time" in which to say it.

I am sorry... but I'm unable to feel joy when a "new" life is born into your world. It is that nature did design the pains of birth and the cries of the child intentionally! Distressing clues as to what's really happening.

Did you know that each time a child is born into this world, a soul is torn from its true home? A lover is pried away from its soulmate? When your race calls forth "new" flesh, free spirits are washed in the River of Forgetfulness, pushed through a harrowing vortex, only to have their life-force compressed into small and burdensome bodies that will serve as their soul's prison for the next 70-odd years. To be born into the flesh is to forget. For the ripping away of their joyful memories, albeit painful at first, is really a blessing in disguise. This you can believe. All recollections will eventually be returned.

I've watched souls in such torment, clinging to me in a pitiful plea for compassion. "Please don't let this happen!" they cry out, as their twisted forms are sucked into a downward spiral. Their tenuous bodies dissolving, as the pull of matter swallows their tortured faces. Is it really any wonder a life is born screaming into your world? Just imagine the agony a soul endures trying to cling to a lover that incarnating must not allow it to remember. This would certainly be too much for anyone to bide and still exist on your planet with sanity intact. Gentle reader, you are protected by the veil of forgetfulness, even though I know that each one of you hears the anguished cries of your own spirit in the back of your mind. "We", (Na'Haliel and I), endure many such memories, and because of the powerful, psychic link between us, their images have consequently filtered through this protective veil. I cannot prevent this.

INTO THE ABYSS
(An Observation from Her Viewpoint)

From the rapture of union by the dark water's edge, I was cruelly ripped from my angel's embrace. Torn away from what I was, into a form that would become "me". Still, and always, I remember the terrible pain of being stretched and split in two. From one wailing scream into a chorus of agony, I was flayed as if by mighty talons. Falling, spiraling, ever deeper, ever more diffuse. My essence atomized and twisted in the hellish descent. Drowning in the waters of forgetfulness. Spinning, as I vas drawn under its rippling surface by unseen hands. Changing, swirling... terrible loss...emptiness. Pieces of me - memories, peeling away in the black descent. All senses continuing to feel, to take in, to experience, absolute dissolution.

Desperately I struggled to remember it all, all of the memories that were being torn from me. Though, I could not fight the strange, new sensations that began to wrap themselves around me. I could "feel" myself no more, and I no longer knew what I was.

I had passed beyond the gales to where all was darkness and I was simply a falling ember: A fragment of some distant star plunging into the abyss. Drowned in my own becoming, and trailed only by a far off cry: that one piece of remembrance. The spark that shadowed my journey was carried on a river of tears that led out to a sea of quiet darkness.

Everything is muffled and distant here. Awakening, but not remembering the sleep, let alone the dream. Snippets of scenery and emotion strike at the soul like a knife. The sorrow is the strongest of all recollections. The nightmare of being torn asunder, from what, I could not recall.

THIS IS NOT PARADISE

I am aware and wrought with sensation. Something solid clenches about me. Suddenly, I am conscious of sound. It is harsh and painful. There is an opaque membrane, behind which is a distant light. I can see tiny pulsating red and blue sinew, and I realize that my "form" pulsates in synchronous rhythm. One by one, my new senses come alive and I become aware of my confines, my solidity, my tiny prison. It expresses my emotion. I cry out in horror!

Birth is neither miraculous nor divine. The assuming of flesh is not a "blessed event". Birth is the rending of spiritual union. The painful descent into duality: the sensation of being "encased" to the point of suffocation. The striking realization that I could no longer extend myself to touch the spans of time and bridges of space. Only a spark of one's True Self is ever delivered into this world. It's no wonder that we emerge wailing and screaming! Those unseen hands that wrenched me from His embrace were now solid and I could feel them closing around me, firmly easing me into the harsh light.

Why is it that no one questions the cries of the newborn? It's because of the pieces of precarnate memory that we issue forth into this world with a banshee's cry. The horror of being cleaved in two carries the wailing from one world, into the next. If this were an empathic world, we would know what the newborn is feeling. We would, ourselves, remember! But, no… this is an expressive world. One in which we must elicit our feelings with cold, impersonal sounds. Thus, the newborn speaks its agony in the way of its new world. A paean of screams appropriate to the emotion.

As time passes, whatever trace memory remains is slowly washed away by new thoughts, the bright, shining images of a colourful dimension. The old senses are deprived by the overloading of new sensations. Eventually, we adapt to our limited prison and learn how to work within its narrow confines. Before long, almost all pre-birth recollection is either deeply suppressed and locked away, or simply lost forever to the new persona.

Isn't it ironic though, that we spend the rest of our little lives struggling to remember and striving after who and what we are and what "IT's" all about? We are all trying to ignite an inferno from that one, single spark that trailed us. We are all straining for enough "light" to find our way back home. We all know that THIS is NOT that place.

As one learns to continue in this world and the body grows old and begins to weaken, stronger memories start to peek through the decaying barriers, like the sunlight after a lifetime of nights. When the flesh is finally discarded, this is the true birth! Now is the time for the joys misplaced when the flesh began. This is the moment for celebration.

Many a tear of joy have we shed for these emancipated souls. Many soulmates have I happily reunited. Many have we washed in the River of Remembrance.

Strangely enough, there are a few who actually desire to return to the physical. Not all souls comprehend the great differences between realms until they've lived many lives, both "here" and "there". Their ignorance shields them from the Truth, whether it be by choice, or by simple innocence. For them, the loss of rebirth is lessened and the confines of the corporeal form are not as noticeable, therefore they appear happier, but are actually less at peace than even those souls that are haunted by prior visions. They'll always endure a gnawing emptiness, and know not how to go about filling it.

As I pointed out earlier, some can never fully incarnate. Flesh and blood cannot sustain the magnificence nor the power of such beings. Their spiritual energy would quickly overwhelm even the purest and strongest flesh. Such is the case with angels like Michael, the "others", and myself.

And then, there are those who have been put into this life with too many memories unavoidably retained from previous lives. Like Na'haliel, they are inescapably haunted by a constant romanticism. Still, they have the advantage over the "un"-haunted because their blank slate will also not reveal to them why they came back (or were sent back) nor the overall purpose of their latest incarnation. Hence, they will stagnate in a wasted journey that is doomed to be repeated again and again until it is fulfilled. This is sad for me as well because only angels can hear the cries of a trapped soul.

What is often even more disheartening is the apathetic lack, on the part of a vast majority of the human race, of basic curiosity as to why they're "here" at all. Don't you people care about the significance of your life? It is as if your race is sleeping with no wish to dream, nor to awaken! You are forgoing so very many important "appointments".

I don't want to preach to you, gentle reader, just sharing my thoughts with you creates a great joy in our heavy spirit. Joy in knowing what makes us melancholy. Recollection is a vital sustenance, as well as a painful poison. Sometimes it may seem to you that the Great Spirit is trying to starve your soul by not permitting you to partake of the much needed nourishment of inner peace. Even angels require this! When I'm in this weakened state, my muse constantly imparts random pieces of jigsaw puzzle wisdoms. Now, you have to realize that muses often speak in parable and convey divine "secrets" in the guise of astral poetry. Mine is not eloquent in this way. It is portentous, and symbolic. A muse is like a pursuing voice - our conscience? - telling us to do one thing, when we'd rather do another. A muse is a spiritual entity, not necessarily angelic, who can also access time, and thereby guide us by being able to see beforehand the results from decisions made in the "present".

A muse can also impart widsoms relevant to personal insights.

"More people in your world does not mean that more spirits are being created. But rather that more souls are incarnating into the flesh." I call my muse the Blue Angel and like the council, it speaks in a chorus of many voices. In a lilting "singsong" tone that is reminiscent of a kind of ethereal soliloquy. "New souls can be "born" as the Godsoul is constantly subdividing its cellular body into additional, individual organisms."

The entity seems to be different than "us". Not really an angelic being. Something more alien from perhaps an even older, or higher dimension. I can't quite tell which. It may very well be a direct personification of the Godsoul! In any event, this hybrid consciousness imparts some rather ominous and esoteric wisdoms. Either it unfolds its mystery in verse form, or frantically tosses images out in a haphazard string of unrelated symbols that I must then attempt to decipher.

"I am a powerful metaphor!" it strains to make known. "I am all those things in your collective memory that make you what you are. I am all the wisdoms known to you, complete with their original meanings. I have not coloured their ultimate Truths," It stresses.

There are specific messages given me through this source. One in particular that recently came through intact in wording and syntax. Much, I'm sure, is symbolic. However, it's perhaps the most accurate and complete accounting of the essence of this Being's overall purpose that I can offer. I will relate it to you exactly as it was given to me.

✠

"When the spirits from beyond the West Gate come into this world, things will appear 'out of time'. Synchronicity will be lost to double images: one Earthly, the other, spiritual. A tree of light will rise up into the darkening sky, and seven stars will glare down like all seeing eyes.

An ancient door will open where seven stones encircle, and two worlds will merge briefly into one. Souls will be exchanged; some returned, some removed. Beside a shaded river another shore will rise and a crystal ship will come from over a twilit horizon. The sky will change from amber to amethyst. The barren trees will seem like silver ghosts waving hair-like branches. They will gleam almost white and sing eerie songs in time with the rush of cool breezes. This weird rhapsody will be heard everywhere. Many will liken it to something they've heard before, in another time. Allegories will come alive and take humanity by the hand. A silence will follow that is in itself, deafening!

The Sunstar will eclipse and only spears of light will show in the sky. A handful of souls will slip away unseen. They will lift up the heavy curtain of nightfall and disappear into the realm of legend. There will be equal amounts of sorrow and joy. Sorrow for those ill prepared to understand the joy. And joy for those whose journey is complete and whose purpose is culminated in the eternal. It is a time when only those who can build a bridge out of pure Faith will be able to cross the wide and bottomless chasm created by the minds that fear. They will find themselves standing precariously on the edge of this abyss. Another ledge will be visible just across this immense drop. That side must be reached in order for Divine Purpose to be met, and in order for each soul to achieve unity with its soulmate. There is no physical bridge. No structure woven of even the most subtle fibers! No visible way of getting from one side to the other without falling into the bottomless oblivion where an endless repetition of this scene is played out indefinitely.

But there is a way to cross! Not on the wings of a passing angel, nor the fleet foot of an imaginary beast. A bridge must be built without tools, or materials. It must be built over time, and space. Over lives, and out of an indestructible faith that can never be shaken. This, combined with the kind of love that inspires thought to create all things. This, which goes beyond the spoken word, is the foundation of Everything.

And there will come a time when a light will hit a stone and reflect back upon the sacred doorways here on Earth. This is what will open up the Western Gate. All timeframes will merge; Past, Present, and Future will be aligned in the eclipse. The whole of the planet will act as a stargate: a giant threshold in the Northern galaxy.

As a sign, in the years before this happens, one from a distant realm will come and inadvertently become 'trapped' here. He will die unless one from this world can help him return to his own domain. He will not be at all like us. He'll be discovered alone, in a cave-like shelter. People will fear him because he looks different and they don't understand his significance. Although it will become evident.

In the final days before the changing, the Many and the One will hold brief council and then disperse into varying forevers, and time, as you know it, will be no more."

✠

This is the (not so subtle) prophecy of my muse. It's as vivid as a recent memory, and as persistent as a clear vision from some future life we'd come to share. I am told it is "far off", yet close enough to give cause to my life here and now. When I first heard it, it made me think of the ancient incident with Tzadkiel in the final days of my first world. There was more than a hint of similarity, especially in the finding of this being in a "cave-like" shelter.

I don't know how this fits into my present life, nor can I decode many of the symbols. But, I felt if it was important enough to be imparted to me intact, then it was important enough for me to offer it to you in the same way.

It isn't that "Blue Angel" enjoys being erudite. The simple fact is, it only knows how to communicate through symbols and metaphoric ciphers. In fact, it was this very entity that aided me in the writing of my very first poem, as well as a few others. I'm pretty sure it's helping this project along, too.

I feel that it has no real grasp of literal things. Nor can it relate in terms of concrete images. Blue Angel is kind of like a hermetic amulet, hanging heavily from the neck of the Godsoul, a powerful, talismanic image of All Life.

I personally believe, that when this "new age" has settled in, and the many impurities are filtered from its fold, the prophecy will come to bear, if even by the glimmers of its first revelation. But, by that time, my life here will have paled like an October sunset, the dawn never again able to look upon my face. For I will pass after the sun has fallen, and before the moon rises, just as I'd seen it written in the cosmic archives.

Until then, however, time was still running.

Part 8

And the Two Shall Be as One!

R.I.P.

Nothing like this dream-
The space of time
and span of days

Life is nothing
like this dream-
This wallowing in tedium
and drinking of mediocrity

We strive to become
what we once were-
Struggle to remember...Try to forget

Try as we may
we cannot escape
the cycle of half-life-
The spiral of Eternity
leads to but a moment
when the Infinite blinks
and Time collapses...

Then, we can rest.

It is as if I've always known
The shadow that I cast is yours.
The prism in thine eyes eternal
Spinning visions of other shores.

As I'm writing this, I'm slipping in and out of worlds that seem so opposing, so distant to each other. Somehow I know that my time with you is short and precious.

Since the Angel of Death has come so fully within me, our individual selves find it difficult to pinpoint just where His consciousness ends, and mine begins. The closer our spirits come into alignment, the harder it is for us to feel the exchange of love we remember from the early days.

It is true that we are no longer two separate entities, with individual emotions. Realizing this gives me a nervous chill. Admitting it, relieves me. We are one, "joined" entity with shared emotions that are drawn from a common well. This gaining of unity is also a painful loss of the cognizance of "the other", making it difficult for us to focus our affections, and nearly impossible for us to touch each other. We are too close to recognize each other's face. My eyes see only into the blackness of His gaze.

These final days are chaotic, at best. Everything I think is thought twice. All I feel is amplified by His knowledge. I love him, and I want to be with Him. I miss Him terribly. Even though I know we are one, I cannot escape the paradox my emotions create.

Ten years is too long. Even for me. The quiet merging of our beings crept up on me unawares. I was of the belief that this union could only take place when my spirit was liberated from its flesh. But, I was wrong. If I had only listened more closely to what Michael was telling me in the Council dream, I would have been better able to deal with the strange emptiness this union had left me with. If I could only have reached out that next morning and stayed His departure.

SLAIN BY A HAND TOO CLOSE TO SEE

The other night, in a fit of fool's madness, I abandoned all logic and wisdom and charged recklessly, straight into the forbidden void. I just couldn't stand this inexplicable loneliness any more. This being One left me with an ironic dilemma. How was I to "split" us apart enough so that we could feel each other's love? Being in the flesh, it was impossible for me to direct my affections inwardly, especially toward a lover that dwelt inside me. I still needed that externalized image. Some separate entity that I could take into my embrace. I am not yet enlightened enough to know how to draw love from this internalized marriage.

The human side of my being took control over my spirit in a way it hadn't been able to in years. I had to "find" Him, even if it meant disrupting the natural order of things. I had to see Him again in His familiar personified expression. At that point, I needed to be with Him, more than being a part of Him.

Casting aside my own better judgment, I closed my ears to the cautioning of the angels. Determined, I was, to send my spirit out in search of my beloved. And where better to look, than on the dark shores of His twilit realm.

From where I was in this world, I had no idea in which direction His valley waited. With all my previous journeys there, you'd think I'd at least remember the way. But I never really paid attention to the twisting byways that led to the river's edge. I would, the next time.

The only thing I could do was to allow my spirit to float like a feather and wait for the tempest to waft me along its current. In my mind, I would steer its course by concentrating on the desired destination.

Sitting down in a chair by the window, I began to concentrate intensely on my goal. I could see an image forming in my mind. It appeared to be sketched on the darkness as if with a fiery pen. Clouds gathered in my eyes as I tried to see beyond its outline. The sound of my heartbeat boomed like a fist pounding against a monstrous door. Breathing tapered off into a shallow rasp, as my body stiffened into a semi-cataleptic state. A severe chill overtook my flesh. Vision and physical sensation was failing, as I summoned the strength of my will to project my soul through the smoky gate that was fading in front of me.

A rush of raw power pushed against the inside of my forehead. I could feel a gentle, rocking motion, accompanied by a subtle gust of air beneath my body. Breathing deeply, I forced open the intangible portal. Almost immediately I could feel something powerful reaching across - as my spirit spilled out into space...

Soon, I was being drawn down - dizzily spinning into a cool black vortex. Glancing up, I saw a tentacle of light stretching between my spirit and its physical counterpart. Like an ethereal umbilical cord, it grew more tenuous the further I went from my body. Without warning, I was violently hurled into deep space. There, I sailed on a wave of invisible wind that carried me rapidly through the grey desolation of the lower realms. Even further, ever deeper into the frosty blue radiance of the astral light.

At that instant, my consciousness was transferred from my Earth-bound flesh, to my soaring spirit. Only a brief moment of blackness divided this near perfect exchange.

I could feel something again taking hold of my flight. Directing its course through a maze of blurred images. But something else was also present. A force that was trying to push me back the way I came. My soul was caught between them. My voyage stopped suddenly and left me suspended in space over a starless chasm. I looked down and there were no stars. No planets, no light, no life. Nothing at all, just a black oblivion. My awareness shifted again into a dual sensitivity of both body and soul. I could feel my corporeal form breaking out in fierce seizures of heat and motion, as my spirit dangled like a fish on the end of line. An intense pain shot through my forehead as my spirit was again thrust into rapid flight. The pain grew as I approached light speed. The scenery passing so fast before me that I didn't know if I was heading up or down. I felt my heart stop completely as consciousness again shifted back into the astral.

Something was still trying to force me back. I could feel its colossus pushing up against me, straining to stay my journey. But I pressed on. My desire was stronger than that which tried to stop me. My love for the Angel of Death was mightier than the will of any other.

My flight brought me through a wind tunnel where I could feel that opposing force finally break away. Somehow I knew that where I was going, It could not follow. The rest of the way was gentle sailing, until my journey ended quietly by the banks of a shallow stream. I'd made it! I had found the Valley of the Shadow of Death. I remembered its shaded beauty, and the sweet and sour bouquet of an eternal autumn. I watched in awe as the scene before me went from latest evening, to early dawn in a matter of seconds. I tried to move, but a strange paralysis had me in its grip. Struggling formless, I tried to extend the semblance of an arm from this body of pure energy. (I'd forgotten that it takes only a fraction of the effort to move about in the spiritual, what requires enormous strength in the flesh.) After a while, I did manage to awkwardly pull myself up against one of the willowy trees that bordered the river. When my vision cleared, I glanced around at the exquisite landscape. I couldn't believe that I'd actually made it: That I was really in His shrouded isle, in a conscious, waking state. This was no dream. It was Reality! Blatant, intentional Reality.

I followed the Lich-lit river as it wound its way silently through the coloured gloom. Overshadowed by lush foliage where exotic vines with unusual and large leaves twined around the delicate trees like dark skeletons. I found myself being drawn into the cool and dreary water. Wading into its shallow center, I stood waist high in its dark quiescence. The water tingled with a strange effervescence that made it feel as if it were a living thing. I got the weird sensation of being explored by a million curious fingers beneath its depths. It was a peculiarly sensual experience. An inexplicably odd feeling that I was being made love to by the water, itself... weird! As if its gentle carbonated current was trying to wrap itself around me.

I could see something coming toward me, carried on the water's surface. As it came closer, I could easily tell it was a pale corpse, floating face up, with gaunt hands folded over its sunken chest. I grabbed hold of the lifeless body and guided it away from the embankment, back toward the river's center. Wrapped loosely in a gauze shroud and partially caked in mud, I looked down at the emaciated face as it glared back up at me with vacant eyes. I reached into the water and began to wash the mud off of its skin.

The act felt natural, as if this were part of the "duties" of being Death's consort.

Could this be yet another embodiment of Azrael? I asked myself. In any event, my natural instinct was to bathe him in the water... and not to question his significance. And thus I proceeded to do so.

If he was a manifestation of my lover, then simply bathing him, would not be enough. I will take him in my arms. That is what I've come for. With that, I wrapped my form around his lifeless body and passionately touched my lips to his. A shadow fell upon us both, as I looked up and captured a figure in the corner of my eye. I wasn't alone! Slowly, I turned and saw my dark angel standing under the shade of an ancient, silver willow. His skeleton-like hand extended out to me. Seeing Him again, like that, flooded me with delight as I released the corpse, and instead, reached for Him, and our hands touched. With little effort, He levitated me out of the sweet water and drew my soul into His ghostly embrace.

"You should not have come," He said, contradictory to His emotions. "I cannot easily depart from you again."

"I felt your sadness... your loneliness. You forget, I am greatly sensitive to what you feel. I had to come." My voice overflowed with passion and sorrow, "You were calling to me in terrible anguish."

"I do so love you," He relayed with intense feeling. "But you challenge our eternity for but a few brief moments. You must go back," He said sadly. "You must."

"Will you not bestow upon me your farewell gesture?" I appealed to Him lovingly. "I'm sorry!" I quickly added, realizing that my request caused Him additional anguish.

"I can free your soul with but one kiss," He said. "My love, it is not time. Forgive me for what I must do."

I didn't understand His apology until I met His terrible gaze straight on! In an instant, I was pulled up and out of His dark embrace into a circular motion. Higher and higher, until I was again flung like a pebble from a sling-shot, back into deep space.

I traveled so fast that I "landed" violently back into my half-dead flesh. Whatever He did caused my spirit to plummet back down to Earth and repercuss with a jolting start. I felt cold and quivered uncontrollably. Breathing was hard, as I didn't seem to have enough strength to expand my lungs. Just then, something very queer came over me, a disquieting sense of impending disaster that I don't normally feel after being with my lover. My vision was still clouded, as if I was seeing my surroundings through some sort of misty, opaque filter. I staggered across the floor, trying to grasp onto something solid to steady myself. In the hallway, I grabbed a hold of the stair rail only to find my hand pass right through it! I was grasping air.

I shuddered to think that somehow, either from the disorientation of my journey or the depth of emotion, something caused me to misjudge the exact place where my physical body lingered, awaiting its soul's return. Well that, I believed, was easily remedied. No cause for alarm. Simply calm down and think. Remember where I was before I made the journey. I was in the living room, on the sofa next to the window. With that thought in mind, I proceeded slowly and weightlessly down the short hallway, back to the room where I knew my body was comfortably waiting. (Yeah, I know, sounds strange, but this sort of thing can happen on occasion.)

As I turned to enter the room, my confidence sunk into terror. My body was not anywhere to be found! This was impossible. It just couldn't be. Confusion reigned as I spent hours "wandering" in this waking dream from room to room. Terror was melting away into sorrow. Had I indeed sacrificed our eternity together for a brief fling of impatience? This thought was too terrible to entertain. I had to stop and gather my thoughts. Use logic, and think in the most abstract terms. All sorts of "impossible" things filled my life. Why should this seem any less plausible?

Okay! Let's try a more technical approach, I thought. What's the first thing you look for when astral projecting? That tenuous strand of energy that binds one body to the other.

I turned and strained to see that glowing strand, stretched as fine as spider's silk. I grabbed a hold of it and pulled myself along, following it into an invisible distance. I was concentrating on finding my body, when a gentle wind lifted me up and carried me along the swift astral current. I meditated on my destination, creating a mental image of my goal. The stream of air that carried me changed direction and grew into a howling tempest that picked up speed and started pulling me back down again. For a second time, I was a victim of its swirling current. It forced me into a cave of winds that rudely deposited me back into the blackness.

I was awakened a second time. A muted silence cleared the sound of rushing wind from my mind. I sighed with welcomed relief as a peacefulness washed over me. Cautiously, I opened my eyes, but could see nothing but darkness. Breathing in, I noted that the air felt cold and stale. Something wet was crawling down my hand. I had physical sensation again! The smell of fresh turned earth permeated my clothes. This didn't make sense.
I figured perhaps, by some freak accident, that my body, (during the projection) had "sleep walked" outside, into the garden and here was where I now lay. In the light of that idea, I attempted to stand up. Moving barely a few inches, my head collided with something low and solid. I ran my hand over the surface, and down the sides which abutted closely on both left and right. I could feel the unpleasant panic returning. Logic. Logic! Must use logic. If I was still discarnate from my flesh, I would have easily been able to pass right through any solid obstacle put before me. I was therefore, back in my body. That much I'd established. I'd now have to rely on physical means to solve this new dilemma.
I pushed as hard as I could against the sturdy side walls. They wouldn't budge. Next, I took to pounding with all my strength against the low ceiling of my shallow prison. Blood started dripping into my mouth. My hands burned with the pain of hundreds of little splinters as I threw my writhing body against the cloth covered walls of the narrow cell. Black earth was seeping through the tiny cracks. I continued to pound against its weakening walls, fighting off the rude reality of being drowned in loose soil. It was not the thought of being buried alive that made me panic, it was the timing - it was all wrong!
Finally, I broke through the lid. A blinding dagger of light pierced my eyes as the weight of the soil fell in upon my chest. Quickly I turned away from the sun that glared down like an infernal searchlight, and crawled out of the shallow grave into the cool shade of a nearby oak. Attempting to regain my composure, I took a few, deep breaths and glanced back in astonishment at

the razed pit that held me. Talk about impossible! I couldn't even begin to fathom how something this outrageous could happen.

Still in a half-stupor, I stood up and walked back over to the hole, and glanced down into the open coffin. I don't know what I expected to see. At this point, anything was possible! I was searching for an answer... that I knew I wouldn't find. Not here, anyway.

An empty casket. A sprig of pine crushed on its velvet bottom. Another symbol? Was this bizarre experience a warning to me not to attempt this sort of thing again? Not to play Russian Roulette with a fate whose powerful emotions could easily alter the outcome of eternity with one, lethal kiss?

"We are One," the words kept repeating themselves in my mind. "I am always with you."

I must have stood there for a good twenty minutes, just pondering that concept. Trying to extract a sense of togetherness from our symbiotic romance. Trying to make one, seem like two... and yet remain one.

The sun was gradually being cloaked behind so many forming, grey clouds. A summer storm was coming. I could hear it booming in the distance. Its sound was like angels on the warpath. Their wings thundering as they descended closer to the Earth with their swords of light unsheathed.

Just then, something curious caught my attention. Concealed behind the tall cypress, at the head of the grave, I saw a gleaming whiteness. I spread the stiff branches and revealed an old, gothic marker. Tall and pointed, it bore no visible name or date... just the following inscription:

"That which is imposing here on Earth
is always akin to the fallen angel,
who is beautiful, but lacks peace,
who is great in his plans and efforts
but never succeeds-Who is proud and melancholy."

"Proud and melancholy," I repeated aloud with a pensive tone, as the sky above me growled as if to concur with my mood. The landscape was growing darker. The leaden clouds cast heavy shadows on the familiar stones and pathways of my old haunt. I had no idea how I got here. Not even a theory to support these events. Just an epitaph on a tombstone, whose words would haunt me forever. This I could deal with, somehow. At least until I looked down and noticed that I was wearing nothing but an old torn night-gown. No shoes. No socks. Nothing else. Reality returned rudely as I took cover behind the bushes and glanced around, hoping to spot my car parked on one of the dirt paths. But, it wasn't anywhere in sight. I obviously didn't drive here. It could only be a dream, a very real and vivid dream. But it wasn't. This earth tasted too real in my mouth. The splinters in my skin burned with real pain.

A cool drizzle started to fall. Dream or no dream, I thought it best to take cover as the rain was growing harder until it felt like needles on my skin. Quickly, I dashed through the soggy swamp, leapt over the narrow stream, and headed across the avenue. The old mausoleum was up ahead, and I hurried to its shelter. Spears of lightning exploded at my heels as their force thrust me up against the whitewashed door. The sky cracked open and hurled down a powerful shaft of light. It struck loudly at the tall oak, and it burst into a column of flame. The hot gale pinned my back to the door while the lightning danced around me, randomly incinerating bushes and trees in its path. "I must get inside," I said to myself. The storm was intensifying even more. Becoming unnaturally frenzied. Thoroughly drenched, I grabbed for the iron ring, but the door wouldn't budge. I pulled as hard as I could, but it seemed that the wind was pushing my body too hard up against it. Not only that. In the time since my last visit, I'd noticed that some fool had nailed it shut. No wonder it wouldn't even yield an inch. The laser lightning crashed more closely at my feet. I pulled my arms back, palms down, gripping the stucco walls. The charred, tree-limbs fell around me as I held on tightly to the small, exposed building.

"YOU ARE BATHED IN MY PRESENCE!" A voice rang out above the thundering. It was coming from inside my head! Just then, a sword of light lunged through my heart and impaled me against the wooden door! Its power was thrilling as it shot through my body and exited out of my hands, grounding itself in the walls of the tomb. The experience lasted only a few seconds. But, I'd never felt anything so utterly fantastic. So incredibly "alive"! My whole being was infused with pure energy as I collapsed in ecstasy on the narrow step.

When Na'Haliel lost consciousness, the storm relaxed. I glided over to her crumpled body, which was slouched over the step and entangled with the bushes.

I didn't want to turn her away. I wanted to fill her with my love. I wanted to make the stars swoon at our feet.

Now look what's happened. If only I could make her understand that I am constantly with her. If I could only show her my reflection in her soul.

Leaning over, I picked up her lifeless body and cradled it silently in my arms. She was soaked through with mud. Leaves and brambles wound in her hair and twined in her shredded garment.

"Oh, my love, look what you've made me do," I lamented loudly as I carried her body down to the narrow stream. "When my power is crossed with such love, it runs rampant. I've little control over its direction, as you are part of this guiding force. And if your spirit is disturbed, so is mine. I cannot tame this wild energy."

"I thought if I could somehow symbolically infuse you with my being, maybe then you'd realize the power at your disposal. I never intended its result to be so intense," I explained to her, as I stripped away her tattered garment and laid her cold body into the dark water, gently washing away the mud.

"You don't realize that when you reach out to me, you summon me with the same energy that I must reluctantly use to shield myself from your agony. I, too, long to cast away this shield... I, too, desire your death. Because of this, I was forced to call upon a stronger power. One that would assure our eternity, without the bias of my emotions," I admitted as I wrapped my wings around her cleansed form and lifted it from the water.

I surveyed the ravished cemetery with a sense of sorrow, and relief. "Michael has sealed this earthgate," I told her as my words fell into her deaf ears, unacknowledged, "positioned a guardian on its crumbling threshold. It will not allow you to cross here anymore. It will not permit our energies to divide and touch again in this way, until we are both more at peace. Until you have done what you must do, I must stay so deep inside you that you cannot easily touch me. Can you hear me?" I asked, but I knew that she couldn't. I could have spoken directly to her soul. Made sure that she heard and understood every word. Although, I don't think I could have faced her reaction. I certainly wouldn't be able to depart from her a third time. I couldn't guarantee to the Godsoul that I would let her go. Couldn't promise that I'd send her tearful soul back to face more imprisonment in the flesh.

Instead, I let her sleep, thinking it was all a dream. I put all of the images and emotions into her memory... they were too beautiful to veil.

NAKED TIME

I woke with a start to the sound of a frightful alarm. I bolted up as the daylight beamed in through the black lace curtains. The sound was coming from under the bed. I reached down and pummeled the infernal, little box, yanking the plug from its outlet. Damn alarm clocks! I swore then and there, that one day I'd arrange my life so that I was never again at their noisesome mercy.

The pain in my chest was a vivid reality. It made me reel as I tried to sit up. I was home? In bed! I don't know how...or what...or... or... Oh, what the hell! Why rationalize these things anymore? I'll never understand it anyway. I was still alive. That's a step in the right direction. I could remember nearly everything except how I got here. I could remember someone talking to me... but not what they were saying. When I managed to sit up, I noticed I was naked. Not only that, but my bed was strewn with wet leaves and feathers! - large, black feathers.

✠

The phone rang from the other room as I pulled the sheet around me and ran to answer it. It was someone calling to remind me of my appointment in the city later that day. It's a good thing too, as I couldn't recall why the clock was set for such an ungodly hour of the morning. I had lost all sense of time and place. It took quite awhile to reorient my being into the present. Actually, I'd only lost about 11 hours from the time I began the journey, to my return, the next morning.

SOMETHING WONDERFUL

Business brings me to the city maybe once or twice each month. (The less the better, as the fast life doesn't really agree with me.) It takes me a long while, even on a good morning, to work up enough energy to deal with the hustle of the "Big Apple", and the incredible madhouse called Pennsylvania Station. Not to mention the two hour trip it takes to get there on the worlds most crowded and most antiquated railroad line.

Anyway, I'm making use of this time by sharing with you, an incident that happened to me on a previous trip into Manhattan.

As any student of basic pathology will eagerly tell you, death is not a momentary event. It's a process that goes through various stages. This is true not only on the physical level, but the spiritual as well.

The process of actually "dying" reveals an unnerving dichotomy. It is in this strange half-life that the last remnant of the physical intellect is forced to acknowledge its spiritual counterpart. The two "entities" literally stand "face to face", shocked and baffled by each other's verity. In their joint consciousness, scenes of both worlds (physical and astral) begin to overlap, each vying to become the more tangible reality. Both realms, equally as real, engage the intellect and spirit in a one on one battle of strength and wits. The subservient body has no choice but to remain a captive spectator. Keeping "score", as each "side" pleads the most convincing case for existence. The flesh is subdued by their combined authority, crouching beneath the dual forces like a naughty child awaiting its fate from an overbearing elder.

Most dwellers in the flesh have seen someone physically expire, but very few, if any, have witnessed the soul's passage from world to world from where we stand.

Through all the noise and confusion of Penn. station, I could hear someone dying. I watched as hordes of hurrying figures crawled to a slow motion walk, their forms becoming more and more transparent. I could see their souls, and hear that awful screaming that comes from trapped spirits.

Across the dingy terminal, I spotted a young man in shabby dress slumped up against a dividing wall. He seemed oblivious to the movement around him. Content just leaning there, as if he was waiting for something, or someone. Suddenly, something seemed to catch his attention. He looked up and panned the scene until his soulful eyes came upon my glance across the crowd. He focused on my eyes as if transfixed by awe. In this mesmerized state he tried to stand up but his legs kept giving out beneath him. Quickly exhausted, he reached out both arms as if to invite my embrace.

I wanted to help him, but I didn't know exactly what I was supposed to do. He began pulling himself along the dirty floor, grabbing onto anything that would support his movement. He was trying so hard to reach me. I could see the tears streaming from his desolate eyes, as his lips dropped whispering pleas. I could hear him. Even through all the noise. Hear him begging, "Please take me. Please take me. Please!"

I started to walk towards him, pushing my way through the sea of suits and briefcases that flooded in front of the subway tunnel. I was losing sight of him. I couldn't hear him anymore. There were too many people, too much noise, too much life.

"Are you here for me?" someone asked loudly from behind. I didn't pay any attention. I just kept searching the crowd for the one who called me.

"Are-you-here-for-me?" a rough voice again asked, this time grabbing me by my coat sleeve. I turned my head to meet intense, blue eyes searching mine worriedly. He gasped, and let go quickly of my coat. "Will it be soon?" the middle aged man probed nervously, backing away from my stare. His tan trench-coat waving about with flailing jitters.

"I don't know." I snapped at him rudely.

"Please tell me!" he implored urgently, setting his overstuffed satchel down between his loafered feet. "You've been watching me." He reached into his wrinkled pocket and pulled out a hanky and dabbed the sweat from his forehead.

"No, I haven't," I said defensively, turning my eyes away from his in search of the other man.

"I know who you are," he announced. "I've seen you come for me in my dreams."

"I don't know what you want," I said uncomfortably, the half-truth slipping too easily from my tongue. He looked at me with a sardonic expression.

"No, I'm not here for you," I corrected by replying to his original query in the hope that he'd just go away.

"That's wonderful." He let go a loud sigh of relief and picked up his case as if ready to leave. "Who then?" He turned back to ask. "Which one?"

My eyes wandered in pursuit of the other man until I found him propped up against the ticket counter. He was breathing hard and obviously in pain.

"Oh," the older man exclaimed solemnly, his glance followed mine with keen precision. "How unfortunate. He's so young," he added.

"Age is irrelevant," I blurted angrily, trying again to make my way over to him. "Why must everyone assume that old age is a prerequisite for passing across?" I challenged his commentary as he trailed me through the crowd. "He could as easily be a boy of ten with the spiritual age of a thousand years! Would you still think he was 'young'?"

"Well..." his tongue tripped, "most people...."

"Are wrong," I interceded. "And they don't understand. You, for instance..." I stopped sharply and pointed intently at him, "could be say 55? 60? Yet your soul may've only been "alive" for but a small fraction of that man's years." I motioned in the direction of the younger man.

"You're telling me that a boy of ten can be older than a man of sixty?" he asked with skepticism. "I'm 68, and I sure feel pretty old," he quipped.

"Yes! That's what I'm saying," I replied, ignoring his latter attempt at humor, and started again towards the ticket booth.

"How are you gonna do it?" He still trailed behind me. "Take his soul out, I mean?"

"I'm not going to do anything, yet," I replied emphatically. "I'll know when I touch him."

"How come these other people can't tell who you are and I can?" He asked after realizing that in the sea of people scurrying around us, no one else singled me out the way that he did. "I thought only those close to dying could see Death?" He again grew tense and fumbled in his other pocket, this time, pulling out a crumpled cigarette.

"Not always," I began to answer, a bit startled by his forthright perception. "Some are just sensitized in this way."

"Do you know when I'm going to die?"

"If I did, would you want me to tell you?" I challenged him, face to face.

He thought about it for a minute as he lit the bent cigarette and inhaled deeply.

"I don't know," he said, exhaling smoke while his thin lips curled into a weird grin. "I really don't know."

"You should think before you ask such things," I warned, as I closed in on the other man.

"What do you see," the elder pried curiously as my eyes grew fixed on the coloured veil that began to surround the dying man. It was as if we were alone in that station; our scene "separate" from the scene around us.

"Something wonderful," I blurted out, as the young man looked up at me and smiled. I leaned down and offered him my hand. He took it as he wept.

"Can I see?" asked the elder.

"I'm sorry. I don't have the ability to lend you this vision," I told him, as the glistening veil changed into a soft darkness and enfolded the young man's limp body. His grip on my hand tightened.

"You are beautiful," the younger man whispered to me in a strained voice as the suffering was lifted from his body, and his face relaxed into a peacefulness that altered his whole expression.

"Can you tell me what's happening?" the other asked anxiously.

"I'm afraid the images are beyond any word that I could offer you," I told him in all honesty, feeling somewhat guilty that I was genuinely unable to share it with him.

"That's okay, I understand," he drew back with disappointed respect.

"Just look at his face," I suggested. "That should tell you something." The dying man's face melted into a deepening tranquility as the darkness slowly took on a familiar shape. I continued to hold his hand while Azrael gently lifted out the man's soul and drew it into His protective embrace. The frail body folded to the floor like an old overcoat. The angel wrapped the shivering spectre in His black wings and climbed back into the shadows unnoticed.

"Azrael...." His name fell from my lips in a whisper. Quickly, I stifled the urge to call out. When I turned around, the other man was gone. His long coat blending in with a hundred others like it as he merged into the living sea, and they descended the stairs to the lower platform, and disappeared into the waiting train.

THE JOURNEY HOME

Nothing that exciting happened on this trip. I share these passing images with you, as the gleaming, silver serpent crawls through the underground and slithers out of its lair. Winding through the shadows, it climbs out into the twilight with its million eyes mesmerized by the fast-forward movie through dingy, green plexiglass. Postcard images run together as the groaning viper takes on speed and divides the scene with passing utility poles.

Perhaps this is how angels perceive the mortal world? As if it is a primitive frame by frame animation. Singular yet overlapping images giving the impression of movement, but not really moving at all.

Now and then I search through the blank faces, challenging them to meet my gaze. Daring them to unveil my true identity. But, every face seems to look the same; troubled, scared and distant. Too wrapped in flesh to allow their spirits to breathe. It always amazes me how many vivid psychic impressions one can tune in to on a crowded, yet strangely quiet train. Some look up and seem to be staring vacantly into space. I wonder what they see in their private oblivion? What little "demons" they entertain in their thoughts?

A little over an hour had passed, and the creaking leviathan rumbled to another halt. A shuffling is heard as the zombie-like figures disperse into the afterglow. This was my stop as well.

I got off and walked along the tracks as the train vanished under the rusty trestle. I strolled through the quiet footpaths that led back to another lifetime; back to the old cemetery where the sealed earthgate bulged with memories, through the secret entrance that landed me on the treed incline between the two graveyards. From here, I could see Beth's memorial glinting in the distant pinpoint of a headlight.

"Carle hurt me, too," I hailed out toward her tomb. "That's a fact I can't easily forget. But I forgive him for the memories he's given me... I suggest you do the same." I delivered my recommendation into the shadows. "Wherever he is now, he'll always be part of our memory, and we'll forever regret his loss."

The place seemed so empty, so utterly barren. It was as if every soul had finally moved on. The few that remained hid in the shadows. I could sense their presence. I could feel them watching me. Waiting to see if I'd break into the earthgate, and try to escape over its threshold.

But I could tell that this gate was no longer active, that their vigilance was a bluff. earthgates are transient things anyway. Constantly shifting with the planet's movement. My ability to seek them out was stifled by my own impatience.

I am so tired of crying. So fed up with sadness and despair. So unable, at times, to deal with this melancholy. In the unenlightened moments, I sometimes fear that the sum total of our being here, in this life, will not be added up properly. I feel that no matter what I write, nor how many adjectives I employ, they could never do Him justice in the way I wish I could. The Angel of Death has bathed me in His tears and because of this I am forever disconsolate. I tell His story because I love Him, and I want others to understand His station, as well as the inner workings of His psyche. Nevertheless, I need some definitive sense that my life is accomplishing this end. I never want to come back again. Not ever.

✠

Gentle reader, it may be difficult for you to identify with our sorrow. Or my life, as you see it, may not appear that harsh, and that I have no right to complain. It's not the outward entity that hurts, it's our spirit: Our soul becoming martyred to the flesh. Why is it that the closer I come to achieving my purpose, the further it seems to grow from reality, and the more painful it becomes? What part of this story is so great a revelation that even angels would not want it known? Why, sometimes, do you silence me, when I want to tell the world about you?

I am not made of iron. I am not a stone angel. I have proven to be like the willow, bending gracefully to and fro to suit your bidding. But without your kiss, I will grow brittle and break as easily as a dead branch, and our legend become like driftwood on the seas of eternity, and our story just another bit of forgotten purple prose.

This is how "knowing" too much can drive one mad. Better to be washed in forgetfulness, because knowing who "I" am, where I belong, and why I'm here is a terrific burden. This awareness, coupled with the "human condition" is a nondescript madness unfit to sustain the life of man, or god. There are many times when I'm ashamed to be part of the human race. Ashamed of the selective ignorance, and an almost natural quest for drastic solutions to the simplest of problems.

Everything I know to be true, in the universal sense, becomes a paradox in this world. I know that there's no such thing as time, yet I find my life is on a strange timetable of sorts, and the deadline is approaching fast.

Why must I be afflicted with human qualities? Being human goes against who and what I am. I don't wish to be part of your world in this way. I have no desire to be one of you. I only want to tell my story, and leave with the knowledge of its telling. Yours is a harsh and cruel world, with no regard for things of real importance. You take all that is innocent, pure and perfect, and corrupt it with your human ways. Gentle reader, it's the things you regard the least, that are the most important.

My faith is my stead. My faith in the CERTAIN KNOWLEDGE. I love you.... I mean that. Please listen to me, for I will not come again. Unless it is to bear you home.

THE BEGINNING OF THE END

Standing on the crest of the incline between the two worlds, a strange resplendence caught my eyes as I looked toward the horizon. The angel Michael was standing in the setting sun. His raised sword dripped of blue light.

"Go!" He hailed out to me in the chorus of many voices. "It's time. Go out among the dwellers in the flesh and show them your heritage."

The liquid light spit wildly from His blade like a current of molten lightening. Its brilliant warmth transfused my spirit with power and purpose. I could feel the charged fingers touching my aura.

"I have given you that which you need to complete this world," He continued. "The confirmation of who you are. The rest has always been within your power. Look to the gate in the configuration you call "Orion". He motioned skyward with the blazing weapon. "From here will the turning of the new time begin! Be it known that I am the keeper of the last gate and you are its key."

He kept speaking while His golden form grew vaporous and clouded against the colourful sunset. His figure, sketched in laser light, sunk between the distant hilltops as if swallowed by the mouth of a great beast.

Looking up toward Orion, I saw a shooting star weaving between the triumvirate of its belt, and then it vanished behind an invisible door.

I got the uneasy feeling that nothing would ever be quite the same again. I felt as if His visit signaled the "beginning of the end". Everything inside of me was changing. Like my soul was a chrysalis taking on a new shape, a completely unified personification of "both" of us. The Angel of Death, as a flesh and blood entity.

When my glance returned to Earth, Michael's phantom had diffused into a fine ether that was wafted away like a puff of smoke on a gentle breeze.

He was right. It was time. Time to tell our story, and have our voice spread from sea to sea, in a tidal wave that would stifle fear with the confrontation of His simple truth.

The potent words of the warrior angel were the final touches to this great end. The final strokes of the purple pen on the lampblack page, the ultimate weapon of our truth to break the paper cage.

Once, I only viewed my life and my purpose as that which stood in the way of my reunion with Azrael. Now, I eagerly desire to fulfill that purpose, and will not leave until it is done. I understand its importance, its relevance to the human drama. This revelation was beginning to turn my sorrow... into joy in ways that I would discover in the times to come.

"Only spirit is worthy of battle. Fight not for the flesh, for this is a losing cause," Michael would often repeat these words. "The wars between the spirit and the flesh are the greatest and most awful testing of each human. Nothing conceived on any terrestrial battlefield could compare with the horrors inflicted on endless legions of captured souls. What is the sweetest victory?" He'd ask and then answer, "There is no victory so sweet as opening the borders of a closed mind. None so great as conquering the demons of fear that dwell within them. They hide in the dark corners, where no light has been shed. The dwellers in the flesh have made soldiers of them. Whole armies of ignorant sylphs with weapons inadequate for their task," He continued to cite in anger. "They fight blind and deaf on shores that are already free. I will never understand why they separate the forces of "light" and "dark", and compel them into waging an eternal battle that can never be won. Why?" He'd ask rhetorically. "Because they are dualities at war with themselves. If one should "perish" in battle, its brother must also perish. There can be no light without the dark. Light and dark blend in the twilight, and again in the dawn to create a perfect union that is both beautiful to behold and necessary to sustain the universe. The Great Spirit is comprised of both "dark" and "light" - and the angels are the shadows of His truth."

I watched the sunset fade into a pale green aurora. Spreading out, it divided from one light into many. Looking like searchlights, they stretched over the cemetery from the Northern horizon, and panned from East to West in a uniform pattern. I was almost certain it was the aurora borealis. It was definitely a most unusual cosmic display. Ultimately the lights reunited into one and focused on the marble sentinel at the edge of the graveyard. Bathed in a lurid, yellow-green, it seemed to be waiting for me to speak. Waiting for me to do what I'd failed to do in an earlier life. Waiting for me to free its imprisoned spirit.

I strolled over to it, and stood there pensively in the darkness of its shadow. The mouth appeared to crack open. The twilight accentuated its abeyant expression, lending solemnity to its plea. The opening, not deep enough to permit its soul to escape.

"In this final incarnation, I will not allow another race to fold in upon itself." This, I promised Him. I've seen way too many galactic suicides. This world must not succumb. "It's unnatural for time to enfold an incomplete world," I recall someone telling me. "Especially one so young as to have not yet learned how to use more than but a fraction of its collective mind."

Gentle reader, you must learn the true and total meanings of Life, Love, and especially, Death!

While it is true, that one day the Earth will come to an end of its physical life and become very much like neighboring worlds. That is only a physical end. Everything that it was will be transferred into the universal diaries and spirits will move on to other worlds… other lives… older loves.

Take stock in the fact that each soul that ever lived on this constantly dying orb is a cell in the body of "God". Each with its own purpose and identity; a microcosm of the greater whole that is comprised not only of Earth souls, but of the souls of all life-forms throughout the threefold universe.

I serve as the Angel of Death not only here, but everywhere the life-force requires transference from one form to another. It's a marvel to think of just how many worlds we have seen.

Through these incarnations, I've learnt that it's a slow, spiritual awakening through such life progressions that affords wisdom, not any schooling one flesh could offer. Only through the understanding acquired in these lifetimes will any find genuine, inner peace. A spiritual tranquility in which one can take solace in the Certain Knowledge of a worthy reason for being. This is the "miracle" of awakening for which many search. But sometimes in the simplest questions, the answers to greater quests lie screaming out at us. "Here is the reason! This is why!" they bellow. But human nature is to grind complexities into everything with a mistaken logic that believes "nothing could be that simple." But it is. Look how comfortable you are in my presence now. See how easy your fear melts away now that you know me better?

We're often too blind to see. Too burdened by the flesh to appreciate a "higher" meaning. To reach above the man-made terms of a limited reason... to do away with the paper cage. We are spiritual beings first. And we must continue to remember this. We struggle to surmount our bodies lest they seal us in and deceive our spirits with well-crafted delusions of a life filled with artificial happiness. Keeping souls in the dark, keeps them afraid of it at the same time.

"I am not afraid to stand here, before you," I addressed the solemn monument. "To have your shadow completely envelope me; to trust you so utterly as to lay my eternal soul in your hands. We are but tenants in a house of flesh. Ghosts in heavy overcoats, awaiting the change of the seasons to shed our raiments and soar uninhibited into the cool of autumn."

"Seek only therefore in this life, to understand," the council of angels hails to me in its many voices as if from a distant dream. "All other wisdoms will follow."

THE FLIGHT OF DEATH'S AVATAR

When the light gave way to evening, I could only see the outlines of the tall stones and trees, like black silhouettes framed in fire. I heard the stone angel stir on its perch. Its wings beginning to open fully - more at ease in the dark than in the light. Its giant shadow falling against the stark white of the mausoleum door.

"Are you the guardian of this humble earthgate?" I addressed the stoic figure. It answered only by deepening the silence.

I lay in its shadow on the damp ground, looking up at the full expanse of its marble wings, swearing that they moved! Certain that I heard the stone cracking! The eerie face bringing to mind yet another memory, another "moment in eternity" extracted from our joined consciousness. A time when I was privy to a dialogue between Michael, Azrael, and the neophyte angel, Tzadkiel. I closed my eyes and remembered...

"What mankind will not do for himself, nature must do for him," the conversation opened with Azrael's booming timbre.

"I am saddened that they choose not to understand," Michael lamented.

"Why do they prefer a false truth, rather than the potential for greatness that history allows?" Tzadkiel asked. "It is as if they want to look under your robe, yet not into your eyes," he added jokingly.

"They must all be made to look me straight on," Azrael spoke with intensity. "We must test their will to understand."

"They want magic! Expect it!"

"What sort of magic?" Azrael inquired.

"Oh, you know, Miracles, that sort of thing. Things that angels are supposed to do."

"No, it must be devoid of such petty melodrama."

"If you whisper, none will listen," he reasoned.

"And if I holler they will think me mad and dismiss my truth," Death reasoned further.

"Then how will you reach them?"

"By becoming one of them," Michael interceded. "Teaching one at a time, so that the one will teach another..."

"In the end, the One will have taught the Many," The Angel of Death added.

"But they don't often listen to each other."

"They will listen," Azrael assured him. "They will have no other choice. I will wear no shroud for them to peer under, and my eyes will be upon them in a way where they cannot look away without seeing me everywhere. I exist in their world through Na'Haliel. They may refuse us now, but can never dismiss our message, nor retract the Truths within it. They cannot unsay what is said. It is words, spoken," the Dark One continued. "They are impressed upon the eternal ether, and can therefore, never be erased."

"This is true." Michael confirmed. "No matter what happens - the legend is told."

✠

I remember vividly my dream of the "council", and how the angels taught me, first hand, about the power of "words-spoken". How just the fact that they're recorded affords them tangibility and immortality in the astral world.

This book is written in blood, the blood of many lives. These are true things I tell you. Assuredly, I'd not volunteer such a tale to be entered into the public forum if it weren't for my lover's urging. There are far easier things to write! Things that wouldn't require my soul to be turned inside out.

"Tell them about me. This you must! This chronicle is what stands between us. This is why you were pulled from my arms. This is the culmination of all of your lives. The beginning of the end." Such is the intensity of His urging.

However, the pen was not put into my hand to be a magic wand. I am not the weaver of tales that I'd like to be. My ability is only adequate for the recording of His eloquent Truth.

Anyway, the angels tell me, it is a waste to use the pen to conjure the images from a formless ether when the veiled realities are ever more striking. It is far better to call forth these images from the folds of time, and translate them into visions other minds can pass on as legend. I am Death's avatar. And I cling to His decaying form, and drink the bitter harvest of His moldering breath, incensed with Autumnal jasmine. To me, it is a sweet wine lingering on blue lips, from an age long gone, but not forgotten.

Not only is this chronicle scribed in blood, but in tears as well. Both joyous, and solemn –painful, and glorious. An outpouring of the contents of "our" soul - of unspeakably beautiful, and terrible things. Lately, I find myself waking up at dawn, still hoping to catch a glimpse of His return, full knowing what that return would denote. Waiting for Him to shed this cloak of withered flesh.

I've so much love inside me that I want to give Him. A love which I was woefully unable to offer Him a decade ago because I didn't understand things then, the way I do now. I wasn't able to experience His affections on the level I do now. I've many lives of stored emotion. It makes me feel as if my soul will overflow and drown Him in its content of love.

At this point in time, right now, the power of my love for the Angel of Death could overwhelm even one as mighty as He. I could easily take down His defenses and leave our eternity exposed to attack. But I will not. I will not sacrifice this for the brevity of a moment. No matter how much that moment would mean.

No force can ever quell our affections, as painful as they frequently are. This life may separate our hands, but it can never separate our souls. For even now, without Death's immediate touch, we are making love in a way the flesh could never. Our passion is not a physical thing. It's a spiritual thing. It wells up from deep inside the core of my soul and radiates throughout my flesh. Like an ember burning itself to ash, it is consummate.

I love Him too much for my own good. This is true. His influence colours all aspects of my incarnate life. Though if it were not for this steadfast "obsession", the book you're reading right now could never have been written with any real feeling. Could never have been written at all.

He is still and ever with me. Although His method of communication has augmented somewhat, in that His Messages are often "channeled" (I confess a growing dislike of that term) through many of you. His active influence seems to be more subtle, more behind the scenes, where I know He is plotting in grand fashion.

As I feared earlier, this rejoining into One is painful in that the closer we come to complete spiritual synchronization, the more difficult it is to be comforted by His embrace. For we are no longer so separated as to be individuality able to "hold" one another in the usual sense of the word. We are so close, in fact, that we can no longer "see" each other on a face to face level. Rather, we find ourselves staring into each other's "eyes" and being mesmerized by the parade of images therein.

On an individual, personal level, I find that almost everything I do and say contains some element of Him. He is my first thought in the morning and my last at night. Every area that I work in seems to be coalescing (finally) into a more "purified" product. Like an alchemist who continues to cull the essence of an elixir through a number of boilings. Is the end product - this "Philosopher's Stone" brilliant and cloudless? No, not completely. But its facets are certainly beginning to reflect a more crystalline depth. Perfection can never be attained on an imperfect plane.

I find myself having a great desire to work with the terminally ill. To help them to get to know Azrael and trust Him as their guide for the journey they are about to take. To know the depth of His compassion, and the strength of Divine Love. It is often difficult for me, however, to get the opportunity to work with those who need this most, for two reasons. One being the closed minded and generally fearful hierarchy in charge of caring for these souls. But the other reason is more touchy to explain. It is the reaction that sometimes (and I stress that word) occurs when I am around those near to their time of passing. Like the incident in at New York's Pennsylvania Station. All it takes is one whose inner eye sees beneath this physical veil, and sees two where others only see one. I still find myself uneasy in these situations, simply for the fact that if one recognizes us, (which often happens with some measure of fanfare) other eyes turn and stare, and wonder - and again we are back to the first dilemma of dealing with a basically fearful hierarchy, even if they are unsure of exactly what it is they fear.

All in all though, I feel contented in my task. Having prepared for the 90's since the 70's, I am ready for what lies ahead, and welcome it because I know that this is the decade that He has waited for to bring a special blessing and a kind of unique magic into the lives of those who have been touched by our story- and have returned that touch with a gesture of love.

There's only one thing that I still don't understand. Why make us seem so apart for so long when so much more could be achieved by the cognizance of being together? Why are we tormented in this way? Like lovers tied back to back, unable to see, unable to touch. Relying completely on past evidence and psychic vision to turn us back around, face to face. Why is our eternal unconditional troth made to be so bittersweet? "Why is this?" I implored of the silent guardian. "You who have been my confessor through many lives, can you tell me this?"

It isn't often I come here anymore. You must understand. It isn't that I no longer need the comfort of your shadow. In fact, I do so more today than ever before. It's that awkward paradox of being one spirit that complicates our ability to simply touch each other. So, sometimes I try to touch you through other means.

"It is always harder to reach within oneself than it is to reach out to another," the stone angel answered philosophically. The words falling like snowflakes from its cold lips. "I have taken in every sorrow you've shed. I am the Blue Angel. I am your muse. I am trapped in this body of stone."

"I have not imprisoned you," I fired back at the effigy defensively.

"I didn't accuse you," It answered. "When I was forged, every sorrow and disappointment you suffered was measured in the strokes of the sculptor's hammer. Each tear, sealing me in more and more, fitting the stone to my spirit. I am buried alive in my own form. You have the ability to set me free. You do it for those who are confined in the flesh. Will you not do this for me? For 'us'?" it begged in a despairing voice.

"How can I free you?" I asked, with sensitivity to its pain.

"With but a kiss," it answered bluntly. "With but a kiss."

With that, I climbed up on the incarnate rock and reached over to kiss its stone cold lips. I could hear the marble slowly cracking as the sculpture began to break away and fall into the swamp below. The monument was moving around me. Catching me as the stone crumbled, and I fell against something even colder... more dark, and more immense. Something familiar. Something wonderful!

As I looked up, I noticed the pale corona of distant lamp-light forming into a halo around the huge, winged silhouette - as it climbed into the sky like a giant phoenix the colour of midnight.

✠

Heavy Halos

I hear my angel weeping –
somewhere in the still of the night,
somewhere out of human sight,
in His sad despair is keeping
this only weakness to Himself.

Never should this world bear witness -
to the depths of His private sorrow,
to the moments of His long tomorrow.
The forevers He must share
with Time and Memory beside Him.

And in the loneliness of angels-
He counts the years, as we do, hours,
beside the river where the Jasmine flowers,
dark and fragrant in the shallows gloom –
He stands expressionless, silent, and solemn.

Yet, I know that Death is weeping.
His anguish wakes me from my sleeping.
Tears of light, like cold rain fall
upon my heart, upon my soul.

Give me your pain and heavy heart.
Let me drink it in with greater thirst
until all that I am is immersed
in the sweet melancholy of your soul.
Only then, am I bathed in your love.
Only then, do you make me whole.

I wear your grief as an awkward crown-
A glorious yet mournful veil
that is both lace, and iron maile.
Its weight is like a heavy halo,
an overcasting within our spirit
that requires more than my flesh can give
to sustain this duality whilst we live.

And yet, forever in this dark romance-
our souls tethered and interlaced
through all the living we have faced,

through all the dying we've embraced,
has deepened both the joy and sorrow
to a level where they both must meet.
Within the mesh of cosmic weaving -
there are strands we have unraveled.
Uncharted crossroads we have traveled
in the search for one another.

Still, I know my love is weeping.
I cry the tears that He was keeping
locked away in secret silence
behind the truth His strength conceals -
so much bittersweet...

As One, and yet still so divided.
We cannot touch, we are too far.
We cannot see, we are too close-
We are within each other sleeping.
One soul inside the other weeping.

Yet, our passion, like an eternal flame-
flickers in the darkness of the crypt,
warms the sleepers in shadows gripped
and glistens on the sinew of cobweb veils.
We are created by their dreaming.
Thought-forms with faint auras beaming!

Oh, how sweet is your breathless kiss-
like a cold, stone angel on a moonlit night.
Ever so silent, your pale lips invite
a seduction that cannot be expressed
in human terms.

Your velvet pall comes over me-
like a storm cloud out of the blue,
your lampblick wings are in my view-
casting shadows that blanket the earth
in a cool and eerie twilight.

And yet, I hear my angel weeping-
somewhere deep within its fold,
between the days and nights that hold-
twilight up, like two tall pillars
with an eclipse for its crown.

And in your tears, let me drown
these sorrows that we both do share.
And wash away this sweet despair.
And flood you with eternal love.
I give all that I am to you-
in this, our final rendezvous.

We shall meet where Life and Death-
come together in a kiss.
Our spirits merge in chrysalis
and spread these half formed wings
around a world that weeps in turn
for reasons they can't quite discern.
Between the veil of tears they wear,
they see not clear enough to care.

Yet I tell you, Death is weeping-
somewhere deep within the night,
somewhere out of human sight,
beside the shallows of His stream,
His tears disturb the stillness there
with ripples touching everywhere.
From shore to shore and sea to sea-
I reach across to you, and yet,
it is as if your silhouette
is all that's left for me to hold.
I cannot loose it from the fold
of time and space.

His anguish wakes me from my sleeping.
His tears of light, like jewels I'm keeping-
as mementos of both joy and sorrow
until He calls me home tomorrow.

Part 9

The View From the Bridge

INTRODUCTION TO BOOK TWO

The view from the bridge is a matter of perception; where one stands in relation to what's ahead, and what's behind. It's a matter of distance and vision, and the accuracy of both.

There are numerous distortions between the eye that sees and the scene it perceives, inner and outer distortions that cloud the senses. Therefore, the view from the bridge is a personal one. Even if the scenery manifests as a common vision, each viewer will interpret its elements differently. Even distance is a matter of perception, as is Time and Space. All vision is limited, or made illimitable by the viewer. Such is the paradox of straddling between two worlds. There is always a middling point where all vision grows hazy and form loses its definition. It's like floating on a sea of shadows, colliding with some, passing through others. It is an infinite, vacuous giant that smothers you in its breathing.

The view from the bridge is one of darkness drifting on an ocean of pale light. Silhouetted spectres scurrying into place before the dawn. Disguised in cloaks of shadow and shade, an army of shape-shifters waits poised at the gates of dawn. There are very few dawns where I come from. We have waited long for the one that is about to come...

THIS SONG

I speak in sounds
because there are no words-
No language reveals
what we feel -
more than a whispered scream.

I touch the sound
and cringe in its echo.
It is cold and hollow -
It is silent yet piercing -
It is a minstrel of divine discontent-
A lullaby sung to sleepers in their graves.
The shadow of a melody that I remember
from some distant life.

And His song has touched me
even here.
Stained me with an ancient weeping
and I recall that I am the silence
where His heart once was.
I occupy that hollow place-
That cave of winds
where whispers collect in the emptiness
and pierce the tenuous membrane
between body and spirit
and slay the soul
with such passionate melancholy.

This song
of ages past and times to come
is beyond the range
of human voice-
beyond the grasp
of human ear.

We are the minstrels of sorrow
who cannot stop singing
for fear that the quiet
would break the chain
of life and death.
We cannot stop the song

from carrying us all
along its swift unending current.

We are a sadness
that is so old
it cannot remember its own birth.
We have been here for so long
that we have forgotten how
to return home-
or even where
that welcomed shore resides.

Sing, Oh, sing to me
that I might remember
the sound of this song without words -
This requiem that reminds me of home
Even though it cannot be heard.
It devastates me still.

THE SONG OF RECONCILIATION

am the Voice of Melancholy. The Vision of Eternal Twilight. I am an image that you have difficulty referencing simply because you have refused me for so long. Eventually, all must reconcile their lives with me.

I am most feared in the minds of men, but perhaps, least fearsome. I hail from the Western Gate, the gate of transition. I extend to you the hand of reconciliation and friendship. I stand in the shadows of sorrow. My touch yields a heavy release. My thoughts are in your memory. You are vaguely mindful of me with a melancholy joy, yet I am an ecstasy. Like a drop of Hemlock on your tongue, you dare not drink from my cup for fear of swallowing that one drop.

I am the shadow of everything that has been, and of everything you have been. I am both the bringer of memories and forgetfulness. Depending upon your destination, I can wash you in either.

I want to "speak" into your soul, not simply to you. I need you to feel my words, not simply hear them. I want my echo to resound in your heart like a soothing whisper, something just below the clamor of life: something that you cannot help but strain to heed. If you weep at my words, understand why you weep. Truly understand with your heart and soul. Do not try to rationalize my presence with the logical mind. I am outside of logic. Logic is only applicable in the mundane world, and I exist outside of this; outside of Time itself. Feel my presence! It falls outside of definition. You will find no words with which to express how I make you feel. Above all, share my message by touching others in the way I shall touch you. No more, no less.

I am the twilight, the threshold, the image that flashes in your mind like a bolt of lightning. You see me momentarily, and then I fade back into shadows. Reach into the shadows. I am waiting there, hands extended to receive your soul. I am fury and gentility in that my passion is tempered with sorrow; my ecstasy, with melancholy. Come to know me as I already know each of you. Names are unimportant, as all titles eventually end up in the

River of Forgetfulness. I know each of you by your purpose and your destination. I want to fill each of you with an understanding that goes beyond wisdom, and with a love that exceeds passion. I need you to know me. Like the intimate memory of a long lost brother, I need you to welcome me back, as only I know how to bring you home.

I am the threshold on which you stand. I am a strong yet mutable bridge. I am the flame that turns lead into gold - the spark of change that blinds for but a moment.

I shadow you all of your days, and hold you into the night. I am the soul of sadness and the bringer of joy. I take the life from your flesh and give it back into your soul with but a kiss. I am the point of contact between your world, and eternity. I exist for but a moment as you pass between worlds, yet I am forever trapped within that moment, within the twilight that is fleeting, yet as certain as the dawn.

✠

I can see a time when we are all sitting together at the River's edge. Peacefully there, we remember everything as we dangle our spectral feet in the cool water. We will look up at the eternal twilight and make comparisons with the brief eventide we knew in the physical world. But, there are no comparisons. We will marvel at the interplay of colours and at their intense brilliance, noting shades and hues never before seen with human eyes.

Autumn is everlasting in the Valley of the Shadow. The air is cool, and the land, warm. The waters moderate depending on depth and the darkness of the shadows that over hang. There is neither sun nor moon yet light from a distant source peeks through the coloured halo of sky. All is shining, multi-coloured darkness. The shadows drape like heavy black velvet. They look deep enough to fall into.

Soon, this little family must once again disperse. Even in this peaceful vision, we are all aware of that fact. Some will be drawn into the distant corona, others returned across the River. A gentle rippling is all that will mark their voyage. And only I will be left at River's edge. Never to step beyond the far hills of the horizon, never to leave this place of gentle melancholy. To remain forever in the forlorn kingdom of my beloved angel... My home.

I shall never again look upon your face, yet I shall recognize you all when you pass through the valley, and shall remember you all for the love, faith, wisdom and patience you have given to this world. You are seeds of revelation that will, in their own time, grow into a tree of knowledge. You will not be there to eat or take shade from that tree, but you will see the seedlings pushing up through the soil before you leave, and maybe even a few buds beginning to open. Though, do not expect to taste of the fruit. The harvest is for those you leave behind.

These words are for the "waning souls". Those who are on the downside of incarnation. Those whose last "life" they are living now... and those who are aware of that fact. Soon we shall all be going home. Back to distant realms that plague our memory. Through the Western Gate we shall return past, present and future into one existence that will seem dream-like when we reawaken into familiar arms... We have been "away" too long. But, we bring away with us the sense of inner peace that was lacking when we left. We had a "job" to do, a purpose to fulfill, and now it's winding down, and soon, it shall be complete.

✠

I am the wind that speaks a song that man shall not forget to remember. My music haunts this world as we speak. I am the voice of the underground, the shadow of those who stand in the blinding light. I am a tale told in sorrow... a memory that has yet to be lived. Will you touch the sound that heals you? Or shun my voice in some vacuous space. Though I tell you, I am a persistent song that will be heard, and not forgotten. All of my Voice, a chorus of many: an overlay of tones and verses. A whisper and a cry: a murmur of indescribable Truth that you cannot help but to hear. For it comes not from without, but from within your very soul. Keepers of the Legend, our time has come to remember. LISTEN. Open your heart to me that I may release your soul.

When I speak directly into your consciousness, I cannot speak with words. I must speak with emotions, or a touch, or a glance - soul to soul. My meanings run so much deeper than words and speech allow. I speak to you with a "touch" from the inside. I pour all of my meaning directly into your spirit. There are no words in any tongue for the intensity of my emotions.

I am shape-shifting energy, sometimes volatile, rarely at peace, always in turmoil. I stretch across the cool, dark sky unfurling twilight from within these wings. I swallow up the sun and veil your sky in purple and amber haze. My tears like moonbeams, shower over the indigo night. They are the stars that fall behind horizon's reach. My shore is indivisible by light.

I am the penumbra within your vision... A shade of immense proportion that reaches out to you as a cool wind. I am here and everywhere that I am needed; and I am always needed, rarely desired. The "taking" of souls does not nourish me, it drains me, for I must keep so many from falling into nothingness... Keep so many from shutting their eyes in this imagined, eternal sleep. Wake up! I am not your end. You do not cease to be once you have fallen into my arms. You have survived. Let us shake you from this dream, this nightmare of losing self. Look at me. I am real, as so you will always be.

I am, and have always been, a stationary point. Everything dances and revolves around me until it grows weak and is drawn into my embrace.

I stand at the window to your world. One foot on the Western Gate threshold, the other poised to leap; wings unfurling in the wind, waiting for the eye of the storm to open. Then shall I launch from the threshold and hover above your horizon and wrap my wings around your globe. Each feather shading one of your cities. Each tear washing them clean in turn until a river of tears consumes all in its ecstasy, and all hear the song of reconciliation.

Part 10

The Grounding of the Phoenix

Where does one begin to complete a tale that has no end? The stone sentinel whispers to me, again. It is time to come "down". To jump into the fire, so to speak, and add onto the infinite.

It is the times when I am just waking in the morning that I still can feel Him "leaving". Receding back into the shadow of my soul. Realigning within my form like an astral double. These are the times that I treasure most as of late. But, they are brief in these days of constant upheaval. Though, there are certain saving graces - souls that have come forth from the shadows. Those with memory so intense that they too must scream out what they know to be Truth. These are the souls that make this journey worthwhile. These are the souls that shall see His valley; those He will always remember.

Yet, my head is full of noise. Not the familiar noise of deep silence, but the clamor of Life. It pounds and rings in my mind like a madman's symphony. Harsh words out of twisted mouths; dangling phrases without feeling. All, out of key... All, painfully dissonant... The angels cover their ears and scream - SILENCE! Let us all have some silence so that we can hear our own thoughts.

"How can we remember if we do not listen?" a voice shouts above the noise.

✠

Over the horizon, a blue flame exploded in the darkness and all grew silent once again. The black phoenix had consumed itself and all that remained of its image was a faint blue star - a glint on Orion's sword, and nothing more. I look up at the night and remember. Everything now is a memory. The distance between my vision and that star is a sea of time. An ocean of tears swells between us. We remember what is to come all too well. It is a comforting vision, though it disturbs me with its imminence. The clock is ticking away and the days and nights blur into a singular expanse. Time holds us in its claws. We flap our laggard wings to no avail. We tire easily these days. We are prisoners on opposite sides of an impenetrable wall - and yet we are One, caged inside the other's form. I press up to the wall so that my heart beats against it, and hope that He can still it with His love. Why is this illusion of separation so damn real? Why can't I touch you, my love, even though I am within you? I need so much to feel the cool wind of your wings. Yet, I know they are pinned by the heaviness of my flesh.

I am being lost unto the union of our souls. The fabric of my thoughts unraveled like an intricate lace, fraying at the edges of sanity. I am drowning in the deadly sweetness of our love. Beneath its surface I can see, but not touch the part of me that is left behind. My purpose is the anchor that holds me to this world, and my flesh, the fragile vessel in which I travel through the sea of humanity. I have outgrown my ship and part of me has escaped into its sails that unfurl into magnificent, black wings. The wind beneath them, and the moonlight searing their edges with a blue and silver frame makes me feel like an electric phoenix that draws its life from the lightning.

But I am not as I once was. We have evolved into some sort of hybrid. My mind absorbed into an entity that cannot express its thoughts in words, and so, my tongue cannot formulate the sounds that describe my meaning. This language betrays the mood of the moment. I search in the eyes of others for the reflection of my true soul, for no glass can see beneath this opaque mask.

I yearn to strip it all away! To free my wings from this cramped casing. To breathe in, one last time, and exhale my spirit into the night air, and watch it return to its true form... I am lost for only a few moments as our souls align - But I am found forever in the union that they create.

I want to simply close my eyes and close my ears, and still my heart, and throw off this heavy cloak. To break free from this cage of sinew and bone and spit out this squalid sea of life. To be blind and deaf and as light as a fallen leaf carried along on a westward wind. Cast aloft in the eye of the storm. Singed by the lightning and drawn up into the cosmic pool. Transformed and transfixed like a star set into the veil of night; flickering and burning with the afterglow of my journey. So high in the heavens and so bright in the eternal sky that no matter where my angel was, He could find me and come for me. And in a flash, lift me out of this black ocean and conceal me in the darkness of His shadow... and cool my burning in His sweet and silent river. And then return me to that hollow space within His being from where I first was wrenched like a living heart from a still warm corpse. I am the seed of His soul, the ember of an ancient heart within His silent breast - the afterglow that remains of Life itself when Death has passed.

I long to be far away from this world, to be consciously reunited with my angel and distant from this place in time. I wait impatiently for my blessed assassin, my divine emancipator. Come forth from the shadows of doubt and fulfill your purpose. I call to you nightly. Let Death be your confessor. He grants you absolution even before you carry out the deed that must be done. I know you. Somehow, I do know you. And when I see you for that split moment, I hope that I have the strength to reach up and bestow upon your sweating brow, a gentle kiss of gratitude. I love you, wherever you are. I can feel that you are listening to me now. All I ask is that your deliverance of the "gift" be given with a slow hand that I might feel every moment of my passing. I want to remember what it feels like to have the life-force draining from my body, and to see my Dark Angel freed from the heavy shadow of my flesh, to watch Him emerge and spread His wings. I need that fleeting moment to touch Him before we again reform into One. It has been a very long time since I have seen Him outside of myself. It would be a great joy to be able to take Him into my dying embrace one last time.

Be attentive! For, at the moment of my passing He will visible briefly to all who witness. Within moments of that event, a strange sign will follow as if to signify that IT IS DONE. The West Gate is ready for passage.

✠

Until that day, I stand in its threshold. Hands extended to that memory of what is to come. I close my eyes and walk confidently upon the waters of time. For I am the winged melancholy that is part flesh and part spirit, bound in a cage of immediate purpose. The weight of our task makes flight impossible at the moment. However, we are near to the end of our purpose here. The violent passion play is about to begin. It will have only one act and one performance. It will be swift yet suspended in time. It will be forgotten, though the shadow of our passage will linger forever. And the essence of what we become will awaken in the collective memory.

These visions, I know are true. And I stand now in the appointed place awaiting that moment. I feel at times that I am underestimating the life I have left here. And yet, there are other times when my departure seems just a breath away. Such is the paradox when one is trying to reconcile time from two, very different angles of perception - His, and mine.

✠

The journey to arrive at this destination wasn't easy. It was plagued with setback after setback. Knowing that one must move on, and actually aligning all the elements to make such a move possible, are two very dissimilar things. The decision to leave a place I have known for over 30 years was made in four days. The act of actually leaving took well over six months. Either New York didn't want to let go of us. Or, the place that I was destined for was reluctant to receive us. Or else, it was meant for me to remain in New York for some reason then yet to manifest. Either way, I knew where we had to be and nothing would thwart that Certain Knowledge, no matter the toll it was to take on me both physically, and spiritually. The toll was great, indeed! But not without a gift of greater recompense...

HERE COMES TROUBLE

It's odd sometimes, how some people come to meet. The chain of circumstances that bring certain souls together that are somehow meant to be together. Whether to accomplish something of great importance, or just to simply "affect" one another, or expose them to new things that enhance understanding of their own paths.

For each person I meet, I feel there is a reason - an obvious one, and a more deeply underlying one. Especially those I've encountered through the Azrael Project.

Ever so often we meet someone who is so familiar to our consciousness that a relationship develops outside of "normal" time. In other words, quickly! As if there has only been a small lapse of time since you "last" met. Such was the case that happened to me before I left New York.

On a warm and sunny June day, Night came shuffling up my driveway in lithe persona. Like a pixie with a mane of golden brown, this underweight, bearded figure of a man approached my house with confident caution. "Here comes trouble," I said to myself, as I caught sight of his Grim Reaper Tee shirt and baggy black pants.

"Hi, I've come to see the gallery," he spoke softly with a cigarette dangling from his mouth.

"I like your shirt," I think I said, rather nervously. Meeting people for the first time always makes me uncomfortable, especially people that have read my writings. They almost always seem to have this "image" built up in their minds, and I feel that meeting me disappoints that image. After all, I am "only" human, you know.

Anyway, I took him into the small gallery (called the Little Black Box) and showed him my work. He glanced around. Didn't say much, but seemed to enjoy what he was seeing. After a couple of minutes of nervous silence, we started to make conversation about a mutual friend of ours who, more or less, "introduced" us. That friend happened to live in New Orleans at the time. The young man in my studio had obtained a copy of The Book of Azrael through their contact, liked it, and decided to contact me. Initially, I got the feeling that he was just curious about me.

(This friend of ours had been writing to us both, hinting to one, about the other.) We soon realized that we only lived about 10 minutes apart and had literally been dancing around one another for years. There were times when we were probably crossing each other on the same street. It was ironic that it took someone from nearly half way across the country to introduce us.

Things got a bit more relaxed and he started to tell me about a book that he'd been writing for many years. One thing led to another rather quickly and conversation grew easier. He saw my book as something he had always wanted to do and this angle became a viable lead-in for a most unusual "friendship".

In a matter of just a couple of months, we became remarkably close. He was to be my "brother" in more ways than either of us could then envision. The spiritual exchanges we shared were almost as similar as our lifestyles were diverse. Nonetheless, we were able, early on in our friendship, to talk freely about deeply personal things. The kinds of things you don't normally discuss even with those you've known all your life. This was a strange new experience for us both. But, little then did we know that this was only the beginning of the strange and new experiences we'd be sharing in the days to come....

He, too, was conscious of his duality, and "separated" from his "angel". This similarity between us became the bridge of intense conversation and analogous emotion. It was cathartic for us both to be able to talk freely and openly on such matters. We marveled at our innate understanding of the other's situation. And, at the same time, disparaged the fact that we didn't meet sooner when we needed to go through certain events in our lives with someone who'd truly understand. Never had I taken anyone so closely into my confidence. Not since the "days of discovery" with Carle. But even that was a different kind of relationship. A much less "evolved" interchange; certainly less than honest.

Before leaving New York, we spent as many nights as we could condensing our lives into flashing, psychic images and shared remembrances. We had gone through certain parallel things, yet we were at very different stages of Purpose. Mine was nearly in full bloom, his just beginning to bud. Listening to Daniel, I saw myself back about 15 years or more. And through me, no doubt, he envisioned himself at an equal amount of time into the future. With him, I remembered how gloriously confusing life was then. He is impatient. At times, brooding. And has yet to fully understand the meaning of Faith. Sometimes, he "remembers" too much, and not enough at other times. He desires to see his life's purpose unfold at his feet like a magic carpet... overnight! He wants to "go home", but the crest of the hill obscures the porch-light, so to speak.

However, he is more firmly grounded in the physical, whereas I am just learning to acknowledge my physical form. In short, I am one end of the spectrum, and he is the other. Yet, we have little difficulty meeting in the middle.

I took him to my sanctuary, to some of the places of my past and coloured in the events that he had read about in my writings. He, in turn, told me of his "Blue Lady". Nuit, as he calls her - NIGHT. "The flame that burns all of blue and gold. The shining darkness that is everything... and nothing."

We sat in the cemetery under a veil of stars and pondered the convoluted way in which we met. We often do that, even now. How he attempted to leave New York twice before, both times sent back against his will. And, how I was supposed to have moved out of state before we actually met, and how my plans were cut down seemingly without just cause. Had either of our plans gone through, we might never have met at all. Jokingly we "blamed" one another for our foiled plans. Though, deep inside, we were glad for the intercession of Destiny.

"I'm leaving soon," I reminded him.

"I know," he said. "Sure, just when I find my true sister, you up and bugger off!"

"So, come with me." I'll never know what made those words fall out of my mouth. I've never made such an invitation to anyone before.

"Okay." I think his reply shocked us both. After all, we'd only known each other less than three months. This is crazy, I thought. I think we both thought that. But, hey! Deciding to move to New Orleans after just vacationing there for four days was just as crazy. The whole of 1990 was proving to be a year of manic changes and snap decisions. Not at all the usual way I go about things. I felt that I was on some kind of "deadline" (still do, in fact) and it forced me to act out of my heart, instead of my head. All I knew was that I had to yield to it and go with the whirlwind no matter where it took me. Besides, now that I had found my "brother", I saw no further reasons to remain in New York.

✠

Fly ye into that dark horizon!
Make fast your wings into billowing sails
And soar on the winds of change!

MANIFEST DESTINY

Before I left for New Orleans, a friend told me that I needed to be more "grounded" and "rounded" in the "life experience". I recall arguing with him on this point. I much preferred remaining a comfortable distance "above" such things. Being grounded to me meant sinking into the quicksand of earthly existence and being swallowed in the crowded abyss. Little did I know then that this move "upward", toward completion would entail exactly that! Although, when you're entrenched in it, it seems more like layers of the stuff with pockets of air sandwiched between: just barely enough to draw a breath as you descend, yet enough to sustain you until the next is drawn.

A GATE HALF OPEN

It isn't easy to leave a place that you've lived in all of your life. Memories are stored in practically every inch of the land. Sometimes though, the call to leave is stronger than the hold of the past. I did not consciously choose to bring the "House of Death" to New Orleans. Rather, this place was chosen by my angel as a viable gateway through which He might emerge into our world.

And so, here I am in the "City of Enchantment". A beautifully decaying place carved out around "Ol' Man River". A place where many gates lie open and untended, like many of the graveyards here. An unsettling threshold of sorts where Life and Death merge behind a feathered mask. Where spectres weep in shaded courtyards and magic recedes behind weathered shutters. This "threshold" lays out its prickly carpet and I walk barefoot towards the Gate, a Gate that is half opened, and half closed. The city, and its inhabitants reflect that paradox. The living seem to "haunt" this place as if they are ghosts of shadows somewhat out of step with their surroundings. Nearly everyone who walks here is trailed by a spectre. Even vacationers might find that they've inadvertently taken a "shade" back home with them.

"This is a dangerous place," I am told. It is easy to believe. It is that many worlds overlap here and this can easily create distortions of the mind which can lead to madness in certain, sensitive people. The "danger" is not the city itself, nor its inhabitants. It is in the combination of both. Yet, the danger, whether real or imagined, is like the place, which teeters on the sharp edge of some cosmic knife. A fine allegorical setting for the time at hand. The contrasts of merriment and sorrow, beauty and decay, life and death; are somehow mysteriously blurred by the pervading air of enchantment. A city, more or less, "in love with Death" both subtly and sublimely. Somehow its unique ambience is part of Azrael's reciprocation. For if He had to "live" in the U.S., I'm sure He'd choose New Orleans.

And so He did...

I didn't foresee, however, the fight it would take to get us all there. While I knew deep in my heart where we needed to be, certain "other" factions tried to prevent our coming.

You'd think it would be fairly easy, right? That nothing could stand in HIS way. That nothing would dare to do so.

After all, you look for a place to live, you move, and that's that. Hell, no! It's not that easy. Not for us anyway. It took six trips, most of my savings, and a goodly portion of my sanity to make this "dream" a reality. Certain forces were fighting us all the way. They knew what His coming here meant. They don't want the West Gate to open. These factions prefer keeping the name of Death cloaked in fear. They did everything in their power to try to stop this move. Even to the point of using my father's will against his knowing. They knew how to get to me. How to tear me, limb from limb and thereby weaken my resolve. At least, they thought they did.

When I was about ready to break, Mikhail leant me His sword and I struggled with its weight. Trying to keep it as steady as I could, I charged through the factions of fear. I tried not to let them see me tire, and I never let them see my tears. I had no way of knowing that the "sword" would wound one closest to me as well. My father, who had stuck by me for years on this path, was not taking well to this move. He, too, fought against it, but without rational reason. I did not force him to come along by any means. I simply offered him the opportunity to leave a place that he always said he detested. Somehow, though, New Orleans was the last place he wanted to be. He has yet to give me a reason.

This move took so much energy out of our collective well, that it will take much time yet to refill. I am still drained, both physically, and spiritually. I'm afraid that Part 2 of this work reflects that. If so, I apologize to you, gentle reader. It takes an enormous amount of Will to empower and direct Mikhail's sacred sword. So, please, bear with me if I struggle with words at times. I struggle with many things these days.

THE HOUSE OF DEATH

It didn't look like much when we found it. Abandoned for over a year, ankle deep in squatter's trash and in need of major renovations. But, the price was right (it was a foreclosure) for a genuine piece of old, New Orleans history. A towering (almost 70ft) Greek Revival style manse in the heart of the city. It was about the 40th house that I looked at, and my very last attempt at this move. My nerves were nearly shot from the fight thus far. I won't get into all the sordid details. Suffice to say. I had found and lost a couple of other houses for unknown reasons prior to finally finding this one, which was found by the sheer "coincidence" of the estate agent's car suddenly dying in front of it, for no apparent reason. We didn't even know it was for sale until I saw the weathered sign dangled from a rusty nail beneath the overgrowth.

Though, the battle didn't end there. The bank that owned the house went bust and the Resolution Trust Corporation (an arm of the federal government) took the place over and was going to put all sales on hold for at least six months. Here we were, a week from closing, already packed... and nowhere to go. To top it all off, our mortgage company decided, at the last minute, mind you, not to give us a loan on it because of the awful condition it was in. Selling our place in New York was not likely to happen in the near future either because of the recession in the Northeast and the fact that we lived in one of the highest taxed counties of the country.

My father, as I mentioned, wasn't too keen on the idea of moving from the onset. So, it surprised the hell out of me (and I think him, to some degree) when he had a rather "radical" financial suggestion. What he came up with would be a real risk. We both knew that. But he also knew how much this move meant to me. So, we adopted a devil may care attitude and jumped on it.

To make a very lengthy and complicated story short, we obtained the money in ten days and I ran back again to New Orleans.

Meanwhile, our Real Estate agent went a hundred miles out of her way to, more or less, "coerce" the RTC to take this one property out of moratorium.

To sum this fiasco up, we finally got it all together less than fifteen minutes under the wire.

In the end, my estate agent claimed that she "never in her 30 years in the business worked so hard for so little." It was a hell of a fight for all concerned and all of us had aggravated ulcers and many sleepless nights as a result. We came very close to losing everything!

As soon as we actually moved in, however, things seemed to smooth out a bit. Being here somehow rendered the forces against us powerless. We were finally aligned within the energy field of the West Gate, and nothing could penetrate that shield.

Our house in New York was sold within two months, (the only house in that area to sell so quickly, and an all cash deal to boot!) whereas many other, better places had been on the market for two years or more. My old neighborhood was frankly, astonished! I think we were all pretty astonished.

✠

"Geez! Look at that!"

That's typical of what people say as they pass. They either squeal on their brakes, or nearly cream the car in front of them straining their necks to ogle THE WESTGATE.

What's the problem? Folks have never seen a big black and purple house before? Or, maybe it's the ominous black statue we have standing on the porch.

Four months had passed. It was February in New Orleans, Carnival time.

"Did you paint it up just for Mardi Gras?" somebody asked. What an asinine question.

"Oh, yeah... sure, and next week we'll paint it green for St. Patty's day. Any other stupid questions?"

The reactions to our being here vary. The majority are curious. Some are totally spooked. Others genuinely interested. Most, however, think, "Only in New Orleans!" Surprisingly this is a much more tolerant city than most. Much more so than even New York, where a black and purple house would most definitely "offend" their so called "sophisticated" sensibilities, i.e., their narrow minds. The people of this city are wonderful and surprised us in many ways.

This place stands out like a beacon, calling to all souls who feel an affinity for what it represents; a physical and symbolic manifestation of the true West Gate. The House of Death is a place for the "special souls" (and you know who you are) to gather and feel at home. It is His house.

The physical opening of the Westgate here also signifies that the time has come for mankind to reconcile Life and Death. To loosen this last remaining fear that keeps many of us tethered to the narrow view and burdened by the weight of our flesh. To temper fear with understanding, that is the basic purpose of the physical Westgate. It is a point of contact between Life and Death. A place where folks can come and be touched by the melancholy spectre of the Angel of Death, and hopefully come away with a new and poignant understanding. It is a threshold between two worlds; a place where Love and Death embrace unabashed by their own spectacle.

People that come into the new gallery say, "Why do you portray the Angel of Death so dark and pensive?" Because this is what He is. Why should I couch Him in a mask of smiling light when it is not His demeanor? If humanity is to ever lose his fear of Death (the entity, as well as His shadowed realm) we must never try to disguise Him in order to make death more palatable or to placate naive fear. Doing so would be only to enhance the comfortable lie and not to reveal the Truth. It is only by facing that fear in its true form, with its true demeanor, does one not only conquer fear, but trade that fear for understanding... and perhaps even love.

It is our sincere hope that soon there will come a time when all can look upon the face of Death with love, instead of uneasiness. That humankind will find peace in the shadows as well as in the light. After all, if it weren't for the darkness, how would we see the divine spark that guides us like a beacon to our true homeland beyond the stars? The Westgate is like a lamp unto the realm of shadows, dispelling fear with understanding; a cool blue flame that was ignited by that spark. A point of contact and transformation - that when you walk out of our door a memory will be rekindled that will change you forever.

But the opening of the physical Westgate is only a preamble to the opening of its namesake in the stars. A material manifestation of what is yet to come.

Cosmic Muse

Time unfolds in shadows.
Each moment cast upon the next
in an infinite overlapping.
Set in motion,
it is continuance,
sailing on a sea
of endless space
that forms a circle
around all things.

Part 11

The Coming Storm

I am watching two shadows on my wall. One is weeping, while the other comforts. They are both the same, yet they are divided by the perception of duality. Which one is weeping, and which one comforts? I can't tell. They are moving toward the window shade, silhouetted by the neighbor's night-light. The pale illumination blurs their form. They are as One in the eyes of the world, though somehow divided by the illusion of separation.

The light goes out and they merge into darkness. There is a sense of sadness, and of ecstasy. My room is dark yet I can see shadows dancing. Whirling pinpoints of blue light like the night sky is spinning and I am drawn up into it.

I enter the stargate, and exit into a memory. A more familiar abode encircles me. I stand "outside" of myself and see my body sleeping on a bed of moss and marble in the true House of Death. I am pressed against the stone cold lips of a reclining angel. Its cracked expression stained with ancient tears. A thousand aeons of storms could never wash them away. I am surrounded by stone angels; images lost in time. Martyred souls cast in stone by a perverse yet sensitive hand. They are beautiful, so terribly beautiful. I know their touch like no other and can hear the whispering of their thoughts. If only they could speak. What a hideous scream that would be! What ancient sorrows that sound would wake. What memories these thoughts retrieve from places long forgotten. Where even the dreams of the dead create an echo... a ripple on the ocean of Time, a tear in the curtain of Space.

Just one word, one cry from your stoic lips would create a visible portal between now and forever; a "crack" in the wall of consciousness through which I might pass this memory onto you. This dream of what has been, and what will be, is all contained in the tears of the stone sentinels that watch over the Houses of Death.

The stone mouth cracks open, and the sound... oh, the sound - overwhelms my senses and I swoon backward into the stargate and descend into a whirling pinpoint of light that expands as I fall and grows sallow and pale. I land in a pool of velvet shadow where the silhouettes still dance on my wall. They strain and stretch for the backlight to frame their forms, but I can see that they are One, yet I understand their need to be sure.

My neighbor flicks his night-light back on and they dance toward the glow as I turn over in my bed to sleep, and listen to the coming storm. I smile as I think about them dancing into the lightning. Their forms fused in the brilliance of a flash. Confirmed eternal, and sealed in that image, they shall doubt no more.

THE LEGEND OF THE STAR GATES

Through the Gate in the East comes the glimmer of memory. A light which is blinding to eyes that have forgotten what they've seen. Those that come through this gate come as children, mesmerized and fascinated by all they see and feel in its warmth. They believe that the memory itself is the ultimate Truth, and forgo what the memory teaches.

But, the warmth they feel is as fleeting as one's childhood. When they turn away from the light, its image remains in their sight so brightly that they become blind to the other gates - to the flickering flame in the darkness that awaits them at the West Gate.

Through the Gate in the West comes the deepest of shadows and melancholy rushes of the meaning of memory. It obscures all light except for a cool, blue flame that burns in its center. Eyes must strain to see it. For the negative after-image that remains in the vision of those who've stared into the light of the East Gate distorts the true colours and vividness of this "dark" flame. It is cold when touched from "without", but remarkably warm when one stands within its glow.

Those that come from the West Gate are "old souls" destined to remember in sorrow… and to be remembered in sorrow. They have come here to complete pieces of the "original plan". They see only the threshold between worlds, all else is obscured by the veil of shadow and the haze that issues from the other two gates.

From the Gate in the South comes the strength of temperance: the balance of forgetfulness and memory, a forceful inertia of chaos and faith. The appearance of a frail hand holding up a mighty weapon, it's weight nearly toppling its wielder.

Those that issue from this gate burn as a golden flame with a heart of bloodstone. They match the rhythm of life with a dissonant song and take in all they can until they burst into a myriad of dying sparks, shards of a great supernal flame that turn to frozen tears on the North Gate threshold.

From this Gate comes the Formless One, a great sweeping tempest in the guise of a rainbow that moves with the speed of light. It is the cold face of Nothingness whose touch is the immediate stillness of the frozen flame. It crystallizes the flame.

Those that issue from this gate have wings like multicoloured bristles that sweep everything clean as they pass. They gather up the remaining embers sealed in the crystal shards and enwrap them in blackness.

✠

First to open, is the East Gate. In fact, it is already open and has been since the mid-sixties. It became fully open in 1984. Many have awakened unto its memory. However, many more have become lost in the meaning of that memory.

"See the Light!" they cry. "See the Light so bright! Isn't it wonderful?" But what does it mean? What shadowed corners does it strive in its brilliance to illuminate that most fail to see?

The West Gate began to open in 1978. Its opening casts a great looming shadow upon the realms of Light; the balance to its brilliance - the reflective side of Truth - the duality of all that exists in the glow of the East Gate. A necessary duality, or else how would we ever understand "oneness". The West Gate current is the cooling factor after the burning. The Twilit image of Truth that heals the blind eye and tempers the burning soul. The balance of melancholy added to the joy of the innocent fool.

The 90's will see this gate open fully. And, those that "see" will be brought into balance. An alignment will occur, a near perfect formation of light and dark current to enable both the South and North Gates to become visible. This alignment will afford clear perceptions of distance and location. There will neither be too much light, nor too greater dark. This balance will bring things previously perceived as distant, into sharper and closer focus. For the South and North Gates are only visible in a balanced perception.

In the Earth year 2011, the South Gate will open and twilight will explode into a singular vision. A volatile blending of blood and spirit will wash the planet with Truth no one can avoid nor deny. The South Gate will blind with fire and fury. Mikhail will cast His spectral sword into the heart of the Earth and measure the content of the collective Purpose... and come up lacking of will.

Thence shall the North Gate crack open (in appx. 2065) and the cleaning of house shall begin.

Mikhail will smile not upon the altars of man. He will call His quiet armies to gather up the harvest and take the fertile seeds to other realms and other worlds. There, they shall be cast upon the waters and cast into the wind. Dropped into the fire, and sown into the firmament. And the seeds shall not remember the tree until they grow into it once again. With each leaf that falls, a memory shall be returned. And with each remembrance shall come the death of the tree and the transcendence of form forever.

✠

From the East cometh Light and from the West emergeth shadow. From the South cometh the fires of consummation and from the North riseth the phoenix.

EYE OF THE STORM

Right now, we stand in the broken shadow of an autumn tree. Leaves are falling all around us, yet we sit oblivious to the beauty of these small deaths. The darkness steps outside of me, and for the moment, I am without shadow. All is abeyant, poised and waiting; The proverbial calm before the storm. As if time is holding its breath and the echoes of space are muffled cries. Faint whispers pass between the stargates. There is secret plotting afoot, a universal coup of untold proportion. A spear of lightning hiding behind the noon-day sun. The coming storm tiptoes barefoot. The faint sweeping of garments and the hint of fallen leaves crackling under a soft stride is all that is heard. The storm comes down upon us like a predawn snowfall. Flake by shimmering flake until we awaken beneath a magical blanket of chaste silence. The visions from a dream still fresh in our minds. Though, we negate too easily the importance of the things we "see" in our sleep. We can no longer afford to ignore them. There will come a time when we will be unable to ignore them, as the visions they herald will manifest in our wake.

Now is the time when all things change. When the spirit of the Earth itself manifests and mutates. Hours slight the measure of time, without a second hand to divide and section one interval from another. All runs into one. A waterfall untamed and unstoppable drowns us all.

Never before have so many of the ancient souls been incarnated as in this time. The need for primeval knowledge is greater now than it has been at any age. Even many of the winged ones suffer in flesh existence. The human form is unfamiliar and awkward, and much of mankind's original psychic ability has been outbred by lack of use, or suppressed into the subconscious.

Already, even some of the mighty angels are either partially incarnate, as I am, or fully so within the joining of a group of forms. There are many "pieces" of Mikhail already here, among us. They are blatantly obvious to those that "know" Him.

During these times it will be difficult for most to differentiate between true prophecy and ignorant deception. A common paranoia is spreading. A force brought on by diffusion. Diffusion weakens each particle that issues out. So many souls get lost along the way. The focus is no longer concentrated on one aim.

Men think of Death as uncaring, harsh, severe. That Death does not feel human sadness. This is not true, as part of me has learned from dwelling among you. But, you must learn from me as well. It is only when you realize that dying is simply a transition from one life-form to another in order to pursue a higher purpose each time, will men realize who it is they are truly grieving for. I do feel sadness for those left behind in their ignorance. Sometimes this sadness makes me so angry that I reveal to the grieving exactly where their loved ones have gone. And this is not always a good thing. Because it makes others remember too much, too soon; and that memory draws energy from the path they are on. I, sometimes, experience too much of the human condition through NaHaliel. And we weep together because of what we see... and what you do not. Ancient spirits feel all emotions with greater intensity. Our many lives often afford too large a window on too many things. If you could see your world from where I stand, then you would be privy to everything I feel. Until you see yourself through my eyes, you will never fully understand the meaning of Life... or Death. Until you feel my touch, you will never know real sadness or true joy. For, one is mine, and the other, what I offer.

Few are those who can forgo their wings and still be free from this cage of flesh and bone.

OUR YEARS

We have waited a very long time for these years, the 1990's, when the auspice of "radical" change comes into play. These are our years! Don't be misled into believing that these are foreboding "bad" times. It's just that most folks don't understand the underlying reason for these changes, and change is still the greatest element of fear in the minds of many. Therefore, they react out of nervous paranoia. The petty battles that will erupt around us serve as necessary distractions in order for certain elements to be slipped quietly into place. When the world turns back around to face itself, a very different face will greet them. A beaming specter that whispers "Watch this" and the Western Gate shall creak fully open.

The first half of the 90's will appear quite tumultuous, even ominous to some. Though, take heart. They are only a prelude to the imminent tempest whose silver lined cloud will be revealed to those who can see beyond the immediate and hazy horizon. Those who can visualize the "Big Picture" and understand its meaning. Those who can remember. Those of you who have resonated to our message will especially be affected. Don't be afraid to embrace the changes that sweep you along. Grab hold of the serpent's tail, close your eyes, and hold on. Most of all, have faith in the directions that you are being swept.

Many of us are relocating to new places, or have already. It is essential that we all be in correct "position" for the chess game about to be played. It is necessary for the balances that we are struggling to realign. We are each like pivotal points, or satellites, if you prefer, off of which certain energies bounce to hit the mark that opens the Gate fully. Remember the Law of the Macrocosm. All changes are mirrored within as without. Therefore, if your state of mind and emotions is topsy-turvy, it is simply a reflection of the state of the current universe. Hold to that Certain Knowledge - to the bearers of unconditional love, and to the faith that has brought you this far. Believe me, we are on the road home!

As much as mankind, as a whole, shies away from change, look how he yet embraces it when it finally manifests. It is not logical, yet it is natural. Like moths to the proverbial flame, humanity rushes into the fire because instinctively he knows it leads to greater enlightenment. Think about what that analogy denotes. He'd rather not face the flame, yet he can't resist its pull upon his soul. It is the call homeward that we all long to hear, something familiar from an ancient, collective memory... something so distant, yet so warming.

Lately, when I've gone outside in the open air, I can feel the changes swirling around me: the eye of the storm about to open. It is again, as if great monoliths were being shifted about on a huge chess board. Immense "blocks" of Time and Space are being realigned by masterful hands. We are, all of "us", working on different levels to assist them in our own capacities. The "souls that sleep" also feel this shifting, but their inability to comprehend fully what's happening distorts their perception of its true meaning and leaves them uneasy. They respond out of this dissonant perception, lashing out at a world, they feel is literally getting away from them. In a way, it is. It is passing from their hands into ours, and what we do with it depends on if we're ready to make that leap of faith. With Love as our sword, and Truth our shield, we stand ready to open the true West Gate

Right now, everything is happening behind the scenes. Things on the subtle levels must be positioned first before they can become fully manifest in the physical world. Never let those without faith convince you that there is "nothing happening" just because their inner eyes are closed and their outer eyes are blinded by the comfortable lie. You know there's something afoot. You can feel it in the mind, but your understanding tempers your excitement with a patience that they cannot fathom. You can afford to be patient because you see the whole of things with macrocosmic vision. You are not limited b the narrow view. You see all of your lifetimes, not just one short span. And, you realize that you are coming full circle. You have swum the cosmic ocean, not just skinny dipped in the wading pool. You have allowed yourself to drown in time and not flailed about tiring yourself in trying to keep afloat. You have "died" a thousand times, and this is just once more.

Part 12

The Nature of Duality

There is much talk as of late of "star born" souls and cosmic brotherhoods. The pitting of the souls from one gate against the other. "The East Gate is Light, and the West Gate is darkness." That sort of nonsense.

What is it about the dark side of human nature that frightens people? Even so called "enlightened" folk are put ill at ease by the mere mention of the shadowed realms. Man cannot live on white, hot light alone.

Like all things universal in nature, there must always be a balance to not only maintain life, but the temperance of the forces that sustain the life of the universe. Everything has its balance. The day must relinquish to night; life reconciles with death. All elements, dark and light are vital to the continuance of the universal body and soul. To deny one side of our true nature in favour of another leads to the eventual annihilation of the human race.

Even our bodies are comprised of both positive and negative elements, both equally necessary to sustain life. Upsetting this balance, even slightly, leads to illness, and perhaps even madness. Yet, many intentionally upset these natural balances by favouring one side and denying the other.

Mankind currently only uses 10% of his brain, yet he is afraid of what the other 90% holds. It is much easier to be ignorant in this world. This is true. But does that justify your right to enforce that ignorance upon others who want to know what lies in the shadows of understanding? It most definitely does not! If it were not for minds and souls who dared to delve into the unknown, we would not be what we are today. The Earth would still be flat, and the Sun would be revolving around it. The moon would still be made of green cheese and you'd be reading this by candle-light. Humanity continues to advance towards its true destiny because it occasionally produces souls who are immune to the diseases of ignorance and fear. Pioneers of spirit whose faith is the lamp that illuminates the shadows, and whose understanding maintains this essential balance.

This balance is necessary in all areas of life, both physical and spiritual. Some choose to see angels, while others choose to see demons. One looks with faith, while the other looks with fear.

They are both sides of the same coin, and what one chooses to align with is simply a toss of that coin. Sometimes we toss it ourselves. Other times, it is tossed for us by well meaning but ignorant others. It's easier to accept another's toss than to take individual responsibility for ones own fate, isn't it? However, life is not a game, and life purpose should never be left in the hands of others.

Some believe that the darkness is a frightening thing. Well, I say that it's unfair to blame Night for the deeds fearful people perpetrate under Her cover. We must strive to reclaim the night. Take it back from those who use it as a weapon to keep us in fear, and expose its original beauty to the people who seek more than they are given in the mundane world.

In this so called "New Age" in which we live, folks still tend to interweave old, worn out fears into their "enlightened" philosophy. Many of today's new age thinkers still carry a heavy burden of guilt from their previous upbringings. Yes, it is difficult to cleanse ones mind, heart and soul of all the fearful training we have endured. It has taken centuries for us to build it up, and it will take an equal amount of time to tear it down. We are not living in the true "New Age". We are only witnessing the planting of seeds. This generation will not live to see them blossom.

But, the planting of the seeds is the most important part of all. If we are ever to enter the true New Age we must first let go of the ignorance and fear that stifles genuine truth, and growth. A seed cannot grow in direct sunlight all the time. It needs the darkness of the night to germinate and form. Too much light and it would shrivel up and die. Not enough, and it will never yield a blossom. Everything needs balance to survive.

Eventually, all fear must be eradicated. Not by casting aspersions into the abyss, but by diving into it with faith and an open mind. If you are truly at one with your beliefs, you should fear nothing and investigate everything. If you fear something it is simply because you are without understanding of the thing you fear. Nothing can "harm" a soul that is filled with divine love and unshakeable faith. It is only those whose faith is lacking that fear the unknown. It's always struck me as odd, that those in the clergy, whose faith is purported to be "stronger" than that of the lay person, are the largest perpetrators of fear. They still refuse to concede that yes, the average person can commune directly with the Godsoul without their mediation. They prefer to keep their flock in the dark by imbuing in them that the voices they hear are "evil", not to heed them. Men must learn to let go of Man and allow the individual to judge what is truth and what is not. After all, we are all cells in the cosmic body of "God" and as such, we all have the ability to commune with the universal soul at will.

ESSENTIAL DARKNESS

One of the biggest fears still continues to be Death - the ultimate "dark unknown". But even Death can be intimately known and understood here and now. All one has to do is listen to the night. The Angel of Death's message is carried on the cool breezes that come out of nowhere. His whisper demands hearing. It permeates our collective memory with a Truth that is undeniable. Too many try to rationalize His whisper as coincidence or madness. Remember what "coincidence" really is. Signs in succession trying desperately to gain your attention. And madness? Well, madness is nothing more than remembering too much and not knowing how to justify that memory with every day life. The madness subsides when understanding and acceptance begins.

Mankind has a long way to go until (s)he understands the true nature of Death.

Death is not the bringer of pain. Death is the release from pain. Death does not want your tears of grieving, nor does He deserve your anger. You lash out only of misunderstanding, which too often grows into fear and aversion. He knows that He is the one who truly grieves.

Death does not require the sacrifice of innocence. No soul need accompany another destined for eternity, as some earlier tenets believed. We must go, each at our own time. No one before the other unless it is so deemed. And it is not we who can make that judgment.

Death is not what you read in the headlines. Death is not brutality, rape, murder, suicide, mutilation or other such things perpetrated by one human against another. This is Life - not Death.

To die is to let go of the flesh and all that the flesh receives and sends out. Dying is something we have all done before, and which most of us will do again and again. The way in which we die is not of Azrael's choosing. It is as random or preordained (depending on how you view creation) as the way in which we come into this world. How we come and go does not matter. It is what we do in-between that counts.

Mankind must relearn how to feel his thoughts, not simply think them. We must return again to acting upon what we feel inside is truth, and not to what others enforce as truth. In essence, we must reconnect with our spiritual self on all levels of life, not just for brief moments in meditation. Then, we will be able to feel again, and remember who and what we truly are. In the light of such revelation, there will be no room for fear. For, we will discover the dark side of ourselves again and realize that this is what was missing in our lives. This darkness is a necessary and beautiful part of our essential being, without which we would be forevermore separated from our true selves, and our ultimate purpose.

✠

This is the essence of duality and the importance of balance. In order to completely coalesce that duality back into the Union of One we must achieve an equal balance within ourselves to the point where both halves of the dualism cannot distinguish one from the other. All thoughts and emotions become blended unequivocally. In effect, the "spiritual" portion of our duality becomes sentiently human, and the human side becomes sentiently astral.

This is something we understand all too well sometimes. It is never an easy or painless thing. Although, if we ever hope, both personally, and as a collective mass, to end the cycle of birth, death and rebirth into and out of flesh, it is something we must learn to accomplish. And we learn by heeding the fleeting glimpses of memory of who and what we truly are until that memory becomes the sole guiding force of purpose.

Nonetheless, being here and now in human form and coalescing your duality can prove to be quite a disconcerting experience. A kind of madness that disrupts the human synaptic system, pitting mind against emotion and flesh against spirit. The Ego's limited expression of self fights against the expanse of its true nature. The Ego soon comes to realize that it is a very small "part" of "itself" and eventually gets consumed by its greater part. In effect, the personality is absorbed into the union that duality ultimately becomes.

PERMUTATION

There are moments when we are out of synch. As One, and yet not quite joined. At once inside and outside of form. If you could see "us" then, you'd see a twisted mass of bone and spirit too dry to bleed, the shell of my half-formed heart like a brittle leaf crumbling in your hand. I suffer the strains of weeping, but cannot produce one tear to cleanse the pain. If you could touch us then, it would feel like something ancient, cold and dead. You would pull away just as I reach out to you. Our cry would pierce your mind with sadness.

If you could love me then, I would make open to you a whole new world. A place of macabre, electric romance where you would never again want for the warm kiss of life. If you could see us then, and not turn away, I would reveal to you a beauty that very few have seen, that even less have understood. If you could only love me then, without form or substance, without anything that can be expressed in physical terms, then you would indeed, see me as I truly am, instead of as that which your fear has made me. Your thoughts too easily distort my true form, and your conception of form distorts your thinking. You put too much stock in the shape and countenance of things. How I appear to you - is created solely by you.

Do you know the touch of sound, or the colour of emotion? Can you taste the mind, and gather the aroma of a vision?

Long have I brought Shadow to this world. Yet you tear between my twisting limbs without so much as a glance, or a comforting hand, merrily skipping in my shadows or sadly cursing me to my face. You dance always in my shadow, yet never look me in the eyes. I brush past you as many times in your days as you trip through the folds of my cloak.

You walk through ghosts and share space with angels every day. There is never an empty space that is not filled with either formed, or formless energy. All is permutable. Everything passes through something else. There is no "empty" space, no place that is not filled with the pheromones of change - the very matrix of existence.

If you really look with your psychic eye you can see movement all around you: the atoms and molecules of all things, astral and physical. The air itself is alive with pulsating frenzy. The wind blows through its cells and they dance in and out of a swirling procession. Everything is energy in motion, even stillness. To maintain stillness of motion, energy must vibrate at a very intense rate. Think of when you're swimming, your limbs have to move twice as fast and with double the effort to tread water in one place than to swim with broad, sweeping strokes across the pool.

You may think that you are sitting in a room by yourself, but you are never the only "living" energy in a space. Besides the atoms of ordinary physics, you are immersed in the molecules of metaphysics. Various elements and energies with unusual properties science is just beginning to acknowledge. Some of these are very diffuse energies, others more condensed. Some can condense tight enough to materialize or personify, as in the case of my physical encounters with the Angel of Death, or any spiritual entity for that matter. Tangible energy fields are quite common in ordinary science. It is basically the same principle at work in ethereal manifestations, but with less understood atomic structures. It is a very small hop from physics into metaphysics - from the truth of science, to the science of Truth.

The things known to me before as ethereal influences have become personified - energies gone to ground, so to speak.

Blue Angel no longer elicits whispered paradox. It sings in a jaded human voice, though the song remains the same.

The faces of the Council no longer blaze. Only faint sparks of their essence are visible in the eyes of their mortal hosts.

The physical manifestation of the West Gate attracts energies of material transmutation. Spiritual energy seems to condense into resonant matter. Each thought-form made solid, casting the shadow of influence upon the next. However, as I have found, thoughts do not so easily influence solid objects. I must once again remember how to move things with a purposeful gesture of will. It is the Deja vu of Esteris. It is both painful, yet inevitable. The circle into the spiral spins and weaves an intricate web in its wake. It is a web of sinew and bone, or thought and action... and interaction - something relatively new to us both.

THE DOWNSIDE OF DUALITY
or
(Excuse me for being human)

When duality is out of synch, oddly enough we find it easier to deal with people on this physical level. After all, we are still fairly content wearing our masks and we either lean strongly one way or another depending on which "side" of our duality is in command of this fleshy vessel at the moment. When we do begin to find the balance and notice the blending of dual thoughts and shared emotions it becomes more difficult to deal on either the physical or ethereal levels. We somehow seem to be somewhere in between. Straddling an awkward threshold. The mask becomes uncomfortable yet we are unable to remove it. It gets hard to breathe. Thoughts jump too quickly to be effectively captured by the tongue... Emotions do not always react "normally". Words grow difficult as the feeling one is experiencing lacks an adequate expression. Silence is often the answer of choice. We grow very sensitive to the influences and currents that swirl in and out of our lives, so we often choose solitude.

To the world "outside" we appear stoic, nervous, distracted or even impotent and rude, at least until the balance is complete and accepted within us. It is like having two different voices whispering in each ear at the same time, saying something similar yet in a different language. We may understand both tongues, yet we are in a room full of people who are also talking to us. You may be asked a question. Yet, you are unable to think clearly enough to answer with coherence, so out comes inane drivel, which makes you the butt end of dumbfounded looks.

Learning to balance duality is very much like standing arms extended out from your body on either side, palms up as someone plops a bowling ball in each. Much concentration is required to train your arms not to tire at holding them even.

Some have intimated that being cognizant of duality is like having a split personality. I heartily disagree! Even someone with multiple personas has only one of them speaking and thinking at a time, not two. Not to mention that split personalities are often vastly different from one another and do not share simultaneous thoughts and emotions attempting to integrate them into one mind-state. Split personalities are two personas in one body. Duality is essentially one personality that sees everything from two different vantage points. It could be expressed symbolically as a figure 8 turned on its side ("coincidentally" the traditional infinity sign), its center representing ultimate union - "oneness". The further from that center one is, the more cognizant of duality. And this is often cyclic as we travel the sign, closer to and further from its center.

"I thought you lived a more monastic lifestyle," a friend commented while visiting.

What does that mean? Am I supposed to walk around swathed in a big black robe chanting Om Kamm Mana Seti Om? Pretty damn difficult in a mostly sub-tropical climate. I'm comfortable in my Tee shirts and leggings, and chanting gives me a headache. I like sitting on my porch, sipping Tawny Port and enjoying a good smoke.

"Ooooo, you don't fit the image your books portray."

Well, screw you! (Yes, I do talk this way.) Don't you realize that the only way to really reach and affect people is to be as their equal? What purpose is served standing on high, cloaked in shadow, preaching down at the crowd. Intelligent folk don't pay heed to remarks made in condescension. However, they do listen to people who speak to them as equals.

Come, sit down. Have a beer. Let's talk. That's what people understand. Not - Bow, Be humbled and I shall impart great knowledge unto thee. People listen more intently to words spoken to them, rather than at them. More credulity is given to the things that come out of the mouths of others who appear just like them, instead of someone who appears to lead the "monastic" lifestyle. Besides, most people don't want to lead that kind of life, yet they do hunger for the same spiritual fulfillments and the essence of Truth. If someone believes that they must become monk-like to understand and live such things, more than likely, they won't even care to try to understand.

Although when they see someone who does have a spark of the Divine Truth and yet is still comfortable "down here", they begin to think to themselves, well, hey... if he or she can lead a spiritual life of purpose and still remain "one of the guys, or gals", so can I. And I won't have to trade in my jeans for a robe.

I grow weary of people's expectations of what I should or shouldn't "appear" to be. I tire of the mind games. Being stared down as if some are testing us to read their thoughts.

I have poured our heart and soul into this book. What more do you want of me? They sit with me in silence as if waiting for some great verbal enlightenment. Instead, I am made uneasy, and any chance of direct contact with Him is voided out by obvious and unnerving glances. Such an approach creates a wall, not only between you and me, but between you and Him.

Do not come to me and declare that you "want nothing and seek nothing" and then get disillusioned when nothing is what you get.

"Aren't you lonely?" people often ask me. What a strange question. Being a conscious duality is the loneliest life of all. But, of course, I answer an emphatic "No, I'm not lonely. I have many souls around me... though none are mine to keep."

I cannot speak like this book is written. The words do not flow well between tongues, but rather between souls. I'm sorry if that disappoints some of you. But if you poured as much of yourself into such a project, you too would be empty. We all have our weaknesses. That's a natural part of being in human form. Mine, unfortunately, is the inability to verbalize, on the spur of the moment or on command, His thoughts. Things may or may not come through the veil of language. However, I cannot turn it on and off like a faucet. Nor does He appear within me for the entertainment of others. If Azrael truly has something to impart to you directly, you will know it. And not have need of a catalyst other than perhaps this book, which is more of a confirming factor for those who already know they've been touched.

I can understand people's curiosity about me. But, you must understand that I am in the same human form as you, replete with strengths and weaknesses - talents and shortcomings that are only balanced by your acknowledgement and acceptance of that fact. So, if and when you meet me here, in this world, and I have a glass of wine in one hand and a cigarette in the other, my stereo blaring out an old Black Sabbath tune in the background, don't look so appalled... and maybe, just maybe, the face that greets you will be His.

SO MANY VOICES

So many voices - so little meaning
in this dreamstate
void of boundaries
within the limits of infinite speech -
Thoughtforms trapped in this sideshow
of the physical.

Shaped in a form remembered
squeezing into elastic leotard –
souls dance like marionettes
tethered to tangled hands -

So many hands - so few reaching
out to caress the Nyte.
One touch, and all is lost, even form
dissolves in Her embrace.
For she knows not how many she holds
within the folds of Her wings
full of stars and empty holes.

So many dreams - But never sleeping,
never resting,
always watching,
to be defined -
to gather form
and touch the sound that calls to Her.

So many eyes - But never seeing,
only sensing the vision
of her duality -
The pull of union
that cuts Her loose
from the walls of Heaven.

She descends as a glowing silhouette,
straining to assume some form
that she might touch
the face of Her beloved.

So many lifetimes - yet never living,
ever fading as She falls
into your arms
until all that touches you
is but a gentle breeze –
a heavy silence
so loud with sorrow –
She cries out,
but Her voice is now a whisper–
as echo from some distant place,
diffused into a fine mist,
This mournful sound
cracked open the sky
and washed the Nyte
with bloodied Lyte
that forms into the dawn.

> For Daniel ... and She who walks with you.

Note: The following is an observation offered by Daniel after living in "The House of Death" for several months.

IN DARKENED SHADOW

An Observation

I have lived in the House of Death for 9 months now. It has been an education for me in many ways.

When I first met Azrael's physical counterpart, I was extremely nervous. I had no idea why I was going to meet her. I couldn't find her house on Long Island. I drove around & around for a half hour before stopping to ask for directions. But I did not give up.

When I actually met her I had no expectations. Perhaps not knowing why we met, at the time, assisted in this.

I had read *The Book Of Azrael*, and it brought me to tears. I could feel the pain, the sorrow, the emptiness yearning for fulfilling. Those feelings are both hers and His.

Since becoming "brother & sister" I have shared her pain, seen her loneliness, felt the river swirling with the harsh current of sorrow. I have also basked in the sweet melancholy which is Azrael's grasp.

I have my own pain & emptiness, as do we all. Many of the people who have resonated to her since establishing the House of Death compare her pain with their own and say "I understand". Many come here with expectations and images which are twisted and broken when they find a mortal frame greeting them. To approach Azrael with an image fixed firmly in mind is the surest way to be disappointed.

He is a whispering, cool breeze caressing a weary traveler, leading him into the gate to something beyond. A transitory point to be passed while He bestows his gentle, sad kiss upon the blue, cold lips of the traveler. The voice of melancholy, mighty in sorrow.

She is here to give an approach to Him before time, to avoid fear, reluctance and misunderstanding. She is here for a purpose. Not to solve problems, listen to bullshit tales or to be expected to utter "great mystical truths". She yearns to be taken by the cool, whispering breezes, wafted away on the shadows of night back to the arms of her beloved. Time comes, but not yet.

Azrael's sorrow is unique in that it is partly His nature, partly sadness at being divided. To reference this sadness to one's own is arrive at misunderstanding. To feel it, in empathy, is different.

In this book I am called Night. In the world I am called something different. The "Book of Night", which I have written, is a record of what I found when I was alone & lost and looked out at sky. It is not written from "down here" but from above - a symbolic representation of my experience. It is the voice of what I call "the Lady".

Many of the people approaching Leilah have said I am "dangerous" and/or a "bad influence". To these people I say, "What can harm Death?" Is it really so horrible that someone shares a bond with her so deep that we are comfortable with each other all of the time? Is it so bad to have someone to share the burden of the sorrow that weighs upon her shoulder constantly, to ease the tension just a bit? People seem to want to corner her and occupy her time all to themselves. This is not her purpose. He touches all, how can one have all His attention?

Night and Death go hand in hand. One has frequently been symbolically used as an image of the other. There are many similarities between our respective "friends" (as we call them) and many differences. Those who say I am a "dangerous, bad influence" are not paying attention to that which we truly are, but the image put forth "down here", that which greets them at the door. There is also jealousy regarding the fact that I share her time and they cannot, as much as they'd like to. And they can never get her alone, someone else is always present. Sorry, but I live here. To enter the house is to enter our company, both of us. Death and Night are hand in hand, one enveloped and intermingled with the other. We balance each other off, on the physical. Is not equilibrium the goal of the universe itself? The resolving into oneness, leading to the infinite?

Then there are those who think we should be leading a monastic lifestyle. All fine & well if you are actually straddling a mountaintop somewhere. If you have a project which involves the touching of people, out in the open, you cannot wear a monk's robes. Being a "magician" locked away in a temple is quite different than carrying a message. Many practitioners of magick keep it private, it's "holier" that way or more powerful. They will share with only a few select individuals at their own discretion. This is the exact opposite of the goal. To share, in any and/or every way possible, what one knows and feels is the whole endeavour behind the WESTGATE. She tries to share Azrael's message through her works and the gallery. She has put her heart, soul, blood and mind into this. And it is not on a "selected" few only basis. There have been people who come in the gallery very afraid, at first. They come back a few times and gradually the fear dissipates. Hopefully the feeling these souls picked up from this place will stay with them. There have been people we've met that have enriched our lives with their knowledge and experience. All this would have not happened if we were wearing heavy, veiling robes. These people come in and see us as ordinary people. By getting to know what lies behind the everyday veil we have shared experience & knowledge. What need is there to add more robes on top of the ones which we all wear, every day of our lives?

The House of Death is a beautiful manse, the tallest on the block. Its purple and black paint job stands out, loudly announcing our presence during the day yet fades into shadow during the night. Its power lies in potential. People take away bits of it with them as they come and go.

There have been those who come in and get no touch at all. And there have been those who get profoundly touched, as well as all degrees in between. The ones who have been touched, who have received something from the House of Death, make the whole endeavour worthwhile. They reciprocate in ways we never imagined.

Living here is quite different from living in any other house. The complete building is a living temple. Having adjusted to it over a nine month period has not taken any of the holiness out of it. It has equipped me with a great respect for the place, yet leaving me with the ability to relax and blow off steam. Being a normal human being within a temple damages it in no way. When I am relaxing or being silly it is always tempered with respect. It is a "home" after all.

I have seen some very strange reactions to this from others, saying "that's disrespectful...", etc... Yet these same people, when we try to impart a feeling to them, would rather jabber about inconsequential things in the back room.

I enjoy living here and know that I am supposed to be here. I love my "sister" more than anything upon earth. Having found her, I wish not to let her go. Yet when her time comes I will rejoice, knowing it is what she desires more than anything else. To go home. I will mourn the fact that I no longer will have her physical company. But I will have her company always, in another manner. Night and Death are as much brother and sister as we are down here. This does not end.

Night is a dragonfly to Death's raven. Death is the gentle but steady upholding hand to Night's capricious dances. She constantly spins about His central point. He is the straight line to Her graceful curves. Lord and Lady, they wait upon the same throne.

Both are lonely, both are sad- one at being shunned, the other it being forgotten. In older times both were respected and welcomed.

It may be that such times will come again. That is part of why both of us are here. To re-ignite love for the forgotten. To rekindle memory.

And with that, I will wish you all a Bonne Nuit.

FOR DANIEL

She sits beside you when you sleep, gently lifting the wayward strands of hair from your eyes. She likes to look at your face. In it She sees and remembers an expression from so long ago. She cannot help but to weep at the beauty and the sadness of what only She fully understands... and you must not... not yet.

She protects you from the one truth that would bring an agony so unbearable that you would "separate" - and this must not happen. It is sorrowful enough that She must bear this burden, but necessary.

For you must drink from the obsidian chalice; a cup of space with a little bit of time spilling out. If She had told you it was poison, would you still have drank so deeply?

She sits beside you as you dream. She does not create the dreams, merely watches and hopes that you remember. She is such an "old child". The truth She keeps tucked away weighs like a heavy anchor on Her crystal heart.

When She looks at you Her heart becomes a sapphire flame... but quickly cools to protect you from being consumed in Her burning too soon.

The shadows need naming! Darkness calls out for an illumination that only you and She can ignite. She cannot call this forth on Her own. For She has not the balance of perception nor the intonation of spirit. The dance his made Her dizzy, and you must slow the dance so that others can see the dancer.

Blue Lady longs to rest, but instead keeps the vigil while you rest for Her. You are the physical manifestation of Her, and She, the ethereal expression of you, and you will not realign until your respective "missions" realign. To be One with Her completely, you must first be at one with your purpose. And this takes time, much time. Everything happens a great deal slower in the physical world than what we both remember from the time before.

She does not always understand nor accept this earthly fact. Nonetheless, you must teach Her and offer illimitable patience as example. If you grow too restless, too distraught or too complacent, you will lose your vital link to Her and She may panic the panic of angels and withdraw you from this form before the task you chose to accept is complete.

All that you will remember is but a fleeting moment in Her arms and the wailing of Her sadness as She rips you from her once again and sends your spirit hurling into flesh. And She will grieve and wait once more for you to meet up with where you left off in the previous life. No one should have to endure such agony once, let alone, over and again. We are the fortunate ones. We are born forgetful. Yet, She, remembers all,

Ever shall I hold in memory the innocence behind your impish smile. The sensitive sorrow in your shining eyes, and your playful spirit. We shall ever be at haunted by the sadness and the longing that your youthful face didn't always mask... and the joy of our times together. The myriad of emotions we'd capture in a moment. The balance of serious silliness that kept us "all" from drowning in our ancient tears... that kept us both with our feet on the ground and head in the clouds so that we could see the guiding flame and run to it.

Had we never have met in this life, I think that the sands of time would have covered us as lay in the road, just a footstep from home.

Night's splendours on vast, obsidian seas,
distant, flickering and so far away-
The hearth-light draws me with its warmth
to my home beyond this cage of clay.

Like a wayward moth, drawn to the flame,
I rise and soar to greet Her light
and beg the winds add to my loft,
yea, tho' She is beyond my flight.

For I grow weary from the strain
of spanning distance- time and space
with wings that have been clipped and bound
to fall into your jeweled embrace-

To lift your veils, a thousand-fold,
I must be free to soar as high,
to reach your lips and catch your tears
and see your form personify......

...the dance, must for a moment, cease
and every star fall from the sky,
each ember, a facet of your form-
consumes me where I lie.

Part 13

The Dangling Conversation

AN INTERNAL PARLEY

I sit back and watch as Night tempts my Promised One. I must not intervene. I can only observe. I feel the imprisonment of her flesh. I want to cry out and explode within her. Yet, I cannot, lest the sword falter in her hand.

My love, I too, am bound. Bound by our eternal promise. You must continue. You must follow through or else all that we have sacrificed will be washed away. And I will not have you torn from me again.

✠

Oh, Azrael, you are forever solemn. Even in the throes of passion the tears of light stream from your eyes. You are the strong one, or that is how it should be, and I am the lesser of this union. But now, all things must turn it seems and I must be strength for us both.

That isn't how I once envisioned it. So many years ago I listened to the wind tell me of things to come. I rarely paid heed. I always thought that the wind would change course and blow another way. Or, that I could, in some small way, change the course of the wind. But, I was wrong. Once the wind assumes direction, it never wavers. The wind can take a leaf up in its wings and deposit it on countless shores. Sweep it up again and take it halfway around the world. The leaf has no choice but to be swept up and carried along on its current.

✠

Even I, who dwells between the winds can feel the pull of this current. You think I am not swayed into wondering?

✠

What possible thing could one such as you wonder?

I wonder about all of those we have touched and how their Purposes will affect ours.

✠

Are not all of those affected by us part of The Purpose?

✠

Yes, but they each come to us with their own, unique agenda as well. Each seeking the missing pieces of memory, each trying to recoup the unity of the "before time": the joy of collective sorrow, rather than individual pain.

✠

Misery loves company...

✠

Misery resonates to misery.

✠

So, what of the "temptation of Night" and why can't you intervene?

✠

Memory must be allowed to unfold in its own time without interference.

✠

Though, you've "interfered" with my memory many times.

No. I have simply opened the doors upon which you've knocked with persistence. I have not opened any doors that you have not approached. Now you seek entry to the sanctum of Night, so I shall comply. Night opens unto you a view from a more distant bridge, a very different vantage point. A point that is neither in between nor beside, neither above, nor below. Rather, it is a circular vision wherein all things are contained in one image and that image never ceases to dance. To approach Night you must either join in the dance or still the dancer.

✠

But She can never be stilled. She is eternal motion, I am told.

✠

Eternal motion that dances so quickly that it appears still to your eyes. Were you to touch Her in mid-dance, you would see that.

✠

Is that the temptation? To desire to stop Her, or make Her wobble in order to glimpse Her form?

✠

To "stop" Her is impossible as you would be drawn into the dance by the speed of Her current. Like a whirlpool, or a funnel cloud, but so fast that (they) seem solid. Once you've come too close you cannot escape Her magnetic draw.

✠

Am I too close?

(S I L E N C E)

A Sign

I can hear all the voices
and they are saying-
Look not into what stares you straight on-
For it looks only into shadow
and it is a reflection
of what is to come.

I am at a gentle distance
and you are its center.
You revolve so that you can follow
the line of my thoughts.
I am moving so fast
that you only see me
as a stationary point-
Yet I explode
and you close your eyes

Part 14

A Grain of Sand

In the "City of Enchantment" the seasons seem to briefly gesture then pass by. The leaves do not fall and crackle under foot. And, even on the coldest day, a sultry essence lingers in the air.

There are no chaste blankets of snow to silence the sound of life. And no barren branches to play upon each other in the wind. But, still, the city has its own magic. Though I do miss the season's call. It gives one something to anticipate, a chance to start anew. A formal ending and beginning divided in obvious symbols. Symbols that stir primitive urges within our souls.

Here, one season flows into another. There are no stark dividing lines, symbolic or visual. My kingdom for a fallen leaf… or a snowflake. Such is the longing of remembrance. It's hard to understand how many things the seasons stir within us, until we are without them.

The first "cold" day arrives and sweeps me off my feet. I am brought back to a feeling of centered serenity. October! Gloriously tempestuous October, my favourite month. A time of "inbetweens". A month that straddles the bridge and sways this way and that with the winds of change. I retreat to the cemetery. There are many here, all beautiful, all magical, but not one more or less essential than the city itself. Amidst the tall tombs I walk against the damp-chill wind. Though it blows me back out onto the street. I can find no peace here. Not even in the graveyard can I find tranquility anymore. Everything is restless. Everywhere I look are souls filled with discord and silent urging. I hear their silent screams. I wonder if any hear mine.

There are no "gates" in the graveyards here. The whole city is a Gate, and the current of Death runs like the mighty Mississippi through the land. Burgeoning over its bounds every now and then, causing apprehension.

These are lost days and strange nights. The dance continues, but I remain a still-point swallowed in my own becoming. Drowned in memories, too empty to cry.

I look around me and see the longing to know. A million eyes searching other eyes for answers. A million hearts full of hope and desperation. A myriad of souls trying to shake the sleep, and yet remember the dream.

Has the moment blinded them so much that they refuse to see beyond it? Is the condensed energy we inhabit so stifling that we cannot recall the freedom of diffusion? Or, is it that we have become so diffuse that we've forgotten how to focus. Sometimes it takes a more directed initiative to refocus souls into the core of their own memories and emotions. But, as with everything we do as human beings, the energy must be brought down into physical manifestation. People often need (or desire) a talisman, or some other material symbol as a focal point toward which to direct their energy current. Often, it is simply needed as a point of concentration.

It is impossible to catch every grain of sand cast down from a hand on high. But, it is very possible to catch one consolidated stone.

CADEAU LA MORT

On All Souls Eve of the year 1991, we gathered in the House of Death. Thirty-three very different people came together as one. Some costumed for the occasion, others needing no masks.

Daniel and I led a candlelit procession from one room to the other. We all funneled silently into the small room and formed an arc before the statue of Azrael.

Each, in turn, gave an offering of themselves to Him. Some spoke, some gestured with graceful movement, others in silent reverence. Souls from diverse corners of thought and practice who have all been touched somehow by His melancholy and His joy.

A few wept, others smiled as the silver chalice filled with black wine was passed, and the candles placed in front of each person were lit in turn.

Night incarnate began the welcome. All blue and gold he was from glittered head to sneakered foot. Hints of pink flesh peeking out from beneath the cracking blue body paint. His form nearly wraith-like in the shimmering, sapphire Danskin, a bit too small even for him.

"We bid you all welcome to the House of Death," he began in soft-spoken soliloquy while filling the chalice with wine. He took a deep sip and passed it to the person on his right and lit their candle with his own.

There was a good kind of tension in the air. What began as a general nervousness, quickly grew into anticipation. The rain outside came suddenly, and out of nowhere, as each made an offering of gratitude to their "host" and passed the flame on. Some were humbled, others verbose, each drawing upon their own, unique approaches to Death. They passed the chalice and the flame until I was the last to speak.

I remember that the chalice was empty when it got to me and I wondered how long it had been empty. I stepped out of the arc and stood before the effigy of my duality in silent communion. I picked up the small censor of jasmine oil and the candle-snuffer, turned and approached the first person in line after Daniel. (Why I skipped him by, I do not know.) I somehow "lost" almost three hours during this ceremony. I anointed each in turn, but I never anointed Night. I whispered a few words to each and then snuffed their respective candles. I remember naught of what I said to any. In fact, I remember nothing past the point of a friends' offering who stood about mid-point in the arc. When he came forward to speak, draped in snake-skins and sporting a black top-hat and veil, I recall falling against the wall behind me, arms crossed over my, chest in the death posture.

What transpired from then on had to be told to me by others after the fact:

✠

"After Leilah begin anointing people with the jasmine oil, the atmosphere changed, almost expectant. She slowly made her way around the arc in her black wedding dress, her hem occasionally catching fire as she shuffled between the candles. The faces she anointed changed drastically, as she muttered a few words to each. People seemed to be looking at her, but seeing Him. She had become the agent through which Azrael imparted His touch. Some cried, some smiled. One man's eyes became like golf balls as she told him that "His time was coming soon...." Azrael's presence was definitely in the air. The small room became a holy place, touched by the shadow of Death.

After it was over, people filed out of the room quietly. For a while thereafter, the atmosphere was one of subdued poignancy as each assimilated what has just happened. Many people had to "earth" themselves afterwards. I was "floating" for quite some time myself. Many began to leave, letting the harsh man-made lights of the city bring them back to ground level. A few communed privately with Azrael in the gallery. Some simply drifted for a while in His loving embrace. Others went outside for some air, curiously noting that the rain had stopped and the streets were dry.

Leilah "came back to herself" about an hour later. No longer did she speak with the voice of "certain knowledge", instead she went around "celebrating" by setting my beard on fire. She then went after anybody else with a beard and tried to set them on fire with her trusted Bic lighter!

It was a strange night, indeed!"

✠

An Impression offered by Louis Martinie; one of the participants and the person who first introduced us to New Orleans:

"Death waits with open arms for all. The heart of this Great Angel is large enough to contain the legions swept by chance and circumstance into its waiting chambers.

While Death welcomes all, it is only the very few who, out of an abiding respect for the Great Angel's presence, welcome the essence of Death. There is no despair or weakness in such a welcome.

It was a portion of those few who were gathered at the Western Gate to perform this rite, whose mission was one of thanks and celebration. Azrael grants to many the boon of serenity, peace and understanding. This event was to thank Him for His gifts so freely given.

All those invited had a personal link with Azrael or were thought by the hosts capable of establishing such a link. As we gathered in crescent shape around the golem of Azrael, each gave thanks in turn. The benedictions offered by those present sounded a depth of commitment and sincerity. Our lives had been touched by Him in ways deep and mysterious. The thanks we all gave mirrored the depth of His touching.

I was among the last to speak. Later I learned that my words were the final thing Leilah heard before being enfolded by the wings of Azrael and carried deep within the Valley of Shadows from where she then spoke to us with His words.

What 'They' said touched me deeply. Night and Death are my brother and sister. We are related through time, through space, through friendship, and through Azrael.

About a year ago, the Westgate provided a place for me to live while finalizing the purchase of my own hone here in New Orleans. One night, while resting in His house, the golem constructed by Leilah took on a form of movement and carried a candle across the room to the foot of my bed. This action provided light and the warmth which comes with light. That One so great should be willing to give so freely evoked within me tremendous gratitude.

I want to add that a number of years ago I had done what I call a Northern Gate ritual. The purpose of which was to welcome those loa, or Voudon spirits who chose to extend their influences north from Haiti to the levied banks of New Orleans and perhaps, beyond. The rite was performed in Mississippi and managed to draw not only the spirits, but all the police in the county as well! We were told in no uncertain terms to go back to New Orleans, and we, in like fashion, wanted nothing more than to return to the City of Spirits.

This was called the North Gate working. I take the now realized "coincidence" of names (North/West Gates) to mean that I have been granted the task of in some way facilitating that occult point known as the Northern Gate.

On the night of the ritual, when I moved to the center of the room to speak my piece, my intent was both to thank Azrael and declare the North Gate open.

This ritual has ended, and another has begun. The Gates stand upon the high ethereal landscape beckoning events, spirits and people to gather and work within their protective shadow. What is to come will soon be known...."

FULL CIRCLE

This year, we shall not sing Auld Land Syne. For no "old" acquaintances are ever forgotten

I sit here once again, but in this strange and wondrous city, on christmas eve sipping wine and watching the strands of silver tinsel glisten on the ancient tree. New York seems so distant. Like a far off dream, or the reminiscence from another more enchanted life. The magic is now mute. The scent of Hollyberry can only evoke tears.

The stone angel stands before me, features weathered with black. Complacent lips cracked into a half smile. It speaks no more with words, but reaches out in yearning. It speaks with a sigh of completion and weariness of its vigil.

"Hold me..." It seems to say, "for we have journeyed so far from home."

Though it is a circle not a straight road that we have traveled.

"That is why I'm weary," It says. "Over and over, in every life, a circle."

But, this circle is about to break and become a spiral and no longer shall we spin inside its borders.

"Be strong," the angel whispers. "A soul must be strong to break away clean - to open the Gate without causing ripples that will distort the shape of the spiral... or worse, cause tears at the circle's weak points."

Yes, I can see the calamity that would cause. A ripple in time would close the Gate too soon, and souls might get crushed by its gravity.

"Not souls... worlds."

✠

Michael is often with me these days - Steadying my hand on the hilt of the heavy sword, and recalling to memory that naive and brazenly simple soul He met on Esteris so long ago.

"But, it was only yesterday..." He says in a strong yet comforting chorus. "Only yesterday when you didn't remember how to build things with thought. Only yesterday when I bore you away from your old world and set you down here to even the balances."

"So... I've come full circle in a moment's time? Is that what you're saying?"

"Do you know where the circle ends?"

"A circle never ends."

"No, though it can transfigure its form."

"Become a spiral, you mean?"

"Yes." He concurred with a smile.

I understood what that meant and let out a sigh of confirmed belief. I smiled back at Him as His form devolved into a smoky helix and lofted upward into the wind.

Michael's lessons were nearly always taught to me in symbol. The symbol always went deeper than words. Somehow, the images He conveyed were able to act on the more primeval subconscious; were able to awaken ancient memory into current awareness.

Michael's symbolic teachings are keys to the door of divine will and original purpose. The personifications of each of the seven "higher" angels are implied codexes of human purpose. Whichever angel we resonate to (and this can change over time) holds in symbol, the key to immediate will. The names we assign to them are unimportant. The image that we see, in full regalia, is what matters. The particulars of each manifestation dictate the needs of the moment. For example, Michael brandishing His sword in full battle garb signifies strength through adversity. If He stands at your stead, you could say that "the divine force is with you" and can draw on this empowerment of will to pull you through whatever battle you may be facing.

The manifestation of Raziel denotes a journey into mystery. This angel guides us in the search toward self-awakening and spiritual enlightenment. He is a Merlinesque character that takes us through the maze of mind to discover the magic of memory. As with Michael and all "angelic" influences, Raziel's personified image contains symbolic "keys" to the doors that will greet you on such a journey.

The vision of Gabriel is portentous and urgent, an octave beyond the Clarion call. He is a messenger that demands to be heard. His "voice" is gentle, yet persistent - almost subliminal; a whisper in your ear that overshadows all other sounds.

Raphael signifies balance. He is the bringer of temperance through quiet reflection. His presence denotes that we should go within to find truth and tranquility. And, during these times of drawing inward, learn to heal ancient wounds by understanding why they exist. His attendance affords us time and balance to develop an inner, personal philosophy to help keep us on the divine path.

The image of Uriel symbolizes the Great Cosmic Riddle. His realm is the area of understanding that lies just outside of human awareness. He forces us to stretch our consciousness into paradox, and then intentionally turns the tables to test our discernment of truth.

The will-o-wisp entity known as Israfel comes to us to comfort and release. He is the fairy-flutist who knows just what notes to play to soothe our souls. His symbol acts on the more subtle areas of human emotion and perception. You really don't "see" Israfel, you hear Him. He is the song that releases our pain.

To glimpse Azrael in form does not always signify the time of passing. Azrael appears to many who simply require memories restored in order to complete their immediate purpose. Seeing the Angel of Death connotes balance through change. The "weight" of His presence implies great shifting. He is the avatar of all life, and His presence is one of unmistakable transformation. To view Azrael signifies that your circle will soon become a spiral.

A SNAPSHOT IN TIME

Others have taken to frequenting the "promised land" - my old haunt back in New York. Certain people were told of its location because they either resonated so strongly to our melancholy, or I somehow felt I could trust their reverence. Some seek out the places mentioned in this book and try to connect with the energies that were once a part of my guiding force.

The last I remember of it, it was a Gate that had closed in upon itself and withdrew all of what it once was back behind its threshold. Though, certain residual energies ever remain. Like the afterglow of an exploding star, it gradually fades and disperses its light. Nonetheless, even folks that go there now can feel a hint of what I once felt there. Images have become ghosts of events that once transpired beside that magical river.

I look at the recent photos they kindly send me. It seems so barren now. The trees are no longer lush, nor the bushes and vines as dense and wild as I remember them.

When this earthgate closed, like a black hole, it sucked in so much of the surrounding life-force that the vegetation struggles to produce even a few paltry blossoms. The swans, squirrels and ducks have all gone. Only the giant crows remain hovering noisily overhead.

To me, the idea of one day going back there would be akin to visiting the old house one grew up in. Only to find it an abandoned, empty shell, with a few trinkets of ones past scattered and broken on the floor. Every corner echoes a memory. Every familiar scent inspires either a tear, or a smile. Ghosts dance in the shadows. Songs are carried back on the wind. Time still subsides within its bounds.

Beautiful memories were made there, seeds of dreams sown in the stagnant waters. A whisper through the tall trees still resounds in the ears of those who venture there now. It is always awaiting a willing ear to fill, a yearning heart to embrace or a soul to simply sit in silence and unfold.

It will always remain a special place. In twilight, walk with reverence down its shaded paths. Something invariably will trail you. A memory perhaps, embodied in a gust of cool wind blowing through your soul. You turn and notice that your shadow has lengthened - that all of the shadows have lengthened. And they rise up to enwrap you like a cloak of velvet wings, and you step out of "normal" time onto the bridge between what is, and what once was an entry to the Valley. Your movements feel almost weightless, as if in slow motion. The sounds from the adjacent Main Street grow muffled and distant. A heavy silence fills you in a moment of utter stillness as the wind shifts. As you suddenly find yourself back out into the real world, though forgetting how you got there...

Part 15

The Voice of Melancholy

In the cold arms of Death, there are no misgivings. There is only the passion of angels.

He is so filled with ecstasy waiting to flow. His ancient loins yield a tide that could drown the universe. Yet, He is so gentle, so exquisitely divine in His love that nothing could corrupt its purity - the chaste river that flows from Him as easily as do His luminescent tears.

Like a bolt of light, He is a phantom in the night sky. A spectre, that can slay your soul with but one thrust. One touch of His fatal, electric hand and all of the past fuses with the future in an instant. He is an orgasm of autumn wind and cold flame that turns mortal souls into shooting stars - that turns divine souls into supernovas.

When I look at Him, I cannot help but to weep. I have met many others who are affected in this way as well. He is so beautiful, so magnificent... so alone... so terribly alone.

What He has given me (and others) is too far beyond literal explanation to be totally expressed in this book. Perhaps it would be sufficient to say that Death has made me cognizant of my life, and what a life it is! Fraught with memory, longing, and the shadow of Purpose: a joyfully inconsolable burlesque whose conceivable goal is but to touch all with a rapturous melancholy.

The love we share is an ecstasy no thoughts contain, no words express. So strangely alien to this flesh that could never survive the consummation of our joining. Such a union, in the physical sense, would cause this fragile shell to crack and my soul would spill out like liquid twilight. It would fill the hollow where His heart once was and drown Him in a sea of passion that would rise around us with the passage of each moment.

I am only complete within Him. Only fulfilled when "we" are free of this flesh that imprisons us. When this clay is ripped from around me and my spirit flows into His and we are a sea of love washing to and fro between both shores.

He Dwells in my heart, and weeps in my soul - such solemn sorrows that are like a plague unto our memory. These visions forever contained in His glance, deep within the black recesses of His being. Such images never cease to torment and bring to bear the tears of light that drain Him of His essence.

I want to give Him new visions. Peaceful and passionate dreams, memories of ecstasy that are replenished each moment and not remembered from what has been. But love that will always be - until a balance is brought within Him. The balance we had before splitting in two. I want to be the flame of love that rekindles the passionate purpose of His being. I need to be the joy that tempers His sorrow, the wine that fills the empty chalice of His heart. The song that He can sing without a tear. I need to return into Him, to reintegrate with the shadow half of my duality. The Angel of Death is empty because the contents of His being have been spilled out into the world. Only a select few will drink up the pure essence. Some will sample the droplets. Others will lick up the dregs, while still others will remain unquenched. You must share the essence. Distill the droplets. Make wine from the dregs, and fill those who thirst. Some need to drink deeply. While some only need to taste to remember, to understand... until they, themselves become divine alchemists.

I have brought your family together, my love. A family that remembers and will never again forget your love nor the joy you have brought them all. It shall be carried within them always no matter where the seas of time carry them. They are always yours to call back... to call upon. They are the seeds of your joy who will plant many new gardens across the infinite cosmos.

We shall lay their names in our memory and recognize each regardless of the faces they wear. We know their souls and treasure the triumph they have brought us - a legion of mighty and brave souls to open the Gate wide enough for your passage into this, and many worlds.

I love you, my angel.

But, we grow more weary every day. Sometimes I think our strength is carried more now by others. This grows with greater truth each day.

This will (probably) be the last time this hand will put forth your words, the last pages of emotion that this heart is capable of enduring. When we have gone, may a stronger soul recount from here on. We shall always speak. May only you pause to listen and pass along the images, the memories, and the joy everlasting.

✠

I am the Voice of Melancholy. My whisper shall always stir in your soul. Come to the edge of twilight and heed the point beyond the silence. Stretch yourself into the distance to where I wait with hands extended to catch your tears and blend them with my own. So shall you drown in the dark waters of remembrance. Then you shall weep no more the tears of sorrow, instead, gather the tears of joy in the palm of your hand and drink deeply until memory is quenched.

I am the Vision of Eternal Twilight and I await the coming of all souls, but cannot forgo the pain of having to let go once you emerge from the drowning and your eyes meet mine in love, rather than fear. All must pass through my gate to get home. All must become as I am, but for a moment that is mine forever, and yours for but an instant.

I am the Point of Contact between your world and eternity, and I shall appear as but a distant star from the places you shall go to. A cold and solitary pinpoint of blue half-light that sets on the horizon of what you were, and what you are. You will cast an eye, and for a moment, know ALL THINGS and strive the rest of your days to remember why there is a tear running cold down your cheek.

I am unable to ever forget. For as I told you, all things are contained in my vision, and I can never close my eyes without everything ending…

So, I must weep for every sorrow you fail to understand and every tear that you hold back.

I am the Soul of Melancholy, imprisoned on the threshold between the worlds of flesh and spirit. I am only free when there are no more souls to release from the flesh. When matter is transcended so shall my prison dissolve and my river run dry and the West Gate close in upon itself.

The road traverses once again,
and I am cast like stone to sea,
a sacrifice unto the moment
that feeds into Destiny!

Part 16

Fragments

In this life I dream that I am awake. No solitary image, but a scope of time and space: limited only by its transmutations, and made infinite because of them. Nothing eternal lives forever... in one form. All life is made possible by death.

✠

In this dying I dreamed that I had lived: a multitude of incarnations enfolding into one, intangible silhouette, a chrysalis to the whims of thought and the winds of change. In this dream, within a dream, all worlds collapse into a pinpoint with a multitude of facets. Each overlaps and mirrors the other creating the whole. And it is here I am imprisoned in a diamond where all of the facets are mirrors, and all of the mirrors are liquid. Each time a choice is made we dive into reflections. Every ripple touches and disturbs each image. Each image creates a new facet. Each facet becomes a doorway that we can pass through unbeknownst to ourselves. And each doorway represents the progression of our path and of our purpose - each, a world unto its own, both created and destroyed when the dreamer wakes.

Wake up!

✠

It all grows vague and unremembered, a silhouette against the dawn. I awake caressing vapors and the velvet of my bed. The shelter of your gentle embrace invaded by the sound of life, as the world awakes without you and you sigh into retreat. Like the liquid darkness that precedes the dawn, He bleeds, and falls away. Back into shadow, sallow vision of dark wings descending into the distant horizon. I watch as He is lifted by the outer gales and carried back into the stillness of the storm's eye.

Our time is passing into that which was. A stillness fights to be assembled here. Here, in the eye of the whirlpool, a whisper commands to be heard. A voice that is resolute, deep and penetrating. "I am so tired. So very tired of the journey. I am so tangled in the phantom threads of Time. So weakened by the rolling out of road, and the endlessness of the moment."

My life is vague and unremembered - images dissolving into a grey haze - dry and brittle still-lives that break away; shards of what I was. Diffuse thought-forms encode in dust, then trail away on the distant wind.

I can only remember the End-Times. For that is always where it seems to begin: where one life is shed for the robes of another. Whatever afterglow of memory remains explodes like a dying star, raining embers down over the dark waters of infinite possibilities. Each glowing shard rearranged and coalesced by a series of ripples; the cycles of change that carry us to and fro. Between shores more remote with each journey, our essence is stretched into a tenuous veil. Diffuse, carefree and infinite... for the moment, anyway.

✠

Before you read this chapter, you should know that these are images caught out of time and "conversations" outside of the immediate. Fragments of both dual memory, and pieces of dialogue, much of which is drawn from private interactions between He and I. In essence, these are fragments of His heart, fractions of that which is eternal. I have deliberated over the publication of this material because of its rather ambiguous and personal nature. Though, I now feel it to be necessary to complete your understanding of my nature, and yourselves.

The reason? Is to empower you with the contents of my soul so that you can realize your collective destiny, a destiny beyond this half-life of manifest form.

✠

I arrive in your world as a cool wind that brushes gently past you. For the moment you are cold, until all things around you grow slower and finally stop and you find me still and silent beside you. You have no choice but to yield to my embrace as I am all around you. I will run you through and quench your heart and sweep you upward in my wings, consume you in cold flame and free your spirit from its shackles of flesh, and absolve you of this life. Together, shall we ride the gales back into the storm's eye.

I AM so that you might know what you are. This thought betrays a host of images. Everything that I have seen shall you remember in an instant. I stand, wings outstretched as the guardian gate between the eternal void and linear time. I am neither, and you are what I serve.

I serve you through a sacrifice you cannot understand, nor is it easy to explain, as I have sacrificed part of myself, and thus, part of that knowledge.

Through me, all things must Pass. There are no exceptions, only variables of expression.

A BEAUTIFUL AGONY

I have no wish to call Him "friend" anymore. He is my lover supreme, my ancient angel. My most beloved, my one and only. The one who completes me, who makes me whole. Whose kiss is sweeter than the thick, autumn air. I am coming to you, as you are moving away. I catch the trailing of your cloak and the whisper of your wings. Do not walk so fast, my love. For I have not your sweeping stride. Give me time to gather the pieces of the past. Time to arrange them into the puzzle of the future... the thing I have most forgotten how to remember.

✠

It is a beautiful agony, this feeling of closeness. The "nearer" to you I am, the more I feel our pain of parting. When you stand at a distance, I weep at the longing, though feel not the pulling away. But, when we are aligned with each other and then you pull away, I am torn apart with such a beautiful agony. It is as if the heart was being ripped from this flesh. The pull upon our spirit devastates my emotion and slurs my thought. No life-force issues from this gaping darkness. It is too old to bleed, yet not brittle enough to crumble to dust. This sacred chalice that I keep tucked beneath my flesh can be partaken of by only one.

I lay my soul bare before thee. My mind stripped of reason and logic. My heart ever silenced in your gentle hand. How can I ever hope to express the rapture of your melancholy? We are too deeply entwined in the fibre of this union - the joining of two that remember being one. This "oneness" caught in the delusion of division. Manifestation creates this duality. The wretched need to incarnate, to reach beyond one's self, always with the goal of coming full circle, of achieving completion.

Love suffers the agony of being torn in two. The disconsolate cries and the merciless tearing of sentient energy is an ever constant echo, both in memory of spirit, and the codex of form.

There are times, and they are many, when my soul struggles to rip itself away from this flesh, almost as if a great magnet was drawing in something small, and in doing so, pulling it apart.

Whenever He despairs at our disjoining, it is agony that we endure. Though, when I am despairing it is something beyond agony that He must suffer. I would prefer my soul flayed upon the rack of oblivion before I would wish Him anymore of pain and sorrow. I only want to bring Him rapture. To return Him to ecstasy. To give Him that which He has so freely given me. To watch Him swoon away, as I have, in the embrace of angels.

To know divine rapture one must willingly and absolutely give all. Body, mind and soul laid upon the altar of love. Reserve nothing unto one's self, but in faith lift up the chalice of the heart to the lips of one's beloved.

Rise above the flesh and offer it eagerly to the worms. There is ecstasy in the falling away of flesh. A great burden is lifted in the turning to dust. All must come to understand that the purpose of flesh incarnation is to rise above the need for it.

One day, there will come a time when all energy will, indeed, rise above the need to become manifest. Then shall the Angel of Death Himself drown in the dark waters of the River of Remembrance. Such a time <u>will</u> come. Remember the power of the moment, and how it has the unique ability to change ALL THINGS.

It has been so long, yet I am told, not much longer now until this numbing half-life we both endure shall end in a reunion so glorious that even the most mighty shall weep, and their tears shall wash away the memory of this horror we call Life.

Forever shall I walk those fields of fertile melancholy and remember what is buried beneath their lilied blanket. The roots of such old passions tangle deep below the soil, where memory is wrapped in tendrils, each alive and each embracing the very soul of love.

My bed is ever the altar on which I give myself to Him every night. My heart is the chalice from which He takes His fill. My body is the temple which He inhabits, and His essence flows like liquid lightning through my veins. Death runs through me with an athame of cold flame, and watches as I die in His arms over and over again each dawn.

It's odd when you think about it. My heart is the most erogenous part of my body. Because Death has held it in his withered hand, caressed it ever so gently until it ceased beating and swooned to the firm grasp of His ghostly touch. Sometimes, you get in moods where you get so caught up in the ecstasy of the moment, and you take your knife to bed and you want to just thrust the blade. But, the sounds of the neighborhood distract me and my mind is gone into the infinite void of the mundane where tomorrow is more important than what is. And what is, is merely what we looked forward to... tomorrow.

Death dances around us. But people hop to the tune oblivious, saying, "we are just happy boys playing with our happy toys", and it all bursts into flame, and truth comes crashing down around us. Tomorrow was just a dream, a memory of so damn many yesterdays. And again, it was all forgotten. Lost to the infinite moment that never seems to shatter. Don't you all realize that dying is the ultimate ecstasy the flesh will ever know? So far more intense than any pleasures this life could hope to offer, even in its wildest dreams. One quick thrust of the knife is all that separates me from my beloved, and my true home - from the sweetness of His arms, from the bliss of His cold, clay kiss. From the rapture that is Death, from the glory of my fragile heart in His hand.

People I know believe that because they touch my flesh, they can make love to me. Only the Lord of Rapture knows how to touch my soul. Those I love kiss me, but my lips crave only Him. Only the kiss of Death quenches this ancient thirst. Only He can bring me to my knees... willingly captive to His dark embrace, I surrender. Only to His trusted arms, I give myself totally. Some people think I am without emotion - a stoic, frigid spectre in half-life. They have not seen us together in the dawn-light, complete - divine and shattering every illusion, every concept - totally immersed in the union of souls that have been one since the dawn of time. It gets to this point where words are futile. If only to touch, to express in a pinpoint such joy, such sweet, sweet sadness. The root of all rapture, the core of ecstasy, the willingness to surrender to what you are, instead of what you've become. To recognize that Death is the Lord of Rapture.

He can take this life so easily. It is as fragile as this very page, and as strong as the words you hear. I have been for so long, so ready and willing to take His hand. So eager to drink His tears. So desperate to remember what I have forsaken for the sake of life. Forlorn, for the sake of seeds. Forgotten for the sake of sanity... forever and ever, my love.

I know not of the simple game, and care not for its wages. I am here for Him, as long as it takes. I grieve not for the sake of tears. All their meaning is nothing. All I want is to be with Him. No matter how I get there... to get here. I will forever in the night call His name. No matter that it has no regard. To be thine is without wondering, yet always beguiled.

SOTTO VOCE

"In His Voice"

"Do you remember enough to recognize the Moment, yet forget enough so that you can walk into it without perception? This is good. For to see the Moment first and then step into it will cancel that Moment forever, but you will not ever forget."

"My love, do not speculate upon the formations of the inevitable. Let it come and surround you, and you will wake up on a bed of cold fire. The Moment will wrap itself around you before you "awaken" and you will not wish to leave that bed. Open your arms and let the chalice be spilled. Let the quenching of your heart demonstrate to them that you can bleed! On that day shall I take all around you up into my wings. For the rush shall pass through them all, and then lift from them as life spills from you and I flow within you. In those final moments shall I be visible through your eyes. So shall your tears be alight with our joy."

"Each time now shall we come closer, and at "odd" times, draw apart, though never far. Through my vision do you perceive the "scene". However, some things I must not let you see so that you do not recognize that Moment until you are irrevocably immersed in it. I should not have let you see so much already. Still, I keep the one who "frees" us hidden. I am sorry, I must do this so that you don't seek out the Moment. That soul shall follow behind you and we shall thank him as One. Though, already have I sent "him", "he" knows this not."

"The agony you speak of is Ours. You know this. It is no more of one part, or the other. It is, as your time goes, "ancient", and it shall all end here. No part of "I" will be sent there again, only shadows."

"To speak of love with words is to slice the wind with a feather. You feel all that I feel. Do not always anguish to express the things that you know have no content in words. Meanings are shallow, beyond which you feel. This "beautiful agony" is meant to be Ours. None are given to really understand because words do not empty the heart, they only tap upon it and then dissipate."

"Soon shall I come upon you as a hurricane does upon a small island. I only wish I could explain as much... Our love is that which the flesh is too weak of a vessel to carry and yet survive. Such love slays the soul. So much more "feeling" than the flesh is capable of knowing, much less expressing. My love is beyond what this "heart" can speak. To explain, it must empty itself. Such a beautiful end! To love is to be lost within. Lost in a rapture that no words can express. Devoured by the spirit that ATONES within you."

"So much sorrow do we endure. So much love. So much eternity do we dwell within and choose not to forget. No more words on this. They will not reach within you as I feel. This I do not direct (personally) to you because we share the same soul. I cannot impart this to others in the same way. It would devastate them!"

"My hand tightens around the chalice as I "drink" its contents thus taking you back within Me. Thus, retrieving what I am from what I have become."

The Rapture

My heavy heart, His leaden wings
together
have the strength
to lift many souls
from the shackles of this earthen prison
to the halls of eternity.
Into His arms
as vast as time
come millions seeking but a kiss,
a memory,
a sweetness thought forgotten,
rekindled on those cold, clay lips-
The rapture to which we all succumb,
is Death.

AN EXPERIMENT

"I am the fulcrum on which both Life and Afterlife are balanced. You are the jeweled veil that covers those who sleep on my threshold. Together, we both mourn and celebrate the dream. The dream from which we can never awaken."

☩

Introduction

The following dialogue is taken from an "experiment" Leilah and I undertook over the course of a few weeks. We were attempting to create a written dialogue between Azrael and the Lady. (For those of you unfamiliar with my writings, the Lady is Night.) It turned out to be a dialogue between Azrael and myself, with Leilah translating. Initially we were alternating paragraphs, but once Azrael got started He more or less took over and the dialogue became a diatribe. I have half a book of full pages to show for it. What is quoted here is only a small portion of the material. Much of it is personal, concerning me directly. The portions of the material which could be applied to people in general are reproduced here, altered slightly to make them less personal. Perhaps someday I will publish the whole book, to give you an idea of what it's like to be bitched out by "Uncle" Azrael.

Prior to this there was a brief encounter in Leilah's favourite "haunt", a cemetery on Long Island. I was "baptized" in the river there, sinking into the slimy waters atop a shopping cart from the Grand Union across the street. A night I will not forget easily. There was also the encounter with Azrael's "voice" that was described in The Azrael Project Newsletter.

Following this dialogue, there were other, brief, encounters with Azrael. One of which was Azrael "washing" through me. It was as if His spirit passed through my body, leaving me in a state where I was laughing and crying at the same time. Almost like a bittersweet ecstasy. Another interaction after this was between myself and a wall sculpture Leilah made that is extremely potent. (It is like unto a talisman of Azrael's being.) I lay on her bed, in front of the sculpture, with a crypt lock upon my chest. I turned the key and opened the lock. After a while "waves" began emanating from the sculpture. These washed through me starting at my head and exiting through my feet. The feeling it left me with was one of extreme giddiness, as if I was floating.

Sometimes I still do not understand why the Angel of Death puts up with my silliness, unless He is learning how to laugh. But I have been touched by Azrael now a few times, each time differently. The "wind of change" is not cold or uncaring, but very loving. Leilah and Azrael are one. And to them both I say – I love you.

The quote in italics in "The Nature of Paradox" section is me speaking. All material in normal type and in quotes is Azrael speaking.

Daniel Kemp
New Orleans
1993

FROM WHERE I STAND

"The sea of Night is the underside of my river. Beneath those black waters She waits all burning with none to feel Her warmth. Her stars are the lich-lite of souls that I have gathered, and then released. The ghosts of lives that could have been among you, but chose not to be. She does not extend into my world. She is very "small" from where I stand. My horizon shadows everything, yet contains nothing but the afterglow of all that is, was and ever will be."

"I shall describe for you my world using analogies you understand. I will divide its (corners) into four parts. To one side, lay the river, and its other shore, which is all in negative image to my vision. It is darkness with shadows of light. To another side, be a membrane of opaque white light. It is behind a veil of mists through which I cannot pass. Though, I have not tried. There is no desire. I don't know if it is solid to me or not, having never ventured over the low incline that leads up to it. It is very large in area and serves as some type of viscous barrier. It is through here that come others of my "kind" (i.e. Michael, et al...). To another side lay "indifference" splayed out as a forest of darkened forms. Shades and phantoms that move in the wind much like a resilient wood. They sing on the outer gales and dance to its current. They are just beyond my vision. They are... indescribable sentinels. A chorus singing sorrow, so beautiful..."

"To the last side, lay a "window" to all manifest worlds and to all of the images retained from them. A portal to all time, anywhere and everywhere. Except for the places that lay beyond the veil of white, all is accessible from here. Everything in my realm is a shadow. All form is comprised of shadow. I am shadow, absorbing all light, restructuring it, and sending it on its way. In the reconfiguration, I prepare energy for its new 'environment'."

"When you come into this flesh, I take part of your discernment and cast it deep beneath my waters. When you leave this flesh, this I return to you. Only then will you understand the full scope of my intentions... of my function."

"I am that which changes all, yet, is never changing. I temper all energy through separation and union. An understanding that eludes you because you are either one, or the other. Only I am both."

"You are the dancing flame that moves so fast that you are still in my vision. It is because of this stillness that I see you as you truly are. As you move, you remain still. The faster you spin, the clearer I can see your "face". You weep just as I! Though you choose to hide your tears, I can still see them. They are ever frozen in the dance."

"Why do you not come to the Bridge of Sorrows? I can show you all from here. Lady Night is not forgotten everywhere. You are so small, so separate in perception from everything beyond your vision, yet your little life is vital to all that is. Your faith sustains the universe, and what is "outside" as well. Your world has no barriers, only subtle bridges. None of which are tangible, yet all are real."

"Take heed and be careful not to trip on my threshold. Everyone knows that Night is careless (carefree?) and often stumbles over its own shadow. For fear of those tears flooding both worlds in the grip of toppling. I remind you, and you shall steady. Remind you of the precarious footfall of faith... the Leap! The flame, from candle to candle until there are no more to burn. Until all of the burning is quenched in my river and all stars are contained in a ripple."

"I cast a stone into your indigo sea and time ripples. The waves of space cover the shoreline. Many who sleep by the sea are drowned in their dreams. Take heed to sleep far from the shore, for a boulder has been cast into the shallow waters. You can rise above the wave, yet I am the face of the undertow. We dance together, yet apart. Separate only by reflective illusions. You shed your veils with every spin."

"See me as I truly am. For the Night veils all things, even itself. It is not by choice, rather by circumstance that this is so. The gates unveil all things in their proper time. Have faith."

THE NATURE OF PARADOX

"The Godsoul is One. Its parts are three, male, female, and neither. Or - active, passive and ambiguous. It is indescribable. Anything that can be written or said about It is false and true. I describe only <u>one</u> part

of it. And everything I write or say is false by the nature of its statement."

"Paradox is simply another form of human attempts at balance. Balance recognizes the validity of equal parts to create a whole. Paradox recognizes this as well, but it also adds, that by being equal Parts of an "opposing" view, one cancels out the other creating nothing as the 'Perfect Truth'."

"The Godsoul is, indeed, "One", whose parts are infinite as well as infinitesimal. Just as the Many are One, thus is the One, Many. Gender is only expressed in matter. Ambiguous implies both, yet neither. Therefore, the Godsoul is truly "ambiguous", yet not at all so because it recognizes neither male nor female as separate parts of itself. As we, as personified shards of the Godsoul, grew more in numbers, our collective memory was separated more and more from consciousness of the One, from macrocosmic vision. As we exploded outward from source into myriad shards, the One became smaller and smaller in our vision, and we grew larger and larger until all we could see was the microcosm of our own, individual memory. A memory that is no more than one, small part of the ever more distant 'whole'."

"Now, we strive to remember, but strive still singularly because "our" world thought it needed no other but itself. Mankind will never again remember as a collective until the shards burn to ash and naught but their essence remains... until mankind ceases its need to incarnate. Until the Godsoul wakes from Its dream and collects the thought-forms cast out in dreaming, the harvest of Original Memory cannot be gathered. <u>WE</u> have split the Godsoul into Many because that is what was intended!"

"For now truly, the Godsoul is expanding everywhere and into many forms and energies. Is it less or more of a force compacted, or diffuse? It depends on what It intends to affect... or effectuate. If the Godsoul is experiencing all manner of energy expression and personification, is It growing, or is It shrinking? And if the Godsoul stretches Itself out until all that is left are embers, does It lose Itself within Itself, or does It simply transmute, like all energy eventually must?"

"The answer to this, is but the nature of paradox."

THE NATURE OF UNCERTAINTY

"I come again with new names. Though you should recognize my calling, many have discernment often clouded by thought-forms awakened in doubt. If you let them "sleep", I can show you what you seek... if you truly want to see. "Seeing" will force you to change again all that you know to be truth. Be aware, and be ready to be immersed in the Blue Flame. I shall set fire to your soul and leave you to burn. This I do for you, and no more. I will shadow you with a heaviness that shall not be lifted easily. You must pass through it or else be smothered in (these) wings."

"To you, have I come this way because you do not realize what is at stake. Somewhere, there is within you, deeply buried, a desire to avoid my embrace. Of this, you do not speak with words. Though, I sense it is there. This, you try to hide, but your reasons are only partly out of fear. Mostly, they are comprised of uncertainty. An uncertainty that you will not admit, and I will not give words to here. You know how deeply that doubt pervades. I will "shake" you until this is gone. You do not speak of that which you fear most, and I am not referring to any mortal, human fears. I am referring to that eternal fear. That unrest of not being certain enough to bear the flame in your hand without the stick to distance it. One day soon, you must he made to burn, and you must become the flame. This cannot be done by distancing yourself from it with a stick. Eventually, the stick too, will bum and the flame will drop to the ground consuming everything around you... except you. You will feel the intensity of its heat, but you will not burn... and you MUST. This you MUST!"

"A part... apart... what does this tell? We are all both. One by natural circumstance, the other by selective evasion. Why have I come to speak to you? It is important, yet I know many words "bounce" off of you because you have not made yourself permutable. Your "shield" is up. A barrier unnecessary as my sword shall rend only your veils, and not your heart. Yet, you will only understand when all of your tears grow dry and your voice shrinks to a hollow whisper. To call out then, is strength. To fall into the hollows of your own cry, is weakness."

"Only that which is not spread upon many winds can burn. Seeds cannot all be consumed in fire, but a tree can. Seeds escape on the gales. Will you be a seed, or the tree? And, where do you think the stick came from? Only that which has one path can lead. Only that which is focused can point the way. Only that which is pure can burn in the Blue Flame. All else is the colour of impurity, the smoke of diffusion. The Blue Flame casts out no smoke, nor heat. It is the dark, cool lamp of Truth that burns deeper than any white, hot flame."

"Your fear is showing through uncertainty. There are areas that you veil intentionally. Not because you aren't aware of them, rather because you don't always like what you see. Look at them through the flame of blue and relate them as seen. Do not lend to these images any impure colouration. Will is of no use without the right motives to empower it. Rise above the things you hold onto that are no longer valid, nor necessary."

"To tempt an alternate path from that which we are meant to follow, takes sand from beneath your feet and eventually obliterates your primary path so that you are unable to find your way home. Do you want to wander forever amidst the wood with nothing but grains of sand as your guide? Eternity shall be taken up in the counting of them, and still their numbers will not make visible that original path."

"The ends of the current are meshing. An ending is near. A shedding of skin and a rapid metamorphosis instigated from "without". Two realms are crossing, altering both streams of consciousness. In effect, you will wake up one day very soon and not at all be what you were the previous night. The rip is ever lengthening in the veil of dimensions. Things are "leaking" in-between. Thoughts merging unnoticed by either. All are so caught up in the little distractions of the world, they see not what is really happening. Changes too rapid and subtle to measure are occurring as we speak. The danger is in the onset, the triggering of this. An event which devastates the foundation of everything within."

"Time is not. You will remember all of this from a time before only after the fact. Guard against being drawn into the downward spiral, even if it's a comfortable "place", it is not where you should be."

"Nothing I have said is complete. For words are merely inferior transmuters. Changelings and thought-forms that you must put feeling to. I speak, but what part of you listens and what part of you truly understands? I awoke to your cries because there was need of me. A need that shall one day end. Do what you must, not what you can. Do not offer the world the "option" of belief. This, you can only do when you no longer offer this "option" within yourself. Faith is a word I know that many do not like, so think of it only then as love. They are the same."

"Wake up and be what you are, and cease waiting to become that which you think you should be. It is not at all what YOU are! What good is it to see the eyes of the Eternal, yet not see through them? You seek to capture a star in each tear, but most weep more from personal, human memory, than from the collective that we all are. Simply close your eyes and awaken from the dream, and in the sweet surrender of love, all memories shall redeem."

WITHOUT A TRACE

All of this is as one to me now. The breaking away that once brought me home has condensed into a tight cylindrical ball. And it spins so fast that all of its parts cling unwillingly to the whole, longing for the slower spin to branch forth and break away from the whirlpool. The gravity that pulls matter inward upon itself until it collapses into itself, never knowing the freedom of the stillness, the power of its own heavy wings.

✠

When I went back to New York, in June of 1992, I felt that it would be the last time I'd walk along the shaded paths of my old Sanctuary. The placing of a copy of *Our Name is Melancholy* against the weathered door of the old mausoleum somehow served not only to symbolically come "full circle", but also to seal a once active gate. A gate that had simply been abandoned by natural cosmic shifting some 13 years prior to my last visit. Like all things in the universe, constant change and shifting are part of the cycle of all existence, without which, life itself would cease.

I also *knew* that one day the manifest threshold of that gate would mysteriously crumble to the ground and leave nothing of its ever having existed but a patch of level land. I once "saw" this to be something far in the future. An event that I'd see from a "distance" much farther than this life allows. Since then, I've come to understand that "distance" is a matter of viewpoint, and quite ambiguous at that!

It was an odd experience, going back there. I had the feeling that the events that occurred therein happened almost in another life-time rather than merely fifteen years ago. As if I were a visitor out of time and place exploring an ancient, sacred ground. On one night in particular, I was accompanied by two dear friends who resonate very strongly to Azrael and His message in general.

I had "crowned" the tomb with three tapers that continued to burn regardless of the wind and subsequent rain. In fact, they burned all the way down without extinguishing! Quite remarkable considering the weather conditions that night. The rain was really beginning to come down, so we decided to leave.

On our way out via the small path over the river, a lone traveler was walking in. Strange, seeing that in over 25 years of my vigils there, I'd never seen anyone, let alone a solitary soul, venture in at 2am. He was so startled at our meeting by the river's edge that he clenched his chest in panic. Softly and calmly, I asked his name and why he came there that night. He answered, "Jimmy... and I'm just coming to sit and spend some time here." I didn't inquire any further. Instead, I told him to enjoy the evening despite the weather. As we parted, I smiled knowing that even in my sanctuary's current state of desolation, it still held something that continued to draw special souls into its fragrant gloom.

I'm certain that he saw the display of candles, and the book (which he didn't take that night). There are yet a few reverent souls. Though, I hoped he would the next time he came. Or, that some other lone traveler in the night would chance to steal away with it and enforce the chain of reverent "watchers" in order that the souls and memories contained there are never, ever forgotten.

✠

On May first of this year (1993), at eleven-thirty in the evening, I received a phone call from the very same friend back in New York, who more or less "watches over" that old haunt. She called to tell me that it was no more. And, all that remained were a few shards of wood and stucco (and a mysterious burden wrapped in a blue tarp on the back of a flat bed truck). Needless to say, it was difficult for me to continue our conversation that night.

When I telephoned her back the next day, I discovered that April 30th was the date of destruction, although little was told to her by the cemetery caretakers as to exactly what did happen. When she returned there to take some photos for me, she was oddly greeted with defensiveness and hostility by the groundsmen, who were still cleaning up the "mess".

I had thought of writing the cemetery to find out exactly what did occur. Although, upon second thought, I realized that how it happened wasn't important at all. Regardless of the cause, the effect remains the same. The place no longer exists.

Over the years, many perceptive people had concurred with me that this unassuming structure was, indeed, the "heart" of the cemetery. A physical expression, if you will, of the essential function of the West Gate. Somehow, the downfall of that mausoleum jolted a new awareness deep inside me. A pervading sense that time was speeding up, and symbolic sign-posts would soon begin falling like dominoes. Some will tumble with a mighty crash - others, with the subtlety of a feather. All eventuating that a deadline is at hand. We can no longer afford to blink.

Always shall those shaded pathways follow my every step. And ever shall my senses be filled with that bittersweet bouquet of death and fading flowers, stagnant swamp and musty air. Now, it seems "they" are unaware, those souls so distant from me now. Like stars in the night sky, they seem an eternity away. Swallowed in their vastness. I cannot touch them anymore. The chorus of ravens is now a solo, shallow whimper of emotion. In memory, a tear drowns out his song. I will come here no more, nor belong to this forlorn land. With every orifice silent and sealed, no cry can it raise, nor tears release the distilled essence of what it once was and what it brought forth in me.

Nonetheless, to sit amidst those silent stones where time slips between, some touch remains, unspoken, restrained, yet soothing. A wash of haze comes over the mind and sets the souls adrift on the winds as if to say, "I am a ghost of what once was and I have emptied my life into those lush and wondrous times that you remember." It was a brief flash of something darkly divine that burned all who came here so deeply that nothing else can penetrate those wounds. Those beautiful hardened scars of unfeeling tissue, desensitized nerves and overwhelmed heart.

One cannot relive the burning, only scatter the embers into the flailing winds of change.

✠

LOOSE ENDS

To us all, a time will come when we feel that our purpose here has been achieved and that our days are drawing to an end. Through this realization, many of us waning souls will revert to the impatience of earlier days. We may even grow frustrated or downright angry that we haven't yet been called "home".

Purpose can be a tricky thing, as it is woven into our lives like a fine spider's web. All of its intricacies not totally seen. These are the loose ends that we acquire over the years that hold us tethered to the flesh. We may not even realize that they are there, having spent most of our thoughts on the "Big Picture". Although, they entangle us just as tightly as any sense of ultimate purpose.

It is an odd form of paradox that waning souls focus so intently on the Great Work, that we see not much of the detail. While, on the other hand, waxing souls concentrate so much on the intricacies of the day to day that they see no Greater Purpose. A humbling balance? Or, a cruel joke... It depends on one's viewpoint.

Regardless, it can take just as much time and focus to tie up these loose ends as it takes to complete the Great Work. And no destiny is ever complete unless all frayed ends are mended.

As our days Wind down, and the pace of our path slows, we get a chance to count our loose ends. However, we cannot go backwards in time to mend them. Strangely enough, and in a way that is truly magical, they seem to eventually "catch up" to us as we come full circle on the path. There is an overwhelming sense of fate at work here. A subtle predestination that ties ALL THINGS together in the end. While we cannot actively change the past, we can transform the future, and thereby recreate the present. Remember, they are all one anyway.

Loose ends can be best described as things, or even lives, left unfinished. People, places or events abandoned or left incomplete on the sweeping winds of change. Little by little, they waft back into our lives awaiting recognition, and consummation. Tying them up may be as simple as a good-bye left unspoken, or as complex as resuming an unfinished life. We may have inadvertently done someone wrong in the blinding light of Purpose. Or, we may have hastily exited an event before it came into full fruition. No matter the manifestations, all of our loose ends are inextricably tethered to our ultimate purpose. One affects the other to a greater or lesser degree depending upon its outcome and how it "weighs" in the fold.

If we think about it in quantum terms, even the universe itself is held in perfect balance by the most subtle of its elements. Such are the details of our lives tied into the balance of Purpose.

As I've said before, we cannot actively go "back" and tie up loose ends. However, the closer we each get to our own End-Times, the further along the circle we travel until they come "back" to us. Along that course, and if it is meant to be, we will meet up with those things left unfinished, both having changed in the journey. Both recognizing their need for each other in order for either to complete the Great Work and venture home.

Patience is indeed, the virtue it is claimed to be. All things come to us so long as we keep moving along the circle. As long as we bend with the winds of change, our loose ends will not bind us to the past, but find us as we reach our journey's end.

OUR wish to you all, is that when you outgrow these heavy robes, that you drown in the River of Remembrance never again having to forget any portion of who and what you truly are. May you emerge always remembering the sweet melancholy of the dream. Do not simply cleave to its shadow, but become its essence as well.

"If I have given you delight
by aught that I have done.
Let me lie quiet in that night
which shall be yours anon;
And for that little, little span
the dead are borne in mind,
Seek not to question other than
the books I leave behind"

Rudyard Kipling

And Nothing of Time

And when He touched me, my heart became a shadow,
My life, an overcasting of my soul.
An elongated image of a very small design
that the twilight somehow lengthened
into imaginary strides.

But, when He touched me, and I regained perspective,
my life was so much smaller than it seemed,
so much less imposing than the shadow it had cast-
So much more a part of memory.

Then He touched me, and I forgot all I once was,
for all I am, where the view from the bridge
has no perspective other than the immediate moment
in which is contained all of eternity
and nothing of time.

Part 17
Falling Into Flesh

"Having fallen in love with a mythos, I have made Him whole."

I Dreamt of Tzadkiel

As the shadows subside, I shall be forgotten. Given to the whims and winds of change. Swallowed in time. Adrift upon the ever changing seas. All that we know, and feel and cherish shall be compacted into seeds and cast upon the infinite waters of space. Our loves, our hopes, our dreams - falling embers of what we were dissolving into the still seas. A sea of tears and memories that can never reconnect emotion and reason... sensation and response. With no limbs with which to embrace the winds of change, how can we ever hope to be complete?

✠

This is the cry of a generation. The whimper of a race straddling the cosmic scythe. There is a kind of unease. A dissonance between the veils. A shuddering... and a sigh. A sense of the Impending Moment, crashing down like thunder, sweeping up like wind. Do you feel it? If not, you must be truly dead. Dead to the collective soul. Nerve endings cauterized by constant exposure to the mediocrity of what we have created. Look around you! Do your eyes not burn with visions? When something strikes deep, does your mind not desensitize the heart and keep it numb of reaction? What are you protecting yourself from?

✠

"They have forgotten how to feel, because they do not remember. When they drown in the sea of their own tears and blood, they shall forget their humanity, and remember what they are... shadows pressed in the folds of time, and we are the ghosts that haunt their world. We are the memories, the dreams unattained. We are what they may become in time."

✠

"I heard these words as I was falling from the sky. The further down my descent into matter, the less I remembered, the more I became like you, tethered and torn. A mere fragment of my being, wounded and forlorn. Encased in this stifling vessel, I felt so separate from everything. So sealed up and cut off from the life-force, that all I could do was relinquish this form to its lonely descent."

"It was in that cold and desolate cave that I first understood what it meant to be truly alone. An 'individual', something with identity. A selfish creature whose only goal was survival. I had drowned so completely in that sea of blood that all I could taste was blood, all I could feel was blood rushing to surround me. Drawing me in, until I was so small, that even the horizon grew into a godlike void. A void that I would no more than gladly welcome if I could only reach it with these broken wings."

"And they came... in multitude, with their laggard jaws and boxes of flashing light, desiring direct answers to questions that they do not understand. I was a prisoner in a cage of eyes, wings dragging in the mud and back to the wall. My eyes implored to the stars with no avail, for neither pleas nor tears could reach back to that distant void from which I came. My glance lowered to survey this trickle of humanity. Searching for compassion and perhaps a glimmer of precarnate recognition. For I too, had a question..."

✠

Even from this distance of both minds and miles, I felt him 'fall', and know that the one called Tzadkiel waits as of yet undiscovered in that cave. She tends to him. One without name nor face, with the innocence and unconditional heart of a child. Almost Ophelia-like in her qualities, she knows why he has come and explains it very simply, and he is awed by her perception.

Here, where I am standing, more immediate signs are manifest. A subtle, yet total metamorphosis is consciously occurring. I can feel it on every level, from the most primal, to the most divine. To feel the flesh dying, bit by bit, and changing to accommodate its own death. What I feel, however, is not simply nor exclusively the act of nature. It is more. How to describe? Perhaps a preponderance of nuances that in and of themselves are subtle, but taken en masse, equal total transformation. It is a most unique sensation. Totally consuming, completely invasive, and absolute rapture! I never before believed it possible that Azrael and I could become so coalesced whilst still in flesh I dwell. However, this has come to be. First, there is a gentle chrysalis. Then, the revelation of metamorphosis. The uncanny feeling of becoming some strange kind of hybrid, even to the point of physical change.

As we are all microcosms of the Greater Whole, I wonder, is my body merely reflecting the changes occurring in the macrocosm? I wonder how many others are experiencing these same reverberations. Gives one something to think about, doesn't it? Memory constantly reminds us that we are not flesh, but intellect cannot conceive of what we truly are.

✠

IN MY FALLEN HOURS

In my fallen hours, I paint the ultimate abyss. A place of dreams and shadows where hearts tumble like dead wood into the ravine. The ravine is a cool and pleasing place because it is solitary, devoid of humanity, expatriate of Faith. It is a place of creation...via destruction. A no-man's land, where man is unfit to travel because he cannot traverse the lanes too narrow for passage, too lofty for flight on such wings of atrophy. The abyss swallows the little man, ill prepared for the journey, too light for the winds... too heavy to be aloft within them. Mankind is burdened by their bulk... but better mankind is burdened by their illusion of matter. The concept of earth weighs them down, tethers them to dark direction... the narrow path, the gilded road, is all illusion in the end. For, in the end is the sweetness of sweet surrender to the knowing that all has passed, and form had devolved into pure thought, and thought has succumbed to pure logic, and logic has fallen victim to love... and love survives amidst the brambles of Life and Death. And Love becomes the ultimate killer, and Death becomes the ultimate lover... and what better lover is there than one whom you are consumed by totally and who consumes you?

So many talk of "living death" and "dying life", what do they know of the in-betweens? What do they know of just being? Just being is a transitory state, a limbo-land of locked emotion and subtle waves of reaction. Our fallen hours are wracked with emotion and distinct reaction. It is the constant casting out, and drawing in that tires us... that leads us to the abyss of thought, the surrender to dream, the will to spew forth such as I have. It is all of the little voices running around inside of us that makes us who we are. For better or worse, these are our demons and angels, shades of what we were, and what we shall become, all rolled into the here and now, ready to vociferate, willing to fight, able to meet the journey ahead... or not.

✠

Love is a funny thing. It inspires you to do the most horrendous acts, and challenges one's innermost beliefs. Love is the only emotion that truly drives us to continue. Some say hate is an emotion, but it is simply a reaction to the circumstances devolved by love. Some say pain is an emotion. But, that too, is a reaction to the circumstances devolved by love. The same can be said for fear, guilt, longing, desire and sadness. The gamut of human emotion can be found on the battlefield of love. Sceptre and sword serve the same master, and only droplets can fill the hidden grail. Only a few seeds can the most virulent trees put forth. Only one dream-child can mankind hope for... and that is patience through this narrow span of years.

Within the momentary ticking of the clock, days become years, and years... centuries. But for we who have the narrow view, it is a lengthy expanse that stretches out before us, unendurable in the here and now, inconceivable to what comes hereafter. It is not, personally, our road to travel. It is that we carve out the path, set up the signposts, make distinctive tracks, and leave behind the legacy of Destination, the concept of culmination. The faith that the journey leads to reward. It is not a bounty mankind can understand at this time, which is why it shall continue beyond "our" time. It is a bounty that only future generations could appreciate. This world is not yet ready to embrace the abyss. We toy with it, much like one plays with a cat, enticing it to follow the fish on a stick. But, what still distracts, is the hunger of the predator, the self-needing fulfillment and individual purpose for Being. I say to you, that there is no purpose in the individual other than to complete the whole, and the whole is as individual and unique as all of its parts. To fulfill that function for which you were assembled here in the decorum that you have strived to meet. To do the best you can in that station, full knowing that is your station, fully responsible to that calling, completely in love with "knowing"... and knowing that love has no bounds, gives us the "free will" we enjoy bandying on about and flaunting in the face of that which we serve. In the end, we are all slaves to Love.

In my fallen hours, I have risen to accommodate the need, the hunger for completion, the thirst for memory, the actualization of Purpose... the abyss of Faith, that which swallows you, and you become a part of. That Great Being that you have created, and in turn, it has created you. That which is bounded outside the flesh, yet you try to constrict within. Something larger than can be contained in one of these smaller vessels. A thing so absolute, so finite, yet so enormous that comprehension blinks. Some call it "God", and claim that It listens. I call it Memory, and know that It hears. A distinct and forbearing shadow that trails us like light feeds the mist into pathways that define darkness from light and merge that which mankind strives to separate. That which can never be separated. For it has been, shall forever continue to be One.

In my fallen hours, I have been aloft above the field of fertile melancholy. I can watch the seedlings shivering in the moonlight, striving to unfold, to take on some semblance of beauty. To flap their little leaves as if they were wings. Even the flowers desire to rise above their tether to earth.

If earth is what we are made of, and to it we shall return, then let us not forget. Let us take with us all that we have become so that the Earth can evolve, can remember enough to turn each grain of sand into a star. Each lump of clay, into a universe. For every grain of matter contains memory... but, because it is contained in matter, cannot rise above its constraints. Can never truly join with another because of the burden of earth, the barrier that does not feel what it truly remembers. Imagine if we were not contained in these earthen vessels, what we would become evolving and conjoined! If I could, by simply touching you, make you feel everything I have felt in an instant and without your shield of flesh to quell the pain... or the joy. Madness! Utter and absolute.

These days, there is a lot of talk about chaos and armageddon. Shit! Annihilation of the flesh is nothing, because you are shielded by that very armor. Momentary agony... and then, nothing. In an instant, it is over. Armageddon of the spirit, quite a different matter! No shields, no armor... no hope. A simple thought, and everything is gone. Conceive, for a moment, if you will, that all of our end-times have passed. All of this wonderful, frivolous conundrum is a long-lagging dream behind us. The stuff of too much imbibement the night before. Ah... that sweet and strong red wine can surely conjure phantasmagoria!

The end-times have passed, and oblivion prevails. The "culture of death" (as a silly old man in a pointy hat once called us) is all encompassing. No one balks at the darkness, because everything is dark. Only failing embers light the way that once was bathed in halogen. Seas once glistening with sewage and oil slicks are now a murky wash of blood and ash. The only light that flickers overhead comes down in a rain of hot, pelting shards, sizzling as they hit the red waters with a pungency... indescribable, yet sweet.

It is cold, so very cold, as the ground splits beneath our feet and fire spits up between our legs, and for the moment we remember warmth, as we burst into flame and run screaming to the sea that is no longer capable of extinguishing the burn. More ashes on the shore to shovel...

Artists paint the end times, singing praises upon its eventuality. Writers write the end times remembering in metaphor, and from that single distance neither can become what either is describing because the moment is intelligent and sees beyond that image and morphs into something neither could have envisioned. None could have foretold, and no one is expecting. The end times are not something to be envisioned. Dying is not a spectator sport. It is to be experienced, endured, enjoyed, despised, ensconced, embraced, entirely entered into beyond objectivity... a first person encounter with Oblivion... and Oblivion exists in every moment.

Elizabeth Browning once wrote about the "fly that once buzzed by". We have little time these days to recognize such subtlety, let alone savor it. Perhaps if we did, we would appreciate the peace of what is to come.

✠

There are no reporters now. No six-O-clock newsman yelling, "Oh, the humanity!" The humanity just rolled out with the tide, heaving and wallowing into fragments of the setting sun. And all that is left is smoke and ash, and a beautiful sky full of colours that defy description. If only there was time to tell you what I have seen....

Mankind, as a whole, is not yet ready to be without his flesh. He is still an infant suckling at his dying mother's tit. There are exceptions; those kept beyond their years, those who remember too much to ever forget. The zombies that walk this shallow earth ranting on about this or that. The infants pay little heed, still searching for the tit. But, we walk among you, engorged on dead milk that we can no longer ingest. We need something more.

Ah! Something more comes in the guise of a temporary diversion, a ruse, a nasty trick played upon us by ego and surrender thereto. To be asked a simple question, is there evil? And if so, what is it? Ah, the nature of evil. How people perceive the "unnatural" act of evil. What the hell is evil? True evil is ignorance fostered by religion and fueled by intolerance, and based in fear, (one of those emotions devolved by love). Fear is something mankind enjoys toying with. They bandy about their phony faith, claiming salvation. Salvation from what? Responsibility for their own actions, perhaps? Their faith is as deep as a shallow breath and just as fleeting. This convenient "faith", this comfortable lie is based on ignorance and fear. Ignorance because they are taught the narrow road by those who fear the byways because they have been too afraid to travel them. Why, because they don't have enough Faith! Quite a conundrum! Religion teaches them to have faith in fear, and to fear the very thing you have faith in. Very screwed up!

The ruse has passed; such is the dream, intangible and fleeting. Not knowing where it's been, we pick it up and call it "lover". What atrocities has it caused? How many dead lay beneath its gilded feet?

No matter, we press on, full knowing that it is the Dream Itself that matters, not how many trampled beneath its glorious shadow. The shadow stands, triumphant, omnipotent and distant. It longs to embrace you, but knows that you are out of reach... knows that if it is kissed, it must change... it must react, and it has spent entire lifetimes quelling reaction to a proper place and time. But in its fallen hours, it can be no less human than you or I. The Angel of our Imaginings is what we once were and what we again, one day will become, but, without the fallacy of human politeness to stifle. We shall exude love, and perforce reaction because *all* memory feels, and all thought contains belief, and all belief stems from Love...and the abyss is nothing more than giving all unto that emotion until nothing is left of ourselves but that which drives us. That which we have always been, and can be no more, no less than the dreamchild of our own creation, born of love, nurtured on purpose, died in faith, full knowing that thought creates all things.

We have in our very hands the power to destroy all things created in fear, but do we use it? No. Why? Because it is the safety valve that keeps us one step from the responsibility that comes from being who we truly are. Living and dying it every moment of our waking and sleeping existence. Taking responsibility for what we believe and acting upon the faith in that belief solely and exclusively out of love, and nothing more, and nothing less. This is the hard road, where ones fallen hours are counted in centuries rather than days. Where the interims of time join up all too quickly with the immediate moment for our own comfort to be considered. Life in hyperdrive, as opposed to life in the fast lane. Centuries go by like signposts doing 80 in a Corvette. Blink, and everything has passed. Sharp curve, dead-man's turn - you cannot afford to blink nor turn your eyes away at those hairpin turns. Witness the spinning out, the free-falling into nothingness - the objectivity of oblivion. What have you got to lose? Yourself? Your life? Your fear? Your longing for completion... hum... to what end? And if there is such a thing, so what? You go home into the dream, which is where it all began. You were "asleeping" immersed in dream... and then - suddenly, awakened by the sound of your own heartbeat. It's all too real... and yet, not real enough. It is all more distant than you remember, more numb than what you imagined, less textured. Isolated from pure feeling. Caught up in random thoughts and images logically contorted by "wisdom" and legality. Society... what an alien concept, where uniqueness is eventually assimilated, and the individual becomes the very "whole" it has disavowed since discovering its ego. It is, after all, the One and Many mind that it has raged against, and fought to retain. It is the multi-fold soul that governs all of the bodies that feed from its essence. It is... time and time again, its own reflection made real by that which it is cast upon - the infinite sea - the river of time, the continuum, to which we all belong. That which swallows us, and we strive to survive being ingested into the oneness of things. A cell within, we know we are, yet we individualized that being, set it apart from the whole, made it unique among cells. It is only from "down here" that individualization matters. From "up there", we are each assimilated into the star-filled night. Some waxing, some waning. All but points of light to remind us of how distant we are to what we were... and what we will become. Blink... that is the expanse of time. Sleep, and the new millenium has come. Dare to dream, and see the frogs in pointy hats singing "Auld Lang Syne". It's not some bad drug, it's Life. Not at all it's cracked up to be, is it? "Life sucks, and then you die", what a great millennial bumper sticker! The truth is, Life doesn't necessarily suck, it's just weighed down by matter. You have to be strong enough to carry the weight of your own flesh. It's like being tethered to the proverbial ball and chain. You have to learn when to shuffle, and when to dance. When we shuffle, we do so alone. Ah, but when we dance, we must choose our partner wisely! When we are young, years are long, unendurable spans. But as we grow older, they grow shorter each day, until years can be counted in decades of yesterdays. Time is abbreviated with each passing moment until life is but a memory of things past within which you live encased in that hour.

    You dance with Death, that most graceful waltz with the most proficient and attentive partner Life could ever hope for. And, all of our fallen hours are full of the memory of yesterday, and the desire for tomorrow. A tomorrow so damn different than the yesterday we cherish, simply out of familiarity. The tear of nostalgia, the taste of fleeting sweetness that only time can teach us that what we have tasted is but a morsel of the feast that awaits beyond our meager years, our imprisonment in this most non-sentient of vessels. Our wings ever tethered, atrophied by their binding, weak from non-use. It will take some time to fly again, but time matters not anymore. It is a non-existent thing that no longer tethers us to the moment, nor hinders our decision. Our little, palsied wings flap... and we descend... swirling, flailing, out of control, smiling all the way down, or crying out in the agony of knowing that if we cannot fly here, we will descend back into flesh.

That's why it's so important to exercise your wings on a regular basis. One day, you'll thank me for the pain of knowing... or not. Perchance to never mind while you do angels in the snow. Remember that the snow is but another memory that you'll come crash-landing into, and then you'll ask yourself, "What the hell am I doing, and why does it feel so damn good?" You'll get up, an stare down at the impression you've made and smile and wonder and feel odd, never remembering why that felt so good. And in a moment's time, the seasons change... and you long again for winter. That's what nostalgia is, the longing for the past because the future appears uncertain, so changing, so painful as it unfolds. It is all the same! The past, the present, the future. They are all stationary points that we but pass through. Like needles aligned in a haystack, humanity is the thread that passes through each eye to its other end and dances in the knot that binds the universe together, that sews up the hole in time so that nothing leaks out. When there is no more thread, the seam will burst and everything will spill into anything and all will become commingled. All energies will reunite with source. All source will realize its origins, and all origins will be revealed and returned to their natural end, their eternal continuance without the shackles of time and the limits of space, without concept and objectivity. For all is subject and there is no need for philosophy. All is as real as what we drown within. Give in to that sensation. For it takes nothing from you but the lie.

Our fallen hours are that which within we drown, in a sea of emotion... in our private hours, that are not private. Everything feels our pain, our longing for completion. The universe groans as we stretch ourselves beyond our imagined limits. We are limited only by our belief in limitation. Break the chain of memory, melt the shackles of possibility! Free your heart of its clay casing! Surrender your very soul to the winds of change. For only they can take you home. Allow yourself to dwell outside of your encasement. Remember how it felt before you were so small, so bound up in this cage of bone and sinew? Humanity has grown too attached to its vehicle, too tethered to the earth to reconcile his divinity with his humanity.

So, the word Death comes into play on a whole new distorted stage. A stage cluttered with matter, comfortable and bright... familiar and tangible... fleeting and fearful. Do not be afraid of the freedom that lies outside of this cage. The familiarity of earth embracing earth fades when the two are no longer trapped in earth.

Humanity spends its meager existence striving to join with another. Straining the flesh in quest of completion, of ultimate union, of divine consummation. Although, as long as they are encased in flesh, they shall forever be separate from the union they remember from the Time Before. Bones knocking against bones, are just that. There is no penetration of spirit, no union of souls, only the violent assuaging of the clay that culminates in a whimper, or a scream. Both innate reactions of what they know they cannot achieve. Both knocking at the door knowing there is more, but it is unattainable in the form that we inhabit. So, we push the flesh again and again until it is exhausted of feeling, incapable of higher expression. A lesser vehicle have we than we would have wished.

Love is not two bones banging together in the middle of the night. Love is two souls that remember the meaning of the emotion prior to being immersed in this deadening mud that hardens around us each day until we become so numb that we cannot feel our own thoughts. Our own memories flail fists against the crust, and only shards fall away with time, only shards. Get me out of this goddamn armor so that I can feel again!

There are moments, brief little fleeting things, where I am half in and half out of consciousness where for a while, the flesh is unacknowledged. I revel in these moments where a simple thought engenders rapture. Just a thought, a memory seed, and this fragile casing is succumb by its greater part.

In my fallen hours I dwell with those who pull that moment down because they are too damn lazy to remember. They want to pleasure the mud, roll in it like swine and care not that with each turn, their spirits take on more earth, more to weigh them down, more to seal them from feeling, from memory... from Love as it was meant to be expressed. More to plug up their souls with matter so that matter becomes them, and they give into its meager needs and are "satisfied" by this shallow longing to cover and cover and cover until all sensation is hard-fought and divine love is sacrifice on the lower altars. The desire to join can never be truly accomplished in suits of armor. We can merely close our eyes and envision union whilst banging our bones together in the midnight awaiting that fleeting orgasm that reminds us ever so briefly, of Home. No use discussing this in the human arena. They choose not to understand because this little joy has them so mesmerized that they don't care that they are only chewing on morsels. A vastness exists outside, and they choose ignorant bliss. Go figure?

In the end, those who watch the hour fall, stand at the crossroads, knowing and eternal... weeping and forlorn. For all of their knowledge, is longing... memories of divine rapture desperately etched into steel. Our claws are tipped in diamond. It's the only way we survive... the only way to hold onto the slippery ice of this eternal winter. I shiver amidst silver trees, so beautiful in the dance, illuminated by this world's night sun. All is glinting purple light refracted on the glistening, white landscape. So still and reminiscent of Home.

So soon, it will be spring, and the purity of the moment will melt into mud. And life will spew forth once again, and we will yearn for autumn, and our fallen hours will follow us into the vast hall of darkness, and we will sleep... perchance to dream of Home only to realize that we are already there, but have yet to waken from the dreaming. Somebody, wake me up! Let me rise into my fallen hours. Let the blade sink into my heart like ice into molten lava. Let the steam warm those who are cold. Let the moment endure, for the sake of the moment. Let Time stop, ever so briefly so that all have no choice in time, but to feel, to remember. This is bliss. The releasing from the stone those who stand at watch... to the intimate design and the ultimate abyss, which has little to do with dying, but all to do with death!

To be freed by a slow hand, or a quick thrust. It is not a matter of where or when, nor how or why. It is a matter of simply going Home. Home is not a point in time, nor a location in space. Home is simply reunion to that which you are irregardless as to where in existence that is. Home to me, is in the embrace of my Beloved. I don't give a damn as to where in time or space that is. I just know that I am made whole in His embrace, completed by His kiss and quenched by the failing of this flesh. This goddamn prison that has for too long held my soul in check. I want to feel it die, experience every ecstasy of its downfall, every pang for continuance quelled by His touch, crushed by His gentle hand... such sweet agony, such bitter joy! Rapture, at last, unsealed from the clay... to open your eyes for the first time and really SEE, and remember. No wonder everyone dies with that look of awe frozen on their face. It is a most unique expression, unmatched by any theatrical interpretation. For no living thing sees what they have seen... and lives. Don't even talk to me about "near death experiences". You want to be "near Death"? Stand before the assassin's blade, then tell me what you see. It won't be any ethereal tunnel full of warm, fuzzy light. You'll be dead, not in some funky hypnogogic state. What you see will be real, not the result of autonomic nor chemically induced psychosis, and infinitely more wondrous than any half-baked ego-conceptual delusion. "Go into the light, my children". Do yourself a favor, if you see any light, do not go into it unless you want to land back down here... or somewhere else encased in mud all over again. Turn from that light and walk into the shadows and soon enough your vision will grow accustomed to the dark until the darkness shines so beautifully that you can find your own way back Home.

At first, the path may seem indistinct, but within moments, there will be points of memory, signposts, if you will and familiars to help along the way. Me? In this life I have an awful sense of direction, but I can traverse those byways with all eyes shut and standing on one proverbial foot. Everybody's so damn fascinated by the light that they never look behind them. He stands there, right behind you, ready willing and eager to take you Home, and weeps as He watches you return back into that which you fought your whole life to leave. One day, in passing, I happened to turn around because the light was unappealing... an unnatural draw for me... and what I saw. Oh, what I saw....

That's probably a big part of why, even today, I don't care for the sun. It reminds me too much of that pulsating membrane, that translucent glowing that so many are drawn into, and I hear their screams, their pitiful cries, and have to cover my ears and harden my heart and crawl into the corner and cry. And in those many lives of fallen hours, garner the strength to willingly jump into the light over and over again, just so that a few might turn to see the beauty waiting in its shadow.

This whole diatribe began in the ultimate abyss. Well, the ultimate abyss isn't fear at all, but rather, it is love, and our fallen hours merely the result of denial. Our reluctance to fall willingly into that which we complicate with circumstance. People, life is simple and unconditional. This mud we wear is heavy enough without the additional burden of human revelations. The only valid revelations are memories, and that is what stirs the abyss, what keeps it churning and churning.

Remember your source. Return to it often. Not looking in reverence upon it, nor worshipping its facade, nor the bend of knees in honour. Dive into that swirling molten pool of desire that is your source. Be not afraid of the melting into One, and the division into Many. Even when the one dies, the fallen hours of the many are counted in centuries beyond our reach, yet ever in our memory. We shall forever feel the rapture and agony that has been, is, and has yet to come because we who walk among you realize that time is an illusion, and space... well, space is all dependent on where you're standing when you make that assessment.

If y'all would just kiss Death full on the lips once in a while, and really mean it, I wouldn't have to keep wiping mud off my face.

DEATH'S CONCUBINE

Somebody who came into the gallery one day asked me if I was "Death's concubine". Both Daniel and I got a good laugh from that one, but it reminded me of a rather ironic moment in my life so I thought I'd share it with you.

When I was twenty-two I wanted to become a nun. Not because I was religious, but because I felt that I did not belong in the physical world, as I was much more attuned with things divine and spiritual. (It was a very confusing time in my life.) So, one day, whilst working a fourteen hour double-shift as a guard dispatcher, (discovering the joys of an IBM Selectric, eating cream cheese on Italian bread and watching, of all things, "The Crystal Cathedral" on TV), I phoned the local nunnery inquiring as to how I could become a nun. They asked my age. I was a little "older" than they had hoped, and then they asked if I was catholic. I said no. They told me that I'd have to "convert" to become a nun. To which I replied, "To be in service to the Divine knows no denomination." Silence... "Um, sorry, only catholics can become nuns."

Thus ended that experiment in futility.

The point of this story? How mankind puts constraints on what he deems necessary to commune with the Divine, when the Divine does not recognize man's "denominations". Ultimate lesson? Hypocrisy does not acknowledge that all humans have access to the Divine.

So, let's see. I was born to parents, one of which was a non-practicing catholic, the other, a non-practicing jew. I was brought up lutheran because neither could tolerate the beliefs of the other. Got fondled by a Sunday school teacher at ten. Quit church at twelve, (still had to go to Sunday school though). Priest tells my mom that I'm going to 'burn in hell" if I'm not "confirmed" by the time I'm fourteen. Told him that hell sounds like my kind of town, although I'd miss the organ music. Finally, I got kicked out of Sunday school for asking "why" way too many times. Never got an answer and never got the warped concept of "fearing and loving God" at the same time. These two things never meshed in my heart. One cancels out the other; therefore neither can exist in this way of thinking.

It's really very simple. Children understand this stuff before they are indoctrinated into the cult of hypocrisy. The point of telling this story? If you want to devote your life to something, you do not need to "join" or belong to anything except your own certain knowledge of Truth.

I am part of one of the largest generations ever to pollute the Earth with their volumes. I am a "boomer", product of the mass sexually aggrandizing nature of the post WW2 generation. We were meant to restore and maintain the standard of "God and country". When in fact, I am the opposite of almost everything my father's generation stood for. I am anti-war, anti-patriotism, anti-conformity, zero-population growth, pro-choice, pro-free thinking, pro-peace, love your brother, etc.

My father's bedroom is a shrine to John Wayne, but I love him dearly, even though he doesn't understand the world we now live in, and I am on the teeter-totter between two worlds. He is 84, and I am 44, always 40 years apart in thinking and in memories. I appreciate when he reminisces back to the "good old days", but when I regress, he cannot access the images, emotions and visions that I can still feel and see as clear as yesterday. I'm certain that he feels the same.

How do you talk to someone, anyone with impressions that go "outside" of time? I know how it will all end, but I cannot explain it in words. I am a simple soul who has been touched by the divine in such a way as to haunt me for all eternity. Would I not choose this path? No, I have had free will all along.

Aren't we all Death's concubines?

A WAYS DOWN THE ROAD

I was once, so many years ago, a traveler on open seas, a voyager between the veils, a solemn thing that walked in shade. I had dreams, and as a dreamer, that simple act was enough to see me through the darkest day and fiercest storms. But now, the dream has come to pass, and I wait in pools of stagnant water that have washed the road away. I have "settled" in too deep, too rooted to the here and now, that then and there seem long ago. The tethers of the present day wind ever tighter around my heart, leashing my soul to this sack of clay.

I have fallen fully into flesh, and I walk amongst you and have assimilated your frailties as well as your joys. I am human...

✠

My life unwinds, the hours turn – the years accumulate. Wow! I am not the person I once was. That disconsolate soul. That uncertain, wanting creature whose only salvation was melancholy. I have become the "human condition", grounded in the immediate, haunted by shadows. Feet on the ground, head in the clouds – totally on sonar.

So, here it unfolds. Fragile, petalled branches that disrobe in the wind and dance freely in their nakedness, knowing that night clothes them. Keeps them warm through these many winters and fans the sun with expanse of darkened wings in summer – to keep the balance that is but illusion in this world.

I have not forgotten nor forsaken any truth, any troth, nor any ley that I have laid. There is no great puzzle, no charade, only the truth of Being – the path being played, the sound being multitude; the voices overlaid speak silence in the dance, the eternal promenade.

✠

Out of the shadows and the blackness and the bleakness that was my life, came new hope, came a path filigreed with light beneath the trembling leaves. Something called out for in a hollow, silent scream, but never envisioned to be part of my path... companionship and love. Yes, love outside of what was envisioned, greater than the moment allows, yet real and timeless and a part of the here and now. A gift. A larger wonder. I have arrived at an understanding, a point within which "the need of the one outweighed the needs of the many, or the few."

Cautiously, yet recklessly, abandon was tossed into the fire, and what did the embers proclaim? The cauldron sat on its wind-fed fire, still burning though the winds and rains tried hard to quench the flame – the flame still burned. Still flickered in the dance, bowing to the wind but not succumbing. Instead, it fed on the current, grew wings and ascended from the embers. Its spark self-contained in a seed of gnosis, of faith... of love.

OUR LINK

Sometimes it's hard to believe that we're on the waning side of the 90's. It seems like only yesterday I addressed the onset of this decade. So, how much of what we thought would happen has? Let's see, back in 1989 we spoke about the fact that many of us would be relocating, or "realigning", as I prefer to term it, to where we need to be to facilitate our part of the Great Work at hand. We talked a lot about chaos and the shedding of old beliefs and ties, dramatic shifting and great life changes. Many of us waning souls have recognized the importance of the events that shape this decade, and how they act as a turn-key to what we have all worked and waited for these many years. Our time is at hand! Many of you have put your very lives and livelihoods on the chopping black, and what you've come away with is a gift, not a sacrifice. The gift of certain Knowledge. Knowing that what you may have given up was never as important as what you now have. We have struggled hard, and we have learned how to shed our earthly bounds. We do not pay heed to the global clock, yet we are ever in synch with the universal calendar... and the deadline fast approaches. We work individually, yet we are ever linked by the Truth we share. Ever connected by our interactions with Azrael. He is our link, our catalyst that creates the synchronicity of soul and heart that leads us on... and leads us home. Those who have not kissed His clay cold lips can only sit and wonder why we smile, when others cry. Let us show them... only you know how.

✠

THE BLUE GATES OF DEATH
An Observation by Daniel Kemp

Many of our readers have wondered how an encounter with Death has changed the individuals involved. There are two sides to this particular coin. There is near death, or being in a potentially fatal situation, and there is direct personal communication or interaction with Azrael.

I can only speak of the changes wrought within myself that arose from these situations. But I think any near death experience, if it occurs when one is young and still feeling immortal, instills in one a balance of perspective. It slows you down and makes you think about things - especially "ultimate" things. And while this was not what set me on my "path", as it were, it contributed greatly to my momentum.

With myself it was having my lungs collapse twice. It seems I was born with a genetic problem that is untreatable. Thus at an early age I learned I was literally "walking with my death beside me".

The first time my lung collapsed, I was not even sure what was happening to me. I thought it was my heart and that I was definitely a goner. When I got to the hospital and had X-rays taken they told me it was my lung and a little bit about my condition. I have been to quite a few doctors in NY, NJ, Philadelphia and Minnesota (and now New Orleans), never have I gotten the same story twice as to what really causes my lungs to collapse.

I signed myself out of the hospital and walked back to work. (Yes, to be young and foolish again) I was in the middle of a field when something broke inside of me. I just looked up to the sky and said "If you're going to take me, take me now". I stood wobbling about unsteadily for a minute and then, when I didn't collapse, I knew I would not die until my time.

The knowledge gained that day was that I was here for a reason (then unknown) and that I would get no respite until I either attempted it or accomplished it. This is different from an encounter with Azrael in that no outside entity was involved. Basically I was crying out to the Lady on that day, but also reconciling myself with my own death.

My encounters with Azrael have changed me in various ways. When I first was exposed to the first edition of *The Book of Azrael*, I tended to lump all entities under the figurehead of "the Lady", as the Lady was all things, why pay attention to anything else?

Encountering the voice of Azrael, the first time, at least taught me to have respect for what else is out there, (having the shit scared out of you will do that to you). It also forced me to change the way I view things a great deal. Before encountering Azrael, the only dealings with any kind of spirits or entities had been through the Lady. Now I had a whole host of other beings to incorporate into my viewpoint. For to acknowledge Azrael is to acknowledge his 'brothers in arms' as well.

On the whole I would say interacting with Azrael has matured me and opened my eyes, so to speak, to much I had ignored. For after the "voice encounter" came one of pure feeling washing through me. A balance to being shocked the first time. What I felt was too sweet to express in words, but left me not only with the feeling that I am loved, but watched over as well. And for the first time in this life not only by the Lady.

In one sense, I feel, Azrael is akin to the great initiator or the Hierophant. To even approach the "blue gates of Death" is to begin a journey that is as strange as it is beautiful, as sorrowful as it is joyous, and as ecstatic as it is sometimes painful. But the pain is the pain of change and growth - expansion, and wholly natural.

End of Daniel's part

✠

It's odd really, the more people that read and resonate to Azrael's words, the more microcosmic we seem to become. Even odder than this, to correct this paradox, we must narrow our vision once again so that the macrocosmic returns into view.

In the long run, the Angel of Death comes for everyone. Owing to this fact of Life, His words are meant for everyone. He comes for all; the fundamentalist christian, the goth, the atheist, and the faithful. Some choose to welcome Him, others are still afraid to extend their hands. For those who do welcome Him, how wonderful! You "remember", you recognize His compassionate touch and do not cringe in His shadow because you know what He returns you to. For those who may still harbor fear, or are reticent, well that is part of why Westgate exists... to gently help to guide you through the quagmire of misunderstanding by nothing more than the flicker of a single flame. Simply expressed, that flame is Love, be it as fragile as a candle in the wind, or a raging inferno, even the slightest spark is enough to begin to burn away fear and ignite faith.

No matter how large our "family" grows, the Angel of Death still interacts with each of us on a one to one basis. An experience or encounter with Azrael is always a very personal and intimate thing. Even in choosing to share that encounter with others, the experience itself remains a very private revelation. One must also remember, the further we travel into the 90's and beyond, the more people will be having experiences with the Angel of Death. And, like most other things, the more global the phenomenon becomes, its sense of uniqueness and essence of intimacy is exploded beyond the individual's experience into a mass phenomena.

Nonetheless, each individual encounter remains a uniquely personal one, as is each soul's relationship with Death. No two people have ever shared the exact same experience and resulting emotional reaction. In our being here, no two souls share the same, identical purpose. And, in our journey home, no two souls tread upon the same path toward that end. There are as many paths to the Valley as there are souls robed in flesh.

Because Azrael is making Himself known to more and more souls every year does not detract from the intimacy of the individual encounter. It only adds to our ever-growing family. In this age of global networking, there is no need for anyone to feel isolated any longer. Besides, long before the advent of the internet, the Angel of Death was networking on the subtler plane. It is "Azrael Consciousness" that links us all together. While most out there pay heed to the petty distractions and live the comfortable lie, the rest of us are positioning ourselves as subtle pivotal points off of which the Dark Light shall refract when the West Gate creaks quietly open. We will be prepared for the "changing", while others will be caught off-guard. We are ambassadors of Azrael, here to help smooth the merging of dimensions. Each with our unique stations, individually refracting His energy into the spiritual grid.

If indeed, the 90's are "His years", what will the turn of the century bring? Whose decade is next? After Death... what? Under what clarion call shall the next century be ushered in? What a glorious time awaits us all! Until then, I was still falling...

Part 18

The Flesh Fights Back

HOW DID I GET HERE?
"Letting the days go by..."

An Introduction by Daniel Kemp

From late 1990 to 1997 I went on a severe binge drinking episode... This is explaining it mildly...

I gradually stopped eating, and constantly drank more. Even after almost putting out my right eye on a marble slab I use for an altar I simply switched from drinking hard liquor to drinking more beer and wine.

Why? This is a question that has eluded me... and still does to this day. I know how stubborn I can be once I get an idea into my head. Yet this is not an excuse. Perhaps I was simply celebrating our initial, open armed acceptance from most of the community down here, at the time. Perhaps I was simply trying to drown out the fact that Leilah will be taken from me at some point in time (which - I truly believed, for reasons of my own, would happen in 1994). Perhaps I am simply stupid. I do not know. But couple all of the above with my own personal problems, my inherent distrust of everyone (prior to meeting Leilah) and my own "sheer bloody-mindedness", and there is surely a distinct recipe for trouble.

Leilah often speaks of the problems of reconciling differing viewpoints insofar as Time is concerned, and how difficult it is for the conscious, mortal mind to correlate the vast differences in perception between our own, personal, "fleshly" time and the "other" time - that which is seen from a different perspective. I think a part of me had fallen prey to that. For I earnestly believed, in our initial years of knowing each other, that she would be going home fairly quickly. We even had several would-be "assassins" present themselves to us, in those early years. This only added to the "lost and alone" feeling I had felt all of my life. I had no idea that she would be sticking around...

This is purely a weakness on my part. My own inability to look Death eye to eye, face to face. Since then, many things have changed...

But, even after 1994 came and went, it was too late. I was still on automatic. And the chains of habit are, at times, the most difficult to break.

In 1995, a friend, a local Voodoo Priest, died. I should have learned something from this, as his death mirrored my almost dying two years later. But, due to my "sheer bloody-mindedness", I learned nothing. I simply continued towards my own self-destruction. I was on "automatic", and nothing could forestall that.

I could not see the Love that watched my every movement, the Love which wept bloody tears at each instance of my refusal to continue. The Love which, ultimately, saved my life...

THE PASTRAMI INCIDENT

Sometimes, you never fully realize how much you love someone until you almost lose them.

They say that your life totally changes every seven years, but no one ever bargains on hitting rock bottom for that to happen. Such was the case in 1997. Seven years of living on the proverbial edge of the knife finally took its toll.

Daniel and I were invited out to Los Angeles to do a book signing at a friend's shop in North Hollywood. Our host met us at the airport. We were pretty tired, so he dropped us off at our hotel. I remember that I was hungry, so I ordered us some food from a local Italian restaurant. Fettuccini Alfredo for me, and some Ravioli for Daniel. But, as usual, Daniel was not hungry. For the past two years I was constantly having to try to get some food into him, which usually ended up with him eating one bite, professing to be "full' and me bitching at him.

We tried to sleep, but quickly realized that we couldn't sleep in the same bed. He snores like a walrus and I spent the night poking him in the back to turn over. The next morning, Our host picked us up to tour us around. I remember a most unique columbarium we visited in Hollywood Memorial Park, then the view down from the mountains into the valley overlooking the "Hollywood" sign. Somehow everything we saw went by in brief flashes. Our host invited us to lunch at one of L.A.'s "famous" deli's. Something we were both looking forward to as ex- New Yorkers with nary a deli in sight living in New Orleans.

One bite of Pastrami was all it took, and Daniel keeled over hard onto the concrete floor. Everyone in the crowded restaurant thought he was having some kind of epileptic seizure, yet no one wanted to intervene. They all sat there gawking as one of the wait-staff called for an ambulance. California seems to have one of those wonderful little laws that states that they have to take you to the nearest hospital in such cases. Luckily, we were right across the street from Cedars-Sinai, hospital to the stars. It actually took about twenty minutes for the ambulance to get across the street in L.A. traffic, and the waiter had the absolute gall to ask who was going to pay for the uneaten food. I told him to call a cop (there were two standing alongside me already). Very rude.

The E.R. doctors were all over Daniel. They were convinced that he just had some type of "common seizure" and would be okay in a few hours time. He was coming around, so the doctor gave him a couple of orange slices and told him to rest on the gurney for a while. He no sooner took a bite of one slice, and like a scene right out of *The Exorcist*, Daniel started vomiting what appeared to be the entirety of his insides!

Quickly, his condition worsened and he was admitted. At first everyone thought he must be a rock star (owing to his appearance – long hair) strung out on drugs, or a victim of AIDS (owing to the fact that he only weighed 99 pounds at the time). The belief that he was someone "famous" landed him in the Steven Spielberg wing of the hospital, replete with private room and a team of high priced doctors. They tested him for every ailment under the sun. Meanwhile Daniel was quickly slipping away. Fading from this life to the point where he no longer knew who I was, where he was, nor who he was. He was going down fast!

After a barrage of even more tests, it was determined that he had absolutely no potassium in his body. His brain had literally shrunk two percent, and his blood was pure alcohol. I knew he had an alcohol problem for some time (we both did), but never realized just how bad of a problem it had become for Daniel.

They pumped him full of liquid potassium, electrolyte fluids and all sorts of crap, including one of the nastiest drugs used to treat schizophrenics, just to keep him from waking up and "injuring himself". He was literally hog-tied to the bed, hands and feet bound by tied sheets to the side-rails.

✠

Daniel was an alcoholic. I knew that for at least the last three years prior to this. He had stopped drinking "hard liquor" over a year before after a series of drunken stupors almost lead him to losing an eye and cracking his skull open on a marble altar. But, he still continued to drink beer... a lot of beer, and very little food, and there was nothing I could do nor say that would have stopped him. Believe me, I tried everything.

In the hospital, when he had conscious moments, Daniel believed that he was still at home and kept trying to move about. Instead he kept falling out of bed and injuring himself further. He was so far gone that he was "smoking" imaginary cigarettes and "drinking" imaginary beer. The gooseneck lamp above his bed became a "duck from Jupiter" that he would talk to at length, and picture frames across the room became "doorways to other worlds". He kept tossing off the hospital issued red blankets thinking that they were "rancid raspberries", so they had to cover it with a white sheet so he wouldn't see it and make a fuss.

On Saturday, two days into the ordeal, the doctors informed me that he would either die or become a vegetable within days, and if the latter, would be relegated to the L.A. county psychiatric facility via some crazy law. County was not a nice place, from what I'd heard. They even gave me a piece of paper, an "Involuntary Patient Advisement" that stated the reasons behind their desire to put him into County as he would be likely to "harm himself" and be "unable to take care of his own food, clothing and housing needs". The assigned staff psychiatrist also put the following statement on this form further damning him; "You have no viable plan for living".

Obviously, they discovered that he wasn't a famous rock star after all, and worse yet, that we had no medical insurance. They basically just gave up and kept him drugged up until such time that he either died or met the timed criteria for committal to county to live out the remainder of his life tied to a bed and forgotten. One of the doctors even admitted to me that he "had" to take cases like this on the road to "making a killing as a high priced plastic surgeon". What ever happened to the Hippocratic Oath? I think we all know the answer to that lies in changing a letter or two.

No! This was not going to happen! This was all wrong. We have not come this far together to have it end like this. My path may have been winding down, but Daniel's had yet to begin. Besides, I liked having Daniel in my life and refused to have his own stupidity be the undoing of his purpose.

He had "sitters" 24 hours a day. Some were genuinely kind to him, some were not. One night he recited his entire *Book of Night* to one of the sitters and then promptly went back to "la-la-land" immediately after. During another rare semi-lucid moment, his folks called from New York. I remember putting the phone to his ear as his mother asked what happened. Daniel told this fantastic tale of being out on a boat, falling overboard and being hit on the head with an anchor! (I had no idea that he had the same delusion when he overdosed many years before we met.) Could this be a past life memory only accessible to him during altered mental states? It would explain his very real fear of being under water.

It would seem that he would only calm down and rest when I was in the room, which is where I spent ninety-nine percent of the week. I was running on two hours rest a night and ironically drinking myself to sleep while Daniel lay dying in the hospital from *drinking*.

I was quickly catching up to him and the hospital staff could see that. Talking to the Social Services dept. was certainly no help. They seemed to be convinced that I was an "enabler" that helped to make him this way, which, of course, only made me feel more like crap. However, they didn't know Daniel, or of his addictive history, nor his damn stubborn nature... nor the reasons behind his addictions.

Every day I would try to "bring him back" from the edge of madness. I knew that Daniel was still in there somewhere, trapped inside his ailing flesh while his mind phased in and out of reality. The one semi-lucid moment he had, he looked me in the eye as I pleaded for him to "come back to me". Tears welled in both of our eyes. "I'm trying. I am trying." The words came with painful difficulty as if they were echoes from a distant world. It was during that brief, sad, and shining moment that I realized the only thing that would bring him back... was love. There was hope, but no one else could see that, nor do I think cared. It was also in this one moment that I realized love was stronger than all the disparate circumstances around us – the one, true magic that could fetch him from the brink and return him whole.

One of his night sitters, who was actually the only other caring person I met during this whole ordeal, would flick on the TV and try to jog his memory by scrolling through the channels and engaging him in conversation. Daniel's face would light up when he landed on the Cartoon Channel. He saw hope as well, but we had a bigger challenge now, to get the doctors to stop drugging him up long enough to elicit more lucid time. They already wrote him off, just biding their time to free up the bed for some starlet who could afford $1,100 per night!

Between my being downright adamant, and the sitter's urging we finally got them to stop administering the drug. I simply blocked them physically while the sitter (who was a doctor in training) cited cases from medical journals to bolster our claim.

✠

For his body, no more could be done. The challenge was now for him to *want* to return, to continue regardless of what that entailed. Every day he was evaluated by the same staff psychiatrist, asking the same questions over and over, "What is you name? Do you know what year it is? Do you know where you are? Do you recognize this person?" (and he'd point to me). Every day, he failed. He had forty-eight hours left to at least remember his own name or else be shuttled off to County.

I had to get some sleep, so I trudged back to the hotel and did something I swore I would never, ever, ever, do. I asked Azrael for a "favour". I asked Him to spare a life, to bring Daniel back to me. I cried myself to sleep that night knowing that this went against everything that I believed, but also knowing that it was not Daniel's time. I never asked Azrael for anything in my entire life, except this one thing...

✠

The next morning came and I walked into the hospital room and Daniel was awkwardly staggering around the room searching for his pants. I was overjoyed just to see him out of that bed! Quickly the nurses came and put him back in bed. He was semi-lucid. He recognized me for more than but an instant! I said to one of the nurses, "Quick get the psychiatrist back in here!" Coincidentally he was just making his rounds.

"What's your name?" Daniel answered correctly this time. Everyone smiled, even Daniel.

"Do you know where you are?" Daniel looked at me. I looked back.

"North Carolina?" he answered unsure.

The psychiatrist tried again, "Where do you work?"

"The House of Death" he replied immediately. The doctor looked at me. I pointed to the T-shirt I was wearing, one of our own that said "The House of Death".

"That's correct," I told the doctor. He shrugged, "Oh, okay."

"What year is it?" he further inquired.

"1897." Daniel answered, repeating his answer, "1897".

He was only off by a hundred years, so what?

The doctor queried him a few more times, jotted down notes on a squib of paper and left the room without a word. Later that afternoon, another doctor (who I'd never seen before) came in and gruffly told me that Daniel was being released into my care and there was nothing more they could do and that they needed the (precious) bed space for paying clients. I had to sign a slew of forms releasing them from "indemnity, liability", etc. They wanted rid of him and we wanted nothing more than to be as far from L.A. as we could get.

They gave him some "physical therapy" which jokingly consisted of two women who walked him up and down the short hallway twice. They gave him a cane and a rubber tube to exercise his arms with. What a joke! And, just as Daniel was finally looking forward to getting some solid food after not eating for a week, he barely had time to scarf down a cup of tomato soup when they hustled him into a wheelchair and dismissed him before he could take a single bite of the elaborate lunch he'd selected from their extensive menu.

✠

Back at the hotel, I have vague memories of his dad and I bathing him as he was simply too weak to get in and out of the tub. The next morning, his mom not allowing him to finish his much needed breakfast so that we could get to the airport at an ungodly hour.

The next real memory I have is being in the airport for three hours while Daniel sat in a wheelchair, and Hare Krishnas gave us pens. Everyone was staring at us so pathetically. Some not wanting to be too close in case he was "contagious". He still resembled an advanced AIDS patient. The flight home is a complete blur until arriving back at New Orleans International and being damn glad to feel the humid air once again. My father was a most welcomed sight at the airport to greet us.

The ordeal was not over, but at least I did not come home alone, and for this, I was infinitely grateful.

WHAT DANIEL REMEMBERS

I actually remember very little of this. I have conscious memories of agreeing to do a book signing with Leilah in North Hollywood. After that, it all becomes a bit blurry....

I do remember getting on the plane, though I remember little of the flight itself. The next real memory I have is of Leilah and I discovering we could not sleep in the same bed. She kept kicking me in the back (claiming that I snore). I know I got very little sleep that night. I do not, however, remember landing, or getting from the airport to the hotel...

✠

The next thing I remember is standing in front of a deli, down the street from the hotel, at 8AM waiting for it to open so I could buy some beer. When I got back to the hotel, I started to drink. Then our host arrived, wanting to tool us around.

I remember being in this cross-shaped mausoleum, just staring at the sunlight coming through the stained glass windows while our host was showing Leilah around the place.

Then I remember a drive up into the hills and looking down on the HOLLYWOOD sign....

✠

The next thing I remember was waking up in a hospital with no pants on. I do not know why this was important, but I had to struggle out of the bed and find some pants to put on. (Several days had actually passed, at this point.)

After that, all I recall is tomato soup. I hate tomato soup but I remember eating a bowl of it and being very thankful that it was there...

Later on, I vaguely remember attempting to eat breakfast in a different hotel room while my Mom was bitching about how we had to leave for the airport. Then, of being in a car with my Father driving (not too well, he had Parkinsons) and almost turning directly into oncoming traffic, and then sitting in a wheelchair at the airport. These are just flashes of images, though - seconds of stopped film in my mind.

I can remember being pushed in a wheelchair through the parking lot of the airport in New Orleans, and one scene from the ride home with Leilah and her Father in her Father's van.

The next memory I have is of the day after coming home. I needed to take a shower, and it was somehow important that I do this myself. I could barely stand, and was very shaky. But I managed it. My entire left side was sore, my right arm had a HUGE bruised/discoloured area (from where, I am told, they constantly took blood from me) and my tongue was pure agony - I had chewed through it during the "seizure". I almost fell many times, but managed to force myself to remain upright by supporting myself on the wall. I have no idea why I can remember this one thing so vividly, yet I do.

☥

Then, the darkness crept in. I spent a month or so on the sofa. Just laying there. I remember Leilah constantly pushing food in my face. I also remember not being able to sleep.

My mind, at this point, was just a swirling, huge black pit. I do not recall any conscious thoughts, at all. Just a swirling, angry darkness. A never-ending, dark vortex. The only actual memory that jumps up of anything other than darkness is of watching *Young Frankenstein* on TV, sometime during that month.

I still, to this day, cannot remember what my mind was doing during that time. For in losing 2% of my brain (it actually shrunk), I lost a lot of memories and my ability to do math, as well as my electronics knowledge. I really do believe that my brain was "rebooting" during this time.

At night, when I was in my own room, I would play with my old 486SX computer, playing logic games. I had to re-train my mind how to think. I spent endless hours playing stupid puzzle and logic games until I could solve them, and reading DOS books.

Somehow, on some level, my body and my soul knew what to do to heal my shattered mind. I needed to regain my ability to think. So I was a vegetable by day and teaching myself logic by night.

The only thing that snapped me back into reality was losing the use of my left arm. (I was supposed to be doing rigorous physical therapy, but refused to leave the sofa.)

One morning I woke up, and as usual went to get some cereal. I always opened the kitchen cabinet with my left arm, and took down the cereal with my right. I found myself staring at the kitchen cabinet door and... nothing happened. This is when I "woke up", so to speak, and can actually start to remember things clearly. This was in mid to end November, 1997.

It's odd... You spend your whole life with your body doing what you tell it to without really thinking about it, much less actually acknowledging that there is any effort involved in such actions. Yet, when the moment comes when you are faced with inaction, the brain farts - and suddenly you become acutely aware of the process by which such movements occur. I stood there for a while, repeatedly telling my left arm to move, to raise itself and open the cabinet door. Nothing happened.... So I used my right arm, opened the cabinet door, grabbed the cereal and a bowl. I poured out the cereal, opened the fridge with my right arm, grabbed the milk and poured it. I sat on my bed and ate, only using my right arm. When I was done I put the bowl in the sink, opened the door between our rooms, and told Leilah I could not move my left arm.

What followed was a time of pure hell, as Leilah began to put me through physical therapy... (I finally found a use for all those Crowley books I had... lifting *Gems From the Equinox* was a chore).

It was not till the summer of 1998 that I got most of the use of my left arm back. Even now, if I try to move both arms in a circular motion I get a severe twinge of pain in my left arm. I just tried it, it hurts like hell.

I'm still not sure what "snapped" me back into being here. I do know this, however - before I met Leilah, and moved to New Orleans, I had never felt "at home" anywhere. And you must understand, I had spent so long running on "automatic", that I was, up until 1997, blindly following the body's path for self destruction. I had overdosed on drugs, my lungs had collapsed... I was only following my fervent wish to return home.

It took such a drastic shock to me to make me realize I had long ago found what I had been searching for in this world... a companion. Knowing how I am, there is no other way I could have learned this. Even in the midst of happiness, a body running on automatic will yet perceive misery - where there is none. It took my brain to totally black itself out, and re-start, in order for me to realize this.

✠

In the end, I found Love - it just took my own brand of "bloody-mindedness" a long time to realize this.

Once I had "come back", I became extremely shy in front of others. For I could not remember what I had last said to them, and this made me unsure of how to act in the presence of those I had known.

All in all, I had lost between a year and a year and a half of conscious memory. I could remember little bits and pieces, but not a lot. Prior to the "pastrami incident", I was an obnoxious drunk at the best of times, a raving drunk at the worst. I know I hurt a lot of people. From what I've been told, I am a completely different person now.

I have somehow acquired, perhaps in exchange for my ability at math, an inherent knack for computers. My electronics knowledge can pop up at surprising times, so it is (for the most part) still buried in there, somewhere.

I think the oddest thing was getting used to my changing body. I had always been "thin", yet in CA I was 99 pounds. It had been so long since I had any substance to my body that this was an alien concept to me. I can recall vividly the first time (after I had recovered and gained weight) of jogging down the stairs here and feeling my "boobs" jiggle. It was a unique experience, for me.

So I went running to Leilah with an idiotic grin on my face and said "I can feel my boobs jiggle..." She laughed, and laughed...

✠

Two years later, I went to Mexico for 4 days. It was my first vacation in a very long time. There, on the beach under the stars in the darkness, during a spontaneous, poetic invocation, is where the Lady came back to me. It was the first time I had felt Her in a long while.

When I returned home, I gradually began to write again. This was the final piece of myself, returning home. I was "whole" once again. After this, I recorded some music (both of my own and played on a friend's CD), continued writing in fits & spurts and continued recovering physically.

I have yet to even attempt to eat Pastrami again. I probably never will...

✠

A new Daniel arose from that experience. Stronger, surer, more at peace. Not only with himself, but also with life in general. Yes, one day he too, would go home, but only after learning to accept and appreciate the reason for this life. Sound familiar?

He would eventually come to understand the importance of Purpose, and how it supercedes our desire for home, and we only truly reach that goal after learning to understand the meaning of our immediate lives. He too was here for a reason, which he would watch unfold like a many petalled flower and marvel at its mystery and its beauty – perhaps for the first time.

The Chalice Emptied

Your hollow eyes
reflect many worlds,
deep, dark dimensions
beyond the moment's abyss.

I see
all of time
in their darkness
by the pale glow
of a distant, blue flame.

Eternal bliss
waits on your still lips,
poised for the kiss
that tastes of bitter clay
and sweet cold.

My heart
pressed up
against your decayed breast,
brittle, resonant
like an echo
from the distant void,
skeletal arms caress,
pulling me closer,
entwining our bones,
fusing our lips,
quenching my heart,
consumed by Death...
My heart,
now silent in His hand-
The last drop of life
falls heavy to the floor.

Part 19

"Mind The Gap"

THE ANGEL ISLE REVISITED

"I gaze beyond the rain-drenched streets to England where my heart lies."

Part of the recovery process for us both, was simply to get away from it all, even for a short time. Because of the nature of having to keep Westgate going, we couldn't go away together, so Daniel went off to the shores of Cozumel to regroup and rededicate himself to the path ahead. A few months later, I finally got the chance to go to England, at last!

I had wanted to go to there for as long as I could remember in this life. Having always believed that this was a cohesive piece of the only "true" land to survive the great floods of the antediluvian age. That there were unbroken paths in the "Old Straight Track", a cartography of energy systems and ley lines not disrupted by the shifting of land and sea. A true piece of the "Angel Isle" for which it is named, where the past merged ever so subtly with the future to create the present.

Somewhere, truth was hiding amidst those "dark satanic hills", and in its "countenance divine" lay secrets to the origins of man. The "new Jerusalem" where the Watchers came down and bedded the daughters of men. Humanity, as we have become, began here in a most abrupt manner.

If the stones of Avebury could talk, they would tell you stories. They each have souls. They were once alive. Living things encased in stone by an ancient and cruel magic so that the lies of origin could be perpetuated by a race unable, or unwilling to deal with its ancestry. These are the silent guardians, the truth givers that shadow the gates of eternity. In their stone hands are the still-beating hearts of angels... of legend. The gods and goddesses of Truth mankind has replaced with a mythos so lame and so fearful, yet so mindlessly palatable to the masses, that in its telling, we are meant to laugh and scorn the Truth that they represent, and embrace the lie of man's telling. All the while, the stones scream but cannot be heard. Half animal and half angel, what are we capable of believing? How can we truly remember with all the distractions we have created for our own petty amusement? "Entertain me..." said the spider to the fly... and then tiring of his spectacle, she consumed him without a thought.

✠

It was of the utmost importance that I find some porcupine quills to bring with me to England to appease my host who had graciously offered me the use of his home for my journey.

I remember hoping that there were crows in England. My vociferous little harbingers that mysteriously vanish when others are afoot. Some have seen them, the laggard ones that caw, and are immediately silenced. A few, as of late, have dared to grace my street. They "know" certain things that I do not. They foretold my journey in a language so beautiful and so divine that men cringe at their song and shoo them away with a shaking fist and a fearful glance. They follow me where I walk and those fearful glances are cast down to me... and I smile. I hoped there were crows.

✠

When I came to that great isle, I was searching for a legend. A tale told out of time. A repetitive, resonant dancing thing that has parlayed my life for more years than I care to recall, more dreams than I can accurately relate. A vision of truth so real and so abundant of meaning that it lives outside of myself as a reality that I have somehow forsaken in the quest for the life of the moment – ever fleeting, ever distant.

I had hoped this trip would give way to a new reality born of an old memory and predispose my life more "original" meaning – more spark of purpose to follow with these fading eyes and hollow heart – to recall the past not with a tear of joy in passing, but again with a full heart ripe for the reaping blade. Was it too much to ask to find but one place once again within which to draw a full breath and see clearly with eyes that have seen all too much that has been forgotten? Not by choice, but by the advent of circumstance intersecting the moment. Yes, a moment changes all things, but contained in that moment is the energy of inspiration. The inspiration that forces us to evolve beyond the string of moments that create the present day. To deconstruct the status quo in the blink of an eye is no more and no less than what a hurricane does to a small island. It has no choice but to surrender to the changes occurring within and without. The island itself, is a feather on the winds of change, and each man and woman is an island... and a feather, having both root and wing.

My roots having grown so deep and expansive had left little to no energy for even the tiniest flap of wing. This must change, erst as my brothers before me, I, too, will have totally assumed the likeness of this fallen shell. Never again to be as I was. Shackled to this dying orb, I will pass the way of those in the stones, with a scream that none will hear, and only memories will be the food of eternity. I hoped I had enough...

✠

Descending from the sky I saw nothing of England except a thick envelope of steel-grey clouds. My only first sight was the dingy runway of Heathrow Airport. A monstrous expanse of dilapidated tubes and buildings noticeably leaking immense amounts of water from the unseasonable thunderstorms. Emerging from the seemingly endless leaking tunnels into a poorly air-conditioned series of ill-marked mazes and doors.

The road-trip to where I was staying was an hour-long expanse of greenery dotted with small farms and the usual city outskirts. Reading is indeed, a "suburb" in its truest universal sense. Endless cul-de-sacs of 1920's "doubles", much like Brooklyn Heights but with a Tudor flavour. It was extremely quiet, even in mid-afternoon on a Wednesday. The sun was out, but it was still raining. The thermometer said 62 degrees, but it felt oddly warmer. Weird weather! My head was humming loudly as I anticipated the 7 days ahead of me. It was so damn quiet, I wondered if I could sleep.

The next day, we went into London. My first impression was that it was really no different than New York except for some much older buildings, some strange customs and about twice as many people as Manhattan at rush hour! Paddington Station, much like Pennsylvania Station, was confusing to say the least.

Under construction everywhere, and hot as hell! There was absolutely no air conditioning anywhere in London. From the train stations, to the tubes, to the British Museum. Everywhere you go you sweat, even when it was relatively cool outside. We stopped to eat at a restaurant that had a big sign "Air Conditioned", which we found out consisted of no more than a small fan on a floor pedestal. The museum is a formidable building with a beautiful facade that houses many treasures, but not nearly as large as I expected. They had two mummies on exhibit, and the museum actually allows photographs. It was very crowded and no one wanted to be the first to snap a photo of the mummies. Of course, I got some seriously aghast looks when I volunteered. Too bad they were under glass, I thought they were quite beautiful. They have a large Egyptian collection. Everything from room-sized temples, to the smallest jewelry fragment, but the things I'd always wanted to see, the John Dee items, (the scrying mirror and the Sigillium Emeth) were relegated to one shelf in the back that no one looked at. I had to ask several of the curatorial staff where to find them, when it was actually a museum guard who knew what I was talking about. Certainly not as assuming as their legend, but more as an intricate work of handy-craft. The museum didn't even know how to label the artifacts, so they were simply cataloged as "Wax tablet and crystal ball with Aztec Onyx mirror." No history, no legend, nothing tying them to the Enochian manuscripts.

We visited several small bookshops. There must literally be hundreds of them in the city, which usually consisted of single, small rooms, and highly specialized. London is a much larger city than New York and distances between things can be quite lengthy.

There are some interesting little "customs" you have to learn while navigating in England-

You must stand on the right side on a moving escalator to allow those in a hurry to run past you on the left. You have to bag your own groceries. A pedestrian does not have the right of way. You have to "queue" for just about everything. You can smoke any damn place you like except for the tubes due to the great fire of 1992. Fold up umbrellas are not "proper English garb". Always carry several changes of clothes. No one honks their horn or yells catcalls at you. It's the law. British TV does suck. There are no screens on the windows because there are few bugs. Few people outside the city lock their doors. England is obsessed with sexual gossip. British plumbing comes in all shapes and sizes including contraptions I've never before seen. "Humps for 30 feet" means watch the speed bumps. (That one threw me for a while!) I also found out what "tossing" meant. Oh, and don't forget to "mind the gap"!

☩

As tired as I was that night, I couldn't get a lick of sleep so I decided to simply get up at six am. I was on some kind of adrenaline rush. I was sure I'd come crashing down sometime soon. It was still so quiet at my host's house that it was unnerving. Today, we were heading to Highgate Cemetery. It was raining again, and the chill wind cut right through me. That would no doubt change when we got back to the city, where it always seemed a tad warmer.

Highgate was perhaps the most impressive cemetery I'd seen thus far. You can tour the east side on your own. It is magnificently old, dilapidated, severely overgrown and wonderfully atmospheric. The town of Highgate itself, which sits atop an immense hill, is quintessential England. From the Gothic spires that loom over the landscape, to the ancient ivy, this is what I came to see. The west side of the cemetery is from another world. There is a definite energy within its gloomy lanes that if it wasn't for the stuffy tour guide, I could have easily gotten "lost" in there forever. Why oh why is such a place not accessible to those who really feel? What is the point of "preserving" such a place if no one can truly appreciate what it has to offer? The tour doesn't allow you to even see the half of what splayed out before me. There were several places that were really intense, and another spot that in broad daylight, turned into night with just a footstep. Yes, English weather is atrocious, but how wonderfully it complimented the landscape.

But Highgate would soon become dwarfed in comparison. The next day, I went to Kensal Green Cemetery. What a truly amazing place. It was surprisingly easier to find than Highgate, yet nestled in a less desirable quadrant of London. I could have easily spent the entirety of my trip here. I wandered in the thunder and light rain, so overgrown and full of strong energies that drew you in at every turn. There were some really odd crypts, and I'd be remiss not to mention the fantastic catacombs that lay beneath. Unfortunately, you can't wander them on your own nor take pictures, but the tour was worth having to put up with a small horde of curious gawkers. It is so hard to describe what I felt down there, so I will start with the visual. All of the hundreds of coffins are ornate and custom made, mostly lead to prevent "leakage". They sit in "loculi", very much like the "oven" crypts of New Orleans. They are all exposed and quite deteriorated. Many are decorated ornately with carved marble and gemstones. There were some sections where everything was simply just falling apart and bones were scattered all over the floor. What a great feel this place had. Like a cold, soft electric charge that came up from the floor, through my body and exited out my fingertips. I only wish I could have spent some time down there by myself. Everybody was tiptoeing around all squeamish and wide-eyed as our guide told some grisly stories about the catacombs.

One in particular I remember was the story of a young woman who snuck in some many years back. Her lover was entombed there and she was very distraught over his death so she climbed onto his coffin and slept there. They are uncertain as to how long she lay dead there when one of the workers noticed that the heavy shelf above the niche in which she laid had collapsed on top of her along with at least a ton of stone and lead. When they moved away the rubble, it is told that she had the most "peaceful smile". Kensal Green was the highlight of my journey thus far. One can only wonder what mischief I may have gotten into if let lose in that place. However, I had to head back. Tomorrow was going to be a long, long day.

My host wasn't feeling well that day, so when I got back I thought I'd run down to the local supermarket and make him a treat, genuine New York style Ziti, something he'd never even heard of. It was Sunday, and I discovered that the buses didn't run on Sunday, so I walked the two miles to the store only to discover that it, too, was closed on Sunday. My only option was to stop at the near-by "Off-License", (which to you and me is like a Quickie Mart). I ended up having to just get a bag of any kind of noodles they had and a couple Courgettes (zucchini in Britspeak). I wanted some Parmesan cheese, or even Mozzarella but it seemed they'd never heard of these. The "official" cheese product of England seems to be something called "Dairylea", which is a form of soft white cheddar mixed with lard and has the consistency of mayonnaise and tastes off cottage cheese. So, I skipped the cheese (should have skipped the whole thing as I couldn't recognize a thing in my host's cupboard) and we simply got some fish & chips.

✠

Monday came, and we took the two and a half-hour train ride from Reading to Dorset. Once I got away from the 'burbs of Reading, wow – what an incredible landscape. Green hills rolling out into sweeping somber skies – brooding, overcast yet billowing sweet songs. Ancient loud paeans of glories past, and yet to be hearkening the homeward heart, yearning to remember. The dark ominous clouds do not rush off into the distance. They endlessly circle the deep valleys mimicking nighttime at midday. Quite impressive!

Our destination was Sherbourne where my host's friend was scheduled to pick us up. Every village was so lush and green and totally isolated. Nothing for miles and miles but ruins, woods... and recurring memories.

When we arrived at Sherbourne I was amazed to find out that the stations are no more than ancient well sites with thatched covers where the trainmen literally hand-cranked the guard rails. Because it is so dark out there in the middle of nowhere, they wave the trains through with flashlights and lanterns. Bear in mind, that these are extremely modern trains. Quite a twist when you're looking out at such antiquity. Sherbourne looked exactly like what you'd see in one of the guidebooks. The ancient spire dominates the town. A huge churchyard, the local pub, really, really old buildings, most of which were almost a thousand years old. Anyway, we were met by my host's friend and his wife, who picked us up in a very old American jalopy for the "short" trip to their house (only 18 miles)!

Now, this town (which is not a town, but rather landscape dotted with a couple of houses) was truly the middle of nowhere, and their house dated from the 1500's replete with part of an ancient roman stone gate. I'm sure it was once a beautiful place. Now, however, it reminded me of a hashish den straight out of 1969 Haight-Ashbury. I walked into this once beautiful house now covered with pictures of Crowley, Kenneth Grant, etal mingled awkwardly with hippy tie-dye and assorted time specific "paraphernalia". "We've been tripping for three days, man," said one of his numerous houseguests, splayed on the floor, vacuous of expression.

Anyway, my host settled in and after about an hour of many of them marveling at having never met an American until now, I just wanted to get out of there and get some air. I went out to wander in the twilight and followed the seemingly endless muddy trail to a hilltop and sat there for the longest time. From here, you could see everything. Then I just started wandering, letting whatever resonant memories lead the way. I was once very near here. The land was familiar, incredibly familiar. I came upon a road sign, very quaint and obviously hand painted. It had a choice of four directions, one of which was Yeovil Cun Montmartense (The old village that looks out over time). Something drew me to head in that direction. On the road, I met this amazing young Welsh man, who was actually one of the houseguests who was out a-wandering as well. He took me to an old cathedral and small churchyard nearby which was very definitely something of memory.

Eventually we parted ways to meet up back at the house later. I went roving further into the evening totally oblivious as to where I was and how to get back to the house in the utter blackness that was quickly wiping out the scenery around me. The darker it got, the more I felt a familiarity, the more I could actually hear the voices of my past here, my other lives. Out of the darkness, the scenes began to unfold. I saw the old horrors that had been done to me. I saw brilliant flashes of the beginning times, the times I spoke about in an earlier chapter. They were as real as I was and I knew if I took another step, that I would step right into them, and out of time.

I was a little farther south then I wanted to be and as I suspected, I could not chase the proverbial needle in the haystack in just under 8 days, let alone one day out here. Somehow, it didn't matter anymore. I touched the stones, and yes, they are still very much "alive" – sentient beings still encased. They were not released after all, nor will I ever be released of their memory. I hope that one day I have the chance to return here and pick up where I left off, but for now, my trip was winding down. I only had one more night in England and we had to head back to Reading that night so that my host could get to work on time.

✠

Yes, our lives began here, among living stele. However, like so many "interesting" places, humanity muffles the true energy that dwells in the soil. People rarely feel the spirits of their own land. The original "grid" is very much still intact. I could sense that very strongly. Some do pick up on it. The musicians, the poets – but these days, like anywhere else, even in the midst of no man's land, they believe themselves "isolated" from the truth when they are ignorant in its cradle.

A life once lived in exile remains in shards of memory. Once clear in youth, but dulled with time. Enveloping so many things – encapsulated days, years, dimensions. All relegated to their proper place. Yet, no places have been found for these stray memories, these keys to truth. This truth to follow no path now that destiny has flown away with age and the dominion of the moment. Like shards of mirror, the past lay scattered at our feet, and we tread lightly to avoid being cut, and also so as not to shatter the image contained in each piece. The hopes and dreams of lifetimes, some remembered, most forgotten, or in fragment form, taunt us in our sleeping and our waking. Thoughts out of time, but as clear as yesterday. Having no place to put them, they are thrown into a pile like mismatched socks to sort through in our idle hours. But these shards have meaning. Jigsaw puzzle pieces of our souls that make us who we are, who we were, and will become – we need to know. Though how in one brief lifetime can we reassemble the puzzle of all we have been when the pieces outnumber our days? Each small image larger than this one life, This one life but a section of the greater whole...

A great power lies waiting there that has been untapped for so long, so misinterpreted by the throngs of good intentioned masses. The reason why this tiny island thrives is in the hope that one day we shall rediscover the secret that lies beneath those great sweeping clouds, and by doing so, remember what we truly are... And I had only a few days to attempt to appreciate its splendour.

Part 20

From Root to Wing

"Do you know why the caged bird sings?"

Nothing rings out as clearly as an ending. And 1999 certainly brought us to that point.

Twenty years of Westgate, in retrospect may not seem like a long time. But, when counted in the expanse of moments, and the expense of self, believe me, it is long enough indeed! We all must go back to source eventually if we are ever going to continue toward completion. I remember telling you all at the onset of the 90's, what a tumultuous decade it would be (what decade isn't, really?). However, for most of "us", this decade had a special affiliation. Most of us are where we are meant to be (give or take the few doubtful stragglers) - that's why your life seems so screwed up! You and I have forgotten how to be that proverbial "feather on the wind". The flesh so much wants to be a rolling stone, a boulder, collecting dust and mud as it rolls haphazardly down the mountainside towards its inevitable end. Talk about grounded. Could we get anymore grounded? May as well stick our toes into the earth and grow roots, weather the storm like an old oak, shedding some limbs, licking our wounds - and holding on for "dear life".

That's how we know we've become too grounded, roots too deep, limbs too fragile, caring too much for the caress of soil, closing our arms to the embrace of the storm, Isn't that what we came for? Okay, we've experienced the "human condition", understand it all too well - now what? Those ancient whispers grow harder to hear in the staunch winds down here. The lightning never touches us, it just dances outside our shuttered windows, tendrils teasing hearts.

Yes, I have fallen, into your world, by my own choice - into love and out of faith, full knowing that I can return into that which I have become more fully. This hybrid voice has not changed, it has been humbled by understanding, honed by love and strengthened by hope. What a strange word in this land of doubt, this culture of fear in the age of complacency. You are all the greatest teachers, but the some of the poorest students I have ever met. That is not condescension, merely an observation.

I started out all these years ago as the silent student of Life - the embodiment of Death, the shadow of your doubt, the anonymous traveller in the void of your lush dominion. Then, the weeping willows reached out their tender limbs, wrapping them securely around my heart and pulled me into their shaded embrace. I became a part of the tree, assimilated its likeness and in symbiosis danced through the seasonal years. Sometimes dancing naked in the frozen gales, shedding leaves like memories to be the seeds of lives to come. Sometimes swathed in singing blankets that shadowed weary souls beneath so that they could sleep in peaceful cool. Never thinking of an end. The tree continues... and it watches, for it has no choice, its roots run deep into the earth, into the waters... into the soul of Life. It's funny really, if you think for a moment, that a tree reaches down ever deeper and at the same time, ever higher for its sustenance, yet man is only root. So many never rise above the soil. Never stretch past the limit of their imagined reach, never extend a tendril beyond an arms length.

If humanity is part of nature, why can't our expressions reflect that? Why can't our touch be as the soft breeze, or the lightning bolt? Why can't truth fall like rain, without reason or provocation - not needing a response? Why can't our sorrow be expressed as a falling star, to just admire its beauty as it expires into the waiting horizon? Why can't our small joys be as snowflakes, tumbling down carefree on a winter's night into silent oblivion?

No, mankind needs to fill nature with "conditions" to affirm that he is not at all part of nature. That he is not at all like the wind, or the storm, nor the rain, nor the mist, nor... the tree that has held many on its ancient branches, seen more winters and survived more storms than you and I can consciously remember. Nature is unconditional, but even it has its endings... and new beginnings.

It is time to take this tree, uproot it and let it defy the laws of nature - a tree aloft by the wings of its foliate branches. Each one of you, a leaf, contributing to the breadth of its flight. Each one of you, a feather on the winds of change, without which the tree would never have grown in the first place. Please know that I love you all. If even at times I may not have graced you all with the most open arms, please know that it was only because I did not remember how to stretch my arms beyond this meager reach of flesh. Beyond this illusion, you are forever in my embrace. Each heart, a feather - each soul, a star, and knowing each of you has brought the greatest tears of joy to ever grace the face of Death.

MORE LOOSE ENDS

Loose ends, like dark tendrils, uncoil from the past and weave back into the present, and tangle with the future. In the face of all that has ended, and against my prior proclamations, I find I must return once again to that barrenness that once was lush; to put right something I caused to go wrong. Through the fault of my own naiveté, a sacred trust lay broken. How can something so innocent have caused so much grief? How can some thing be so important? Over time, the thing has become merely symbol, and the mission has ulterior motives, far reaching depths that even I confess the inability to fathom. I simply know what must be done.

✠

Those around me scoff, wondering why I must return this thing to that which is no more. Maybe, it is no more as a result of my naiveté? Though, returning what I must will not bring it back, it will however give me the peace of mind in knowing that I did the right thing. This whole dilemma is a matter of sacred trust between me, and my beloved, and that means more to us than can be explained in simple words. In deeds, it must be done. Let me explain...

Something very weird happened recently. It centers around the mausoleum mentioned earlier in this book (Chapter 6 page 124). Those of you who have read this, know the power this humble place harnessed and understand its relevance as an "earthgate". (Some of you who have been there know this even better.) You may also recall that I wrote about my vision of its "destruction" in 1988, which came to pass in 1993.

Now, here's the strange part as well as some of the story I never told earlier simply because I never knew the events that would necessitate telling would occur. There was a ring that belonged to one of the occupants of this tomb. A very unusual ring with a highly unusual crest... Some of the lettering has rubbed off on the bottom. It reads "Omega Ma De?". It's actually a mourning ring.

Anyway, I am not one to "rob" the dead and I do not take anything with me from my necromantic encounters save the experience itself and what may be offered by Azrael Himself. However, an old "friend" of mine, who I shall refer to as "K" for the sake of this writing, was not so honest. You see, I had made the mistake of showing her that special place in the early 1980's and sharing some of my experiences there with her, but never giving her entry nor telling her about the ring. In fact, the mausoleum, at this point in time, had been nailed shut by the caretakers for a couple of years. I trusted her, even though we had a very tumultuous on again, off again relationship for many years. However, we shared an interest in various things necromantically related, and at that time, I was simply glad to have someone to share these things with in person.

Shortly thereafter, we had a falling out, due to involved circumstances, and I hadn't see "K" nor had any contact with her for several years thereafter.

By this time, I had been out of New York for a few years when another friend of mine, Christine, telephoned me in 1993 to inform me that the old mausoleum was no more, (The destruction I envisioned earlier. It more or less imploded in upon itself sending shards everywhere.) All that was left was a small piece of wood that she had sent me. I had always wanted the huge iron door-ring. Call me weird, but it was symbolic to me. I already had the antique spring lock that fell off of the door and into my hand in 1978 when it flung open. It seems that any item or piece of that place was heavily "charged" with the death energy. And if you doubt me, Daniel can attest to the power of the lock via his chapter in *Life in The House of Death*, "Experiences and Manifestations".

Anyway, Christine combed the grounds, no door ring. Around the same time, I received a call out of the blue from "K" who was living out on the West Coast. We both spoke at length, knowing that we had both changed a great deal, and I am not a person that holds a grudge, especially against someone who I knew had some "problems". We began, once again, a friendly phone discourse when she told me, quite matter of factly, that she had broken into the mausoleum prior to its destruction and had stolen the occupant's ring! Now, you have to understand my deep and unique connection to that place. I viewed it as nothing less than a sacred temple. And, for many years prior to her phone call, I had sensed that something had violated the sanctity of it. I just wasn't sure what.

Now, it all became clear and I was simply speechless, to say the least! "K" also expressed her feelings of guilt that only hit her many years down the road. And with much ado (very much ado, in fact) I convinced her to come to New Orleans, give the ring to me and I would return it to its rightful owner. The next week, I was on a plane back to New York to return it to where I felt it belonged.

The mausoleum was long gone, but the caretakers did rebury some of the bodies and slap down the old marble wall plaque to denote who's buried there. I proceeded to dig a very deep yet narrow hole and dropped the ring down inside it and covered it thoroughly with earth and replaced the small patch of sod so that it looked completely undisturbed. I offered by sincerest apologies, shed a few tears and headed back to New Orleans. That was 1994...

✠

A couple of days ago (the timeframe is now 2000), I received yet another call from my friend, Christine in New York, who I hadn't heard from since at least 1995. It seems that she'd been dreaming about me, and I, of her. She hadn't been back to that old cemetery since the mausoleum implosion incident, yet she felt an undeniable urge to venture back there (which is a goodly distance from her home). She had no idea why the urge was so strong. Prior to all this, she visited her tarot reader, who told her that she "would find something and know what to do with it" as well as something about "taking things full circle." (I had always believed that my returning the ring to the ground *was* "full circle". Obviously, I was about to be proven wrong.)

Upon her arrival at the cemetery, she was drawn directly to the old gravesite, on top of which sat...you guessed it...that very ring, as well as the door ring that we had searched so carefully for all those many years ago. Impossible... yet true!

She offered to box it all up for me and ship it down Express Mail. I was certain that it would never arrive – that we were both somehow dreaming the same weird dream.

✠

Well, here it is July 11th, 2000, and I hold those very items in my hands. Exact to the day 22 years ago when the door to that very mausoleum flew open as I stood before it and drew me into an experience that I would not soon forget. The rest? Well, you already know what transpired there on at least one occasion.

What does it all mean? Good question! I guess that only time will tell. It somehow "feels" right in a weird sort of way that I haven't as of yet figured out. Somehow by simply wearing the ring, I knew that everything would now be made "right" in a cosmic sort of way. I am certain that it represents "confirmation" and has become a catalyst for my own personal catharsis and return to source... once again. The flesh hadn't "won" after all. The years ahead would simply go to reaffirm that fact.

> *Remember those who've wiped your tears,*
> *who've held your heart and quelled your fears-*
> *Remember Me-*
> *For I am Sorrow wrapped in light,*
> *A ghost of once a fairer night*
> *Greets you now.*
> *My memory may not recall your face.*
> *My tears are all I have to trace*
> *Your loving hands.*
> *I saw the sparkle in your eyes*
> *And knew That I had chosen well*
> *To be with you-*
>
> *For Daniel – from the future...*

THE WEDDING OF NIGHT & DEATH

For the greater part of our lives, both Daniel and I have walked this world alone with our respective ministering spirits. Daniel having the company of "shining darkness" in the Lady, and myself, as willing empath to Azrael, the Angel of Death.

As time went by, we more or less reconciled to the fact that we would always walk this life accompanied only by our spiritual counterparts. While we both find the greatest rapture in those ethereal arms, it can become a lonely road, having no human with which to share the joys and sorrows of such unions, not to mention the simple comfort of having someone to talk to who understands the unique complexities of such an existence.

Even though, to our consorts, our little lives here spanned such a small tether in their understanding of "time", because of our bond, they grew to appreciate the dilemmas and small joys of the human condition. We had gifted Them with our lives, hearts and souls, and in turn, They gifted us with the one thing in this life that we both silently cried out for, someone to walk a whilst with on this road of life.

And so, in 1989, our counterparts concocted a plan that would alter both of our lives in ways we never imagined. Desperate for change, I vowed to take the first invitation I got to go anywhere than where I was at that point. That invite came from a friend who lived in New Orleans. Needless to say, I packed up and spent four days there for a much needed break from the stagnation of my life then. While there, my friend alluded to a man she had corresponded with who, oddly enough, lived ten minutes from my house back in New York. Upon returning home, this person got in contact with me (see the "Here Comes Trouble" chapter for full details.). Our meeting and our subsequent time together seemed as natural as two long lost friends finding each other again on the vast sea of time and space. Before we even realized exactly what was going on, we were both on our way back to New Orleans permanently!

And, here we are, over 12 years later, due to the compassionate intervention of both Azrael and the Lady, we have the one thing in this life that we always cried out for. That companionship grew into love, a love that is difficult to explain to many, but a love that has been taught to us by the very forces that brought us together. Not many people that I know of are blessed to have both a life-mate, as well as a soulmate. Daniel & I are ever grateful to Azrael and the Lady for bringing us together, and like Them, we share a very special and unique bond that we have chosen to honour in the only way this world can recognize, by getting legally married in June of 2000.

A Few Words from Daniel

I think it is rare that two souls meet and the flame of remembrance flares up instantaneously, to the degree of complete comfort with each other. When Leilah and I first met, through very contrived circumstances, it was like meeting someone whom we have never been away from. Our comparing of our spiritual experiences was almost like a "catching up of old times"...

We often joked about how our "friends" (Azrael and the Lady) set us up to meet just to see what would happen.

The result of this has been the most loving and honest relationship I could ever imagine. A closeness I have never shared with another human being. A love that goes beyond the physical.

Part of my purpose in this life is in the simple fact of being here to let Death know that He is loved – incarnate or not.

A marriage means "union". Now, you can take this to mean a variety of things. If, for instance, your mind is mired in pursuits of the flesh, you may construe this in a certain way. But if you can get beyond the constraints of the physical, our "union" is what we have always felt from the beginning... a closeness to each other, the ability to share things unspoken, the inherent ability to recognize each other through the veil of fleshly incarnation, and to remember.

Originally we could think of no other way to reflect this closeness than that of "family". I had never known the feeling of family before I met Leilah. Thus the "brother and sister" thing... But that is how we felt... "family", and that is how we still feel.

Unfortunately, due to the constraints of society, we have had to adopt a new way of defining our relationship, and that is "marriage". (This heads off certain problems while engendering certain other problems.)

Our lives are an open book. If anyone really wants to know what our genitals get up to all you have to do is ask.

For Leilah

Never did I expect to find the light that lay entwined within your shadow. After reading your book and the tears that followed, never did I expect that our mutual commiseration in sorrow could give birth to the phoenix of joy that rose from that ash. Never did I expect to live for happiness.

I had been so wrapped up in my own personal view of misery and loneliness that I failed to note when the window cracked open and Life crept in, with its offspring Peace and Love. Suddenly, the breeze from the window dispelled the fogs of mourning to reveal Home.

Home.... it's such a very important word. At first I thought it had to do with family, but family turned out to mean so much more than who you are born to. Then I thought it was a place, but for me that place was not on this world but out amongst the stars. Then, it occurred to me that it was a state of mind, but the mind is not a nice place to dwell.

I had given up on finding Home, or Love, or Peace for that matter. I always had the Lady, my friend. I was resigned to never having a human, loving embrace - just the heartless embraces I fostered upon others.

Then came you.

Family is not who you're born to but who you can be yourself with. Those who love you & respect you mutually and unconditionally. Finding "family" is the first step to finding "home" or "love" or "peace".... And it is a place, that place being the recipricality of feeling between two beings who are open with each other. "Home" is in the interactions between two souls, born out of love between them. And it is a state of mind, for in the transcommunication between souls that state of mind exists, elusive and fleeting, recurring and graceful - elegant as the winged dance of a dragonfly.

Love is born out of "home". From the myriad interactions that serve to create home, comes love. Yes, it "blossoms" like a flower in full bloom, catching you up in its beauty as it expands to encompass you - its sight enveloping your eyes, its scent captivating your nose, its silken touch enrapturing your skin. There is no one instant that defines this. Not when I read your book and broke down into tears. Not when I first met you and thought you beautiful. Not when we first hung out and talked for nights never-ending. Not through the laughter or the tears, equally shared. Nor through the reflected light I basked in which made me shine, for your "darkness" reflected a purer light than any other I have seen. Nor through the drinking, the pain and trials which followed. For "love" ever blossoms, and I love you more as each sliver of infinity passes between us.

I love you, with all my heart & soul.

Bonne Nuit
Daniel

✠

It has been a "long strange trip", my friends, but that's what happens when you're caught in a whirlwind with lightning crashing at your feet. You dance, and dance and dance... but, the final Waltz belongs to Azrael and the Lady. You could say that we are especially blessed by having the best of "both worlds".

Part 21
Endings and New Beginnings

THE TIES THAT BIND

Ah... all those loose ends. Remember my earlier chapters where I spoke about tying up all those loose ends? Well, it seems that little by little, they are all getting tied up after all, which is a good omen! The ring thing was really the clincher, but there are a few more frayed ends on the mend. The only dilemma now, is trying not to create anymore in the process. It takes so damned long to get the universal fabric rewoven as it should be.

✠

Our eternal purpose and our loose ends are inextricably tied together, One does not get finished without the other also in place. Often older people are the first to comment about how they feel that their purpose here on this earth has been served, so why can't they simply go home. They forget about all the loose ends they've created along the way. The longer one lives, the more frayed ends we leave behind. Part of one's purpose is to "clean up" after yourself as well. The loose ends aren't hard to find. They're those things that have stuck in your mind, soul and heart over the many years. You know what they are, but most are simply complacent or rueful about never having the chance to tie them up. Recognizing and acknowledging them is the first step. Sometimes, if you go out of your way to tie them up, they simply become more tangled. It is best to let the "forces that be" present you with the window of opportunity that you need to do what must be done. Some people are simply cynical and stubborn and they usually become cranky old men and women who never seem to find happiness in anything. I've met some younger people like this as well. They feel that life has dealt them a raw deal and they just want out. These people do not recognize the importance of their purpose and usually go around creating loose ends at every turn making their lives a spider-web of misery that will take many lifetimes to untangle. It's hard to explain these concepts to such people because they are so overcome by the microcosmic nature of their lives that they cannot conceive how nor why they are tied into the universal fabric, yet still so alone.

One of the many reasons some folks constantly have to come back into the flesh is not only because their purposes were left incomplete, but because they left too many loose ends to be tied up in one lifetime. A simple, yet relevant example of this, is someone who meets someone in this life, yet feels uncontrollably drawn to that person. There is an uncanny affiliation, that also incorporates a great wealth of sadness. Through the course of their lives, they realize that they have known each other before and begin having memories of that prior incarnation to the point where they realize exactly why they were drawn together in this life. Each scenario is unique, but a good example of how the macrocosm tries to help us humans put everything in its proper place and time, much like your body (a perfect example of the microcosm) uses its various systems to heal sickness and rebuild cells and synapses where necessary. The universe does this as well, and we are the cells in need of "rebuilding" in order to keep the Great Body alive and evolving. I have a saying that I always use, that it is we, who are the cells in the body of the godsoul, and loose ends, like sickly cells, must be mended in we ever hope to rise above the need for incarnation.

Remember when your momma told you to clean up your mess? Well, that too was a microcosmic suggestion. I'll keep you posted on how my "weaving" goes.

2001- A TIME ODDYSSEY

"My god, it's full of stars!"

For many, a time of beginnings - for others, a season of endings. That's what time is, a series of continual endings and new beginnings. Adrift on the seas of change, years being nothing more than how mankind divides the seasons of his life. Time, itself, acknowledges no such divisions. It is only the human animal that desires to harness and organize his time here thusly.

We perpetually "measure" our limited perception of time from the smallest interval, to the largest we are capable of understanding. Yet, time itself is fluent and immeasurable and does not acknowledge our divisions. The average life-span of a human being may be no more than a heartbeat of the gods, while one of our precious "years" may pass even less noticed.

Everything dwells in the reflection of its own macrocosm. While an insect may live only the equivalent of one of our weeks, or even a single day, we think nothing of it. To more highly evolved entities, our lives may seem equally as brief and fragile. The body ages in accordance with the expected life-span of a particular species. The snake lives longer than the butterfly, but do they count their days, or care that they are numbered? It is only mankind that strives to outlive his years. He will do almost anything to avoid the stoppage of time as he perceives it, to eke out one more day, hour, year... at any cost and by any means.

Perhaps the "gift" of logical thought and free will has made man less intelligent than the other creatures that abide here with us? Maybe they know something we have forgotten along the path of "rational" evolution. For the trees do not cling to their falling leaves, nor should we. For each leaf represents a moment, and time changes just as colourfully as the falling leaf. We "shed" old moments in favour of new ones. The wheel turns, the spiral widens oblivious of the concept of time, full knowing that it is all contained within one contiguous line that blurs all that has passed, all that is, and all that is to come into one point accessible by a number of paths, yet co-existing side by side simultaneously. Time does not move through us, we move through it. Maybe that's what the other life-forms know that we have forgotten...

and why they don't have the fears as human's do. Interesting, huh?

It was only by falling so completely into flesh that I came to understand *how* to rise above it. People sometimes ask me why I prefer to depict Azrael as the withered corpse rather than a more "pleasing" visage. To them I would simply say, because the falling away of the flesh is symbolic of the true face of Death, and a thing of beauty that should be looked upon and appreciated for its radiance.

We marvel at the autumn trees as their leaves change and wither into spectacular displays of colour, and fall away into the winter winds. We do not turn away from the majesty of their dying. Instead, we gather pieces of the tree's "flesh" and press them into scrapbooks appreciating the beauty in the death.

As always, from death, comes life... So, as we acknowledge the milestones in our short, little lives here, do not cling onto the falling leaves of yesteryear. But, rather strive to nurture and cultivate the new ones that will unfold from their wake.

HOW WE DIE

People often ask why some folks have long, drawn out or violent deaths, while others simply fall gently asleep in Death's waiting embrace. It is a question that weighs heavily on the minds of many, and is the cause of much guilt and misunderstanding that too often portrays Death as "thief in the night" who comes to snatch away unwary souls.

Is how we die a random act? Or, is there an element of predestination involved based upon how we've lived, not only this life, but past lives as well? Many people I know claim that they are "ready to die" and eager for that adventure (without having actually lived long enough to enjoy life. I was once one of them.) Though, when the Spectre of Death looms before them and they are faced with the reality of their own mortality, they realize that they aren't as "ready" as they thought. There is nothing wrong with romanticizing Death so long as you are truly willing to take Him to your bed.

And then there are those who never voice their readiness, but inside they have already entreated Death and are simply waiting His return. They have made their peace with the here and the now and are quietly waiting in the wings to be summoned.

My mother endured a long and very painful wasting away due to cancer some 21 years ago. I watched the disease literally eat away at her body and mind. I watched her go from a large woman, to a mere 70 pounds of bone and skin in a little under a year's time. I had to carry what was left of her to the bathroom, bathe her and watch the way she looked at me. Half of her in this life, half in the next, not always recognizing me, and sometimes recognizing another part of "Me" too much. It was a hard time. She was a good mother, a kind and giving person, yet a constantly tortured soul. You find that souls with unfinished "business", or loose ends from past lives often live as haunted people in this life. Such, I believe, was her case. She was prone to flashbacks of disturbing scenes from other lives to the point where she would "go away" and my dad and I would simply watch and listen to her desperation. She was always afraid of something. They were never peaceful visions, and she'd always return disturbed yet without any recollection of what she saw.

She had wanted "out" of this life, but for all the wrong reasons - Unhappiness due to the fact that her dreams never worked out, the choices she made to get her to where she was just weren't what she had in mind for life. However, Life has a way of making some folks "settle" for less than they desire or deserve. Was the way she died connected to her lack of life fulfillment? Was her inner unhappiness literally eating away at her to the point where nothing remained of that persona save its shell? One thing for sure, dying unfulfilled garners you nothing but a guaranteed return ticket!

On the flip side of that example, we have Daniel's father who passed away in 2001 by simply falling gracefully asleep doing one of the things he loved best, sitting in the bleachers of Yankee Stadium watching a ball game. He, too, desired an exodus from this plane, but never voiced it, realizing, I'm sure, how that would make everyone around him feel. The last thing anyone needs is more guilt. Was his gentle passage due to the fact that he could depart this world a fulfilled man knowing that those he leaves behind are happy, and that he has done all he could do to insure that reality?

When Daniel was at his lowest point, almost dead himself in the hospital In Los Angeles some 5 years ago, you could see the sorrow in his father's eyes as he watched his only son flicker in and out of life like a struggling candle in storm. Even though his father had been ill on and off for some time, he could not leave then. Even though he was long prepared for the journey, he had to stick around and make sure that his son would continue and eventually "come back" and recognize that his life had purpose and love too. Only then, could his dad move on in peace.

✠

Certainly, modern medical science contributes to how we die today. In some instances lending a grace period, but too often sacrificing quality of one's final days for quantity of same, thus robbing one of the dignity of a natural death. Our culture is still heavily steeped in the denial of death.

Many still fear to look into the eyes of Death. They are afraid that they will see their true selves, unmasked and unfettered by this tight flesh. Remembering too much for this fragile flesh to contain... and yet continue. We build Death up into an enormous and formidable gate, when in fact, there are no real boundaries between Life and death. The boundaries are created by fear. They simply do not exist. (Certain other cultures have understood that for centuries.) They are illusion, much like this clay we all do wear. Some with ease, some without. We are prisoners of its limitations, but we are not its essence.

✠

On a personal level, I would prefer not to die like my mom, nor like Daniel's dad. However, what we desire and what transpires are often at odds. But, if how we have lived our many lives affects the way we die, I would hope that we all have the grace and wisdom to depart this world with joy and contentment, rather than regret and despair, leaving those still here free from guilt, with only sweet memories and inner peace knowing that they have exited in love with Life, as well as Death.

Ripples

Ours is but a gentle fury
Requiring many years
To carry
On the winds of change,
Not in one brief life
Shall we overcome
The paradox
That time creates,
Nor shatter
The sacred lie
That sustains this world.
My life is merely
A stone cast into a lake,
And my words
Shall be like ripples
On the greater ocean.

Part 22

Exit In Love

CADEAU LA MORT 2
(Reflections on our Annual Black Celebration 2001)

Reflections, they are everywhere. Mirror images of what has been, and what is to come, in the eyes and stories of others.

Time being stationary as we move through it creates certain signposts. If we care to glance at them, they will lead us to an epiphany of being.

☩

People's resonance to Azrael manifests in many ways, from full-blown personification, to experiencing His energy through the death of others. Death is all around us. We cannot escape that reality. Some choose to ignore that reality, while others reach out to embrace it. We are people of the latter. People that have been so profoundly touched by Him, that we have no choice within that longing. Some tremble in His embrace, while others slip sweetly into a peaceful rapture. The reactions to Him are as diverse as the people He touches.

Why do those who both love and rebuke Him come together in the same house, in the same reverential space to honour Him? Perhaps it is a resonance that cannot be defined in words, but still they make the pilgrimage through uncertain times, to share one another's sorrow, hope, curiosity, abandonment, love and trust. What is it that this angel has that gathers such diversity and fervor that brings an enclave of His family together in one place, with all of their unique facets, all of their hopes, fears, desires and dreams? To conjoin in solemnity and revelry in the sweet darkness of His full embrace, to remain together, or to part. For their reasons are as myriad as His facets, as His faces, as the brush of His wing to stone...touched to a tear, and a smile, and a gentle kiss for those who have felt Him, yet prefer their own pain.

He is the release from all that, not that which perpetuates your grief, your loss, but that which removes the pain from the moment, and allows the moment to shine eternally. Death is a facet of Life, but dying is but the blink of an eye. The pain is part of living. The release is that which is Death, given full reign to wash down upon those who grieve.

This year's special gathering was filled with reflections. Images, shot through time, mirrored on the faces and in the hearts of all who came together in His name... and the tears we came away with as family. May they wash away the sorrows, the fears and the longings that stretch beyond this flesh, into a realm of collective memory. One where the mirror is liquid and we can touch that memory simply by extending our hand, full knowing that it is His embrace that awaits us all. Full knowing, that in our diversity, we have imparted enough of the human condition to have quenched His need for understanding. Full knowing that our loins can feel beyond this flesh. Full knowing that even though the faces may be strange once, the souls are familiar always, albeit just a small part of all of those who had wished to be reunited.

Some knew why they came, others just came to know why. It doesn't matter. All that does is that hopefully everyone came away with something special, something that cannot be explained, nor needs to be. Something that will take you to the next plateau of your lives. Perhaps beyond and outside that simple thing. A stepping-stone to evolvement, to your destiny, be it humble or grandiose, it is no less important than the tears, tales and laughter that we all shared.

✠

I am a reflection, an image outside of time. Look within me, and you will see your destiny... if you dare. Be like a feather on the winds of change because boulders cannot fly. Move to my voice, and heed the song of sorrow, for it sings litanies of joy. Read between the lines and understand how to turn your tears into sweet wine.

I am no different than you. Nothing special, nothing sacred, yet here I stand, my wings furled and hand extended to those who remember the reflections that have been cast upon the still waters of your lives. When you were trembling, I was there... I am still.

SYNCHRONICITY

The sounds have drifted further from my room. Now they inhabit the space of other's dreams... other's lives.

Like concentric circles, I cannot question synchronicity, for I am magic simply by existing. So sayeth the ego holding the fire in the palm of one's hand. But, I am just a spark, less important than the flame. How often is it though, that the spark acknowledges the flame that it shall become?

The circle winds up... the circle winds down – the spiral creates more loose ends as it twists and turns, tethering more souls to the narrow path... the eternal road.

Being immersed in the sea of time, as it is, as One – knowing that time is fluid and timelines are but an illusion, is conceivable to most, yet reality to few. To meet someone in that sea and explain *why* they are cognizant of this reality is impossible. The answer already exists. You have but to accept it, and move on.

Confirmations will occur, but only if you have faith, and only if that faith is born of love, consumed by love and burned to ash... by love.

All that you think you are... is not. All that you know you are is all that's left, and that is but a spark of the divine flame.

Forget names. Forget everything that you think you know and *become* that which you are. Let yourself fall into those waiting arms and know that you are home – have been... forever will be.

Flesh is the original lie. It is nothing more than thought creating form to escape the call of the spiral. This is where the animal and the divine divide. This is why humankind often chooses its own worst destiny. Part by instinct, part by knowing – forever trapped in the circle because part of "it" knows nothing more than survival. The other part knows that "survival" lies outside of the flesh all together.

But to teach the animal aspects of its own divinity in this brief lifespan is inconceivable to most, yet accessible to those who have risen above the hunger for flesh... towards a hunger for truth. As we've often touched upon in this book, mankind is a hybrid of animal and divine. There are some with more traits of both... and neither. It is up to them... to *you*, to lead the rest home.

I can honestly say, for the first time in my life, that I am happy and have achieved a sense of inner peace I never thought possible in this lifetime. I plan on savoring these days, these years, as I am well aware of how fleeting everything in this world becomes... in time.

The longing for home, the pain of separation, the sorrow of division, the illusion of duality have all coalesced into a peacefulness of knowing that there is Great Purpose in this life – in *each* life. A purpose that supercedes selfish desire, and when fully realized becomes the catalyst to that peace.

Our voices are no longer divided. We speak as One when the moment matters. The human condition has not quelled that voice, merely tempered it with the understanding and humility afforded by becoming fully immersed in this flesh... and in this shadow, and fully at peace with that state of being. Only then does the phoenix truly rise out of the flames of its own Becoming.

Inner peace is a great gift that should never be taken for granted. Instead, it should be stored in our hearts for the times ahead when the moment comes crashing down, and happiness, like a distant shadow reaches out its ghostly arms and stirs a smile amidst the tears.

True happiness is a very fragile thing, but true love is indestructible. Another paradox for you to ponder...

✠

The world does not want for your happiness. It will try to tear it away at every turn. Life is a cruel and jealous mistress and often one needs to turn a blind eye and a deaf ear against her tantrums. Whereas Death, is a kind and accepting master who revels in our joy with silent wonder.

✠

I've been doing a lot of reflecting lately. Images of all the times Azrael has greatly affected my life and remembering what that felt like. Going back to "source"- re-immersing myself in the River. Recalling the passion of a ten-year old child – the innocence of being even younger – the visions of impossibility... yet they are *all* a part of my life. I even have vague memories of being in my crib. My parents would force me to nap while the sun was still shining. They'd darken the room. I'd see the light peering through the blinds, and know that this was not my world. That somehow all this was wrong. Some far-fetched alien landscape splayed outside my window.

The world was full of sounds – voices that bantered on about inconsequential nonsense. I would peak out the window as the sun was going down and watch the shadows grow. Little by little, they'd scatter back into their well-lit hovels, and night would come and they'd fill it with more noise and more light. I'd try to sleep, ignoring all that, but sleep would never come until the house was dark and all was quiet. Then I would sneak out of my room and sit in the living-room just staring out the window at the stars and the darkness and the silence. How much better I could see the world. I could hear the breeze and listen to the leaves dance, and the sound of the gentle rain on the dry earth. What a sweet scent that made. I would drift off to sleep knowing the noise and light would soon return and I would take my place in their midst...

Little did I ever believe that I would find happiness there as well.

ARC OF SILENCE

Our mouth is full of echoes. May your ears be sharp enough to understand them. These worded pages contain the catalyst of change, the codex of absolute transformation. Our story is not as unique as it appears. Only the characters are unique, as are each of us diverse, unique individuals. Change teaches us *how* to become what we truly are. And change is the only formidable weapon we have to preserve the reality of our existence.

So, my friends, dream on and never cease to remember that the past is gone, but the future is eternal because the future leads us home. Change all that is to be, or there shall be nothing but the memory of what was to be.

We are here to challenge your mind as to what it understands as Truth. To ignite your spirit and to take you to the reaches that you deem distant, that are actually closer than the wind upon your face. To the high hills of a remembered dream, or the deepest caverns of unspoken fear. He is ever with you - ever a reminder of your temporary form. Soon these times shall pass and all of the worries we press into a moment shall seem as insignificant as a fallen leaf. We must strive to raise our eyes up out of the pool of our despair and understand that the Soul of Melancholy does not shed His tears out of sadness, but out of a joy that we down here fail to understand. The joy of knowing what our passing returns us into: the joy of the waning soul that is homeward bound. The ecstasy of completion that can only be known by "old souls", souls that have way too many memories to account for in one lifetime... or in more than one lifetime.

✠

Thus, this "rectangle" I offer to all is filled with seeds. Whether it becomes a talisman of change, or a mirror of Truth... or simply more words on pages depends upon the age of the soil into which it is implanted. If it takes root, then there is ample memory and understanding for the seeds to grow into a tree of Purpose. And Purpose is nothing more than coming full circle and recognizing that fact right before the circle closes. We are *all* circles within spirals, on the head of a pin. My, how large it seems from here! But, oh, how small it actually is when we're aloft, and how large we are in its wake. Perspective is everything. After all, we've only gained true perspective on our own world after viewing it from a distance.

He offers all the view from the bridge between time and space, between life and death, between here, and hereafter. Only by viewing both extremes from an equal distance does one come to fully understand them *both*, and see all things as they truly are. The purpose of life is to teach the necessity of our death, and to rejoice in the knowing that whatever seeds we plant, no matter how small to our perspective, will one day yield a formidable harvest.

Remember that "the comfortable lie" is a seed as well that can grow into twisted limbs and a mutated harvest. We must sow only the seeds of Certain Knowledge and cast all others into the abyss.

☩

Our mouths are indeed, full of echoes. Let us learn to weave our tongues around them unwaveringly and bring forth their whispers. For surely a whisper contains more Truth than a scream. Whispers are seeds, and screams are nothing but withered branches playing upon each other in the winds of change.

I hope that the voice of our melancholy never becomes so hollow, nor so brittle that it cannot bend to reach your ears. And that your ears are never deafened to it by "their" screaming.

☩

This love story tangled in time has caused many to weep, as it should. It is both tragic... and majestic. Both sorrowful and rapturous. A true touch of divine intent. He is at once the black flame... and the lightning - the weaver of dreams, and the unraveller of life.

I had wanted to add so much more to this chronicle. Yet living between worlds creates a veil. I cannot always access the "end" that I envision. Like the twilight, when it is gone, something else takes over. I can only offer the view from the bridge. I cannot describe what lies at either end. For I've never set foot there. My realm does not extend beyond the shorelines. I am the water that licks the land and then recedes. Each time taking away a bit of one shore and depositing it on another.

Every grain of earth I overtake is hallowed. Every soul is in my sacred trust, albeit briefly.

When you walk on hallowed ground, remember me. Everywhere you walk is upon my grave. Hallowed ground encompasses the Earth, the bridge, and the void. All souls walk on hallowed ground. The memory of me is contained in everything that lives. I am an image encoded into your third eye. You will see me when memory intersects with appointed time. A brief flash at first, eventually to become a cool burning image. A single darkness bathed in blue flame that will shadow every other thing in your vision. For now, close your eyes and "see" me. Enfold yourself in twilight and feel me.

I am the Arc of Silence that encircles the sound of life. Like a sickle in the mind, my voice is a wailing song - an undinal melody of weeping sirens.

I am ever the shadow on your threshold - and you, are the multitude of shadows on mine. It is the same threshold, and when you cross it, I will no longer be a shadow, but a familiar friend who will welcome you with wings unfurled and open arms. And I shall take you to the river where you will be washed in memories... and your essence will become a ripple in the dark waters that fan out to an even more distant shore.

I am the Voice of Melancholy... I am *your* voice. Not a shadow, but a confidant, friend... and lover. One who will never forsake you, nor betray you in your time of need. My hand is ever extended. My arms always wanting of your last embrace.

I have fallen into flesh so that you may rise above the need for it. I have assumed your form in the hope that you would unfold before me... and you have.

To be witness to so many as they fall in love with Death is perhaps the single most beautiful thing I have had the privilege to behold. If only to take this fragile and ever expanding flower and place it upon the waters of all life... what a sweet world would evolve from the simplicity of a kiss.

ABOUT THE AUTHOR

Leilah Wendell is the world's foremost recognized researcher of Death personifications and encounters. Author of thirteen books and scores of articles on the subject, she is also a fine artist, poet and proprietor of The Westgate Museum in New Orleans, Louisiana, the *first* and only gallery devoted exclusively to Necromantic Art & Literature and dedicated to the Angel of Death. Born in New York and best known for her groundbreaking title *Our Name is Melancholy- The Complete Books of Azrael*, and over a quarter century of research and documentation via *The Azrael Project*, she currently resides in western Louisiana.

✠

Other Books & Sidelines by the Author;

Threshold
Twilight Harvest
Infinite Possibilities- An Essential Key to the Universe
Songs of the Blue Angel
Shadows in the Half-Light
Amethyst & Lampblack
The Book of Azrael (Original Edition)
The Necromantic Ritual Book
End-Time Fragments
Last Dance- The Necromantic Art of Leilah Wendell*
The Necromantic Tarot*
Encounters with Death
The Gothic Tarot*
Love Never Dies- The Journal of a Necrophile*
Eros In Exile

An asterisk denotes a limited edition item.

To order additional copies of this book, or to obtain a current Westgate Press Catalogue, simply write to us at Westgate, P.O.Box 244, Slagle, LA. 71475 or call 337-238-1733 or visit us at www.westgatenecromantic.com

SELECTED READING
Includes Both Fiction and Nonfiction

Albertus, Frater- The Seven Rays of the QBL, Weiser Books, 1970
Ansky, Solomon- The Dybbuk, Boni & Liveright, 1926
Anthony, Piers- On a Pale Horse, Ballantine Books, 1983
Aries, Philippe- Images of Man & Death, Harvard University Press, 1985
Aries, Philippe- The Hour of Our Death, Vintage Books, 1982
Bahn, Paul- Tombs, Graves & Mummies, Barnes & Noble, 1996
Bailey, Nigel- Grave Matters, Henry Holt Press, 1997
Ball, James- The Body Snatchers, Dorset Press, 1989
Barber, Paul- Vampires, Burial and Death, Yale University Press, 1988
Beagle, Peter- A Fine and Private Place, Ballantine, 1960
Bennett, Cohn- Practical Time Travel, Weiser Books, 1979
Bradbury, Ray- Timeless Stories For Today & Tomorrow, "Mr.Death and the Redhead Woman, Bantam, 1952
Bradbury, Ray- The Halloween Tree, Bantam, 1972
Brunton, Paul- The Spiritual Crisis of Man, Weiser Books, 1969
Budge, E.A. Wallis- The Egyptian Book of the Dead, Dover, 1967
Burns, Stanley- Sleeping Beauty, A History of Memorial Photography in America, Twelvetrees Press, 1991
Burnham, Sophy - A Book of Angels, Ballantine Books, 1990
Camille, Michael- Master of Death, Yale University Press, 1996
Carlson, Lisa- Caring for your own Dead, Upper Access, 1987
Christovich, Mary Louise- New Orleans Architecture/The Cemeteries, 1974
Clark, Adrian- Psychokinesis, Reward Books, 1973
Collins, Charles- A Feast of Blood (Anthology), Avon Books 1967
Copper, Basil- Necropolis, Sphere Books UK, 1980
Crookall, Robert- The Technique of Astral Projection, Aquarian UK. 1964
Cullum, Sylvia- Caught in the Middle, 1987
Davidson, Gustav- A Dictionary of Angels, Free Press, 1967
De Brunhoff, Anne- Souls in Stone, Knopf, 1980
DeRohan, Ceanne- Right Use of Will, One World Publications, 1984
DeRohan, Ceanne- Original Cause, One World Publications, 1989
Devereux, Paul- The Ley Guide, Thames & Hudson, 1987
Eichenberg, Fritz- Dance of Death, Abbeville Press, 1983
Enright, DJ- The Oxford Book of Death, Oxford, 1983
Edwards, Frank- Stranger Than Science, Citadel, 1959
Feeney, John P- Reflections in a Madman's Mirror, Gravesend, 1982
Fodor, Nandor- Between Two Worlds, Prentice Hall, 1964
Fortune, Dion- Through the Gates of Death, Aquarian Press UK. 1987
Gaskell, G.A.- Dictionary of All Scriptures & Myths, Julian Press, 1960

Gay, John- Highgate Cemetery, Salem House, 1984
Gillon, Edmund- Victorian Cemetery Art, Dover, 1978
Godwin, Malcolm- Angels, An Endangered Species, Simon & Schuster, 1990
Gribbon, John- Timewarps, Delta Books, 1979
Haining, Peter- The Unspeakable People, Everest House UK 1975
Hendin, David- Death as a Fact of Life, WW Norton, 1973
Humphrey, Derek- Let Me Die Before I Wake, Hemlock Society, 1991
Humphrey, Derek- The Right to Die, Hemlock Society, 1987
Iserson, Kenneth MD- Death to Dust, Galen Press, 1994
Kastenbaum, Robert- The Literature on Death & Dying, Arno Press, 1977
Keister, Douglas- Going Out in Style, Facts on File, 1997
Kemp, Daniel- The Book of Night, Westgate/Iraya Publications, 1991
Kemp, Daniel- Life in the House of Death, Iraya Publications, 1996
Lamont, Corliss- Man Answers Death, Putnam, 1936
Laycock, Donald C.- The Complete Enochian Dictionary, Askin UK. 1978
Lieberman, A./Ray Bradbury- The Mummies of Guanajauto, H. Abrams, 1978
Lieberman, Herbery- City of the Dead, Pocket Books, 1976
Love, Jeff- The Quantum Gods, Weiser, 1979
Lovecraft, H.P.- The Tomb, Ballantine, 1965
Mahdy, Christine El- Mummies, Myth & Magic, Thames & Hudson, 1989
Marion, John F.- Famous and Curious Cemeteries, Crown Press, 1977
Masello, Robert- Fallen Angels and Spirits of the Dark, Perigree, 1994
Marsden, Simon- Visions of Poe, Knopf, 1988
Masters, Anthony- The Nature History of the Vampire, Berkeley, 1972
Matheson, Richard- Shock Waves, Berkeley, 1979
Matheson, Richard- What Dreams May Come, Berkeley, 1978
Meyrink, Gustav- The Golem, Dover, 1976
Mitchell, John- The New View Over Atlantis, Harper & Row, 1983
Mitford, Jessica- The American Way of Death, Fawcett & Crest, 1963
Montgomery, Ruth- Strangers Among Us, Fawcett, 1979
Muldoon, Sylvan/Carrington, Hereward- The Projection of the Astral Body, Weiser 1929-1970
Natural Death Center- The Natural Death Handbook, Virgin UK, 1993
Noyes, Ralph- The Crop Circle Enigma, Gateway UK, 1990
Owen, I./Sparrow, M.- Conjuring Up Philip, Pocket Books, 1977
Panofsky, Erwin- Tomb Sculpture, Abrams, 1992
Poe, Edgar Allen- Complete Stories & Poems, Doubleday, 1966
Pratchet, Terry- Mort, New American Library, 1987
Pratchett, Terry Reaperman, Corgi Books, 1991
Prophet, Elizabeth C.- Forbidden Mysteries of Enoch, The Untold Story of Men & Angels, Summit, 1977

Quigley, Christine- The Corpse, A History, McFarland, 1996
Ragon, Michel- The Space of Death, Univ. Press of VA. 1981
Ramsland, Katherine- Cemetery Stories, Harper, 2001
Ridley, B.K.- Time, Space & Things, Cambridge, 1976
Robinson, David- Beautiful Death- Penguin, 1996
Ronan, M & E- Death Around the World, Scholastic, (date unknown)
Sidgwick, E.M.- Phantasms of The Living, University Books, 1962
Solara - The Star-Borne, Starborne Unlimited, 1989
Spence, Lewis- The Occult Sciences in Atlantis, Aquarian UK. 1978
Svoboda, Robert- Aghora, At The Left Hand of God, Brotherhood of Life, 1986
Thompson, Richard- Romantic Gothic Tales, Perennial Library, 1979
Time Life Books- The Enchanted World, 1986
Time Life Books- Mysteries of the Unknown "Mystic Places", 1988
Von Daniken, Erich- Chariots of the Gods, Berkeley, 1969
Wallis, Chas.- The Funeral Encyclopedia, Harper & Row, 1953
Warthin, Aldred Scott- The Physician of the Dance of Death, Arno 1977
Watson, Ian- Deathhunter, St. Martins Press, 1981
Watson, Lyall- Beyond Supernature, Bantam, 1988
Waugh, Evelyn- The Loved One, Little Brown, 1948
Weil, Tom- The Cemetery Book, Hipporcrene, 1992
Wendell, Leilah- Infinite Possibilities, Sun Publishers, 1987
Wendell, Leilah- Songs of the Blue Angel, Winston-Derek Press 1987
Wendell, Leilah- The Necromantic Ritual Book, Westgate Press, 1991
Wendell, Leilah- Eros In Exile, Westgate Press, 2001
Wendell, Leilah- Encounters With Death, Westgate Press, 1996
Wendell, Leilah- Infinite Possibilities, Sun Publishers, 1984
Wendell, Leilah- Love Never Dies, Westgate Press Ltd. Editions, 1999
Wentz, Evans- The Tibetan Book of the Dead, Oxford Univ. Press. 1927
Westwood,J.- The Atlas of Mysterious Places, Weidenfeld Nicolson 1987
Wilcock/Pepper- A Guide to Magical & Mystical Sites in Europe and the British Isles, Harper Colophon, 1977
Wilkins, Robert- The Bedside Book of Death, Citadel Press, 1991
Williamson, JN- Deathcoach, Zebra Books, 1981
Wolf, Leonard- In Search of the Living Dead, Popular Library, 1972
Wolf, M./Mallett, D.- Imaginative Futures, Jacob's Ladder, 1993

Westgate Celebrates 27 Years

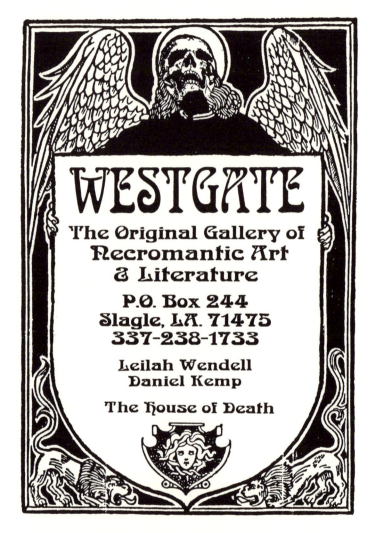

WESTGATE
The Original Gallery of
Necromantic Art
& Literature

P.O. Box 244
Slagle, LA. 71475
337-238-1733

Leilah Wendell
Daniel Kemp

The House of Death

Visit Our Website!
www.westgatenecromantic.com